FAMILY ASSESSMENT

Buros-Nebraska Series
on
Measurement & Testing

Series Editor

JANE CLOSE CONOLEY

Managing Editor

LINDA L. MURPHY

Buros Institute of Mental Measurements
and
Department of Educational Psychology
University of Nebraska-Lincoln

FAMILY ASSESSMENT

Edited by

JANE CLOSE CONOLEY
ELAINE BUTERICK WERTH
University of Nebraska-Lincoln

BUROS INSTITUTE OF MENTAL MEASUREMENTS
University of Nebraska-Lincoln

RC
488.53
.F36
1995

Buros Institute of Mental Measurements
135 Bancroft Hall
University of Nebraska-Lincoln
Lincoln, NE 68588-0348

The paper used in this publication meets the minimum requirements of American
National Standard for Information Sciences—Permanence of Paper for Printed Library
Materials, ANSI Z39.48-1984.

Buros-Nebraska Symposium on Measurement and Testing, 1992
Family Assessment

ISBN 0-910674-38-8

Printed in the United States of America

Contents

Preface

Assessing families suggests both interesting measurement issues and significant clinical applications. This volume is a collection of important papers to explore the topic in some depth.

Some of these papers were first given at the Buros-Nebraska Symposium on Testing and Measurement. Others have been written especially for this volume. All are outstanding examples of scholarship in this very thorny area of psychological measurement beyond the individual. We commissioned papers that examined the history of measurement with families and to cover family issues that are of particular interest to both clinicians and researchers.

The book is divided in three sections. Drs. Halverson and Carlson introduce our topics in two important chapters. Halverson provides readers with a discussion of quantitative measurement of the family from multiple perspectives. He provides a brief, but comprehensive, overview of the history of family assessment by exploring the development of techniques and instruments used for measuring various aspects of the family and interactions within the family system. Dr. Halverson identifies the major shortcoming of the evolution of family assessment as being the development of "too many measures measuring too many constructs."

Dr. Carlson explores the theoretical and practical issues in family assessment. Using family systems theory, Carlson explores the assessment process highlighting the different purposes served by clinical and research assessment procedures. Whereas structural adequacy in measurement is essential to the goal of research in verifying theory, clinicians' use of assessment to guide treatment calls for the functional or treatment utility of measures through the multi-function, sequential family assessment process that leads to decision making and evaluation. A multisystem-multimethod approach to family assessment is recommended by Dr. Carlson to guide family assessment.

The second section of the volume explores the assessment of particular family dynamics. These include aspects of marital quality, assessment of sibling relationships within families, constructs and measurement techniques associated with family health, and special challenges associated with assessing families from diverse ethnic and cultural backgrounds.

Dr. James Bray's chapter is an in-depth look at the theory and measurement of family health. He views the health of the individual from the ecological perspective of the family, both in terms of the development of individual health/adjustment and maintenance and resolution of problems. Bray acquaints the reader with the basic assumptions of systems approaches to families and to family health. He reviews research and theory regarding healthy family functioning and issues to be addressed when studying families. Bray provides an organizational framework for studying the family that includes: status, process, affect, and organization.

Although previous chapters illustrate the challenges inherent in family assessment, Dr. Jane Close Conoley and Lorrie E. Bryant's chapter suggests that assessing ethnically diverse families further complicates the measurement process. Cultural sensitivity, the array of constructs examined in multicultural family assessment with a variety of populations, and adequacy of measurement techniques are analyzed and suggestions are offered to clinicians for the utilization of valid assessment procedures. Conoley and Bryant argue against the use of ethnic glosses and suggest that clinicians view families in the context of their specific family systems as well as from the perspective of their cultural norms. Identification of family membership and roles of family members are discussed within the context of various cultures.

Michelle Schicke's chapter is an exposition of sibling relationships as they relate to psychosocial development and family structure. The research literature on the characteristics and the quality of sibling relationships is reviewed and issues involved in the assessment of these relationships are discussed. Schicke's investigation illustrates the multiplicity of influences on any one individual in the family system in his or her relationship with other family members. The birth of a sibling, birth order, quality of interactions among siblings, combined with other relationship variables and individual characteristics such as gender and temperament, influence and are influenced by parental involvement and response.

Dr. David Johnson provides a critical review of the assessment of marital quality. In doing so, he offers readers a thorough understanding of the constructs used to define marital quality, the measures designed to assess those constructs, and the methodological issues of marital assessment in life course research. Johnson explores the issues involved in defining marital quality and examines three perspectives currently used in its conceptualization: marital adjustment, subjective evaluation of marital quality, and marital quality as a set of traits.

The third section of this volume explores family assessment issues with particular targets of concern including the effects of divorce on children, the influence a child with disabilities has on the family dynamics, and methods to assess the effectiveness of parent training efforts with parents who have aggressive children.

Dr. Paul Amato explores current issues in the measurement of parental divorce on children. Methodological and measurement flaws are identified and suggestions are offered for improving research efforts directed as assessing outcomes of divorce for children. Amato offers a distinction between research that examines how divorce affects children and research that investigates how children cope with the effects of their parents' divorce. Research has mainly focused mainly on the effects of divorce, little research has been conducted regarding children's adjustment. Amato addresses each conceptual framework separately, offering insight into measurement issues associated with each.

Elaine B. Werth's chapter focuses on assessment of treatment effects for families who have aggressive boys. Her work is timely in its analysis of parent training as a treatment of choice for facilitating change in both parents and acting out youngsters. With current concerns about youth violence at high levels both clinicians and researchers are interested in creating and measuring effective approaches to remedy this intractable problem. Werth's chapter illustrates the complexity of attaining attendance at and compliance to treatment and identifying the most appropriate targets for measurement.

Dr. Marjorie Padula describes the many concerns faced by families who have a child or adult with a disability. She critiques the major paper and pencil measures that have been used for family assessment with reference to the special concerns of families who have a member with a disability. Some of the perspectives she raises include the negative focus of many items, the lack of voice given to the person with the disability, and a tendency in some measures to consider family dynamics only in relation to the person with the mental or physical challenge. Dr. Padulla also provides a comprehensive set of constructs that must be investigated if such families are to be helped to access appropriate resources and improve their quality of life.

Overall, the authors have tackled very big issues. They have illuminated issues associated with measuring more than one person, that is, creating constructs that define systems and interactions. They have considered these measurements from both clinical and research perspectives. Finally, they have created a framework that captures normal developmental milestones for families and families in reaction to significant stressors. It is an important work that continues the Buros Institute tradition of being at the cutting edge of measurement concerns.

Jane Close Conoley
Elaine B. Werth
Summer, 1995

Section One

Family Assessment: History, Theory, and Applications

In this section a more unified research effort in family assessment is advocated by Dr. Halverson. He urges the constructs most important in the study of families be identified by shifting from the study of isolated components of the family to a more global view of family functioning. There is a lack of attention to the nomological net of constructs. Multi-trait and multi-method analysis is recommended to produce useful information regarding the family.

Dr. Carlson continues this critique by highlighting the influential role of theory in the development and use of family assessment measures and methods. Carlson traces the development of family assessment by discussing the influences of sociology, systems/communication theory, ecological psychology, social learning theory, and the emerging influences of behavioral genetics, developmental psychology, the close relationships model, and the social relations model.

Measurement Beyond the Individual

Charles F. Halverson

University of Georgia

This chapter has several goals. First, I will briefly review the history of measurement as it applies to family assessment. This history has been recounted by many and is available in many recent publications, so I shall be fairly brief. Second, I will discuss family measurement in terms of important issues still facing the family measurement field—issues that are not, in my opinion, being well addressed at this time. And finally, I will attempt to weave these various threads into some speculations about the future directions that family measurement might (or maybe *needs*) to take.

I will confine this discussion to quantitative measurement because the available space does not permit any extensive discussion of the growing area of qualitative research. I will confess that although my biases permit qualitative research to be complementary to quantitative research, I believe we will always find it necessary to use quantitative measures when we entertain questions involving comparisons across

Author Notes: Portions of this chapter are based on material contained in a chapter by Karen Wampler and Charles Halverson that appeared in *The Sourcebook of Family Theories and Methods: A Contextual Approach* (1993). Edited by P. Boss, W. Doherty, R. LaRossa, W. Schuum & S. Steinmetz (Chapter 8).

Thanks go to several anonymous reviewers who considerably strengthened the chapter. The work was supported in part by Grant MH39899 awarded to C. F. Halverson.

families or when we desire generalizations to populations with certain defined characteristics.

Let me be clear about what is meant by quantitative research methods. Quantitative measurement is simply the assigning of numerical values to abstract, theoretical constructs that constitute the core of family theory. Further, my emphasis is not on measures pertaining to individuals but rather on *family* measures—when a *family* relationship is measured or a set of relationships in the family are measured (See Draper & Marcos, 1990; Huston & Robins, 1982; and Thompson & Walker, 1982, among others for discussions on individual- vs. family-level measurement). Note that the distinctions made about family versus individual measurement are independent from *types* of measurement (e.g., observations, self-report, diaries) as well as *data analytic techniques* (e.g., combining scores from different family members, using dyadic codes, etc.).

When discussing the measurement of relationships we can for our purposes summarize a definition of relationship as clearly involving more than one individual over time (Wampler & Halverson, 1993). When considering the conceptualization of *family* relationships, we must also take into account the idea that families have a specifiable past and an expected future—that is, the relationships are intimate and extended as opposed to casual and brief.

Before I discuss history and issues, I will mention just one brief aside about family theory and its relation to measurement of family constructs. For most family researchers in the past, there has been a conscious attempt to link broad, theoretical positions to certain types of measurement. For example, symbolic interactionists have demonstrated a strong commitment to qualitative, grounded methods, whereas behaviorists have verified their commitment to observational data by focusing on behaviors, right down to microcoding small behavioral sequences in family interactions.

My position is that measurement cannot be formulated without theory—such a theory is not a *global* theory, however, but rather a set of theories about constructs that will dictate what measures we should collect to identify each abstract construct. This theory about measurement stems from a "multiplist position" (Houts, Cook, & Shadish, 1986) that advances a measurement pluralism where *every* abstract social science construct is best measured from multiple perspectives—no one measurement system (self-report, observational, short-term, long-term, etc.) is adequate to measure any complex construct. Every construct's meaning is more than that indicated by any one measure, source, setting, etc. I will return to this notion of "construct building" when we discuss some of the shortcomings of current-day family assessment. (See also Bank, Dishion, Skinner, & Patterson, 1990; Patterson & Bank, 1989.)

HISTORY

In our recent chapter on quantitative measurement we proposed that the history of family measurement coincides with the history of the scientific study of the family (Wampler & Halverson, 1993). It has culminated with the multiagent and multimethod strategies that are increasingly being used today.

MEASUREMENT OF MARRIAGE VARIABLES

The earliest attempts at measurement of marriage were almost entirely based on self-reports and focused on indicators of either satisfaction or marital adjustment (Burgess & Cottrell, 1939; Locke, 1951; Locke & Williamson, 1958). Revisions of early measures by Spanier (1976), along with Gottman's (1979) research indicating the centrality of marital adjustment and satisfaction for marital functioning have led to many measures of the core evaluative constructs of marriage. For the most part, they are self-report and individuallybased measures that are widely used today in nearly every study of marriage.

In the area of marriage assessment, there has been what could be termed a growing methodological dualism with the rise of observational studies of marital interaction in the late 60s and 70s, continuing to the present. Beginning in the 60s at the Old Child Research Branch (where I had a new post-doctoral assignment), Harold Rausch and his colleagues began the study of filmed marital improvisations (Rausch, Barry, Hertel, & Swain, 1974). Later, his colleagues Bob Ryder and Dave Olson began to use adaptations of the old Revealed Difference technique along with such innovative assessments of interaction as the color-matching test (e.g., Olson & Ryder, 1970).

Latter-day clinical psychologists have continued to refine the observational armamentarium over recent years (e.g., the Couples Interaction Scoring System [CISS], Gottman, 1979; the Spouse Observation Checklist [SOC], Weiss & Perry, 1983; and the Marital Interaction Coding System [MICS], Weiss, Hops, & Patterson, 1973). Ironically, these two traditions in the marriage assessment area are still relatively non-cross-fertilizing, existing in parallel tracks; both viewed as valid and sufficient in themselves. With the rise of video and high-tech coding procedures based on video records, we seem to have a proliferation of custom-coding systems, designed for special uses. As we shall see, this parallel system and the proliferation of measures has not clarified the marriage measurement field.

MEASUREMENT OF FAMILY VARIABLES

Measurement of family variables has had a somewhat different history, with observational coding systems arising early from the small-group work of Bales (1950) and others. These early studies focussed for the most part on the verbal interactions among parents and their children. Many of these studies, like some of the marriage observational studies, were laboratory based and used various techniques to elicit interaction (e.g., Revealed Differences, card sorts; Reiss & Klein, 1987; SIMFAM, Straus & Tallman, 1971; Building Houses, Halverson & Wampler, 1993).

Although self-report measures of family functioning have been around for many years, self-report measures of the family really did not become widely available until David Olson and his colleagues began to create and make available a wide variety of questionnaire scales, most notably the Family Adaptability and Cohesion Evaluation Scales (FACES) with its associated circumplex model of family functioning (e.g., Olson, McCubbin, Barnes, Larsen, Muxen, & Wilson, 1985). This instrument, more than any other, has become the benchmark for family assessment. Olson has reported over 600 studies using one of the versions of FACES; the researchers continue developing its norms based upon different family forms, ethnic groups, and studies on cross-national differences in adaptability and cohesion. Clearly, FACES is a popular instrument. The only other self-report instrument that approaches it in popularity is the Moos Family Environment Scale (FES; Moos & Moos, 1984).

MEASUREMENT OF PARENT-CHILD VARIABLES

In the area of parenting and parent-child relationships, self-report instruments of parenting practices and attitudes like Block's Child-Rearing Practices Report (CRPR, Block, Block, & Morrison, 1981) have been developed along with observational measures of dyadic interaction in the family—observation of parent-child and sibling interaction supplementing the observations of husbands and wives, (see, for example, the Family Interaction Coding System, Patterson, 1982; the Family Interaction Q-Sort, Gjerde, 1986). These observational measures allowed investigators to conceptualize parent-child relationships as bi-directional (Bell, 1968; Sears, Maccoby, & Levin, 1957). The use of both self-report parenting measures and observations of parent-child interaction allowed investigators to realize that parental report is often inconsistent with self-reported attitudes. (See Bradbury & Fincham, 1990, for an extended discussion of this issue.)

Sibling and intergenerational relationships have been increasingly measured in recent years (see Bengtson, 1989; Brody & Stoneman, 1990). Interestingly, the sibling measures are self-report, interview, and observational whereas nearly all measures of intergenerational relationships are one-respondent self-reports. Below, I have quoted a passage from our recent chapter on quantitative family measurement that directs the interested reader to one or more of the many reviews of quantitative family measurement (Wampler & Halverson, 1993).

> The reader is referred to the following publications starting with the most comprehensive: Touliatos, Perlmutter, and Straus (1990), Jacob and Tennenbaum (1988); Fredman and Sherman (1987); Grotevant and Carlson (1989; family and parent-child); Filsinger (1983b; family and marital); O'Leary (1987; marital); Skinner (1987; family self-report); Forman and Hagan (1983; 1984; family self-report); Sabatelli (1988; marital self-report); Filsinger and Lewis (1981; marital observation); Gilbert and Christensen (1985; marital observation); Markman and Notarius (1987; marital and family observation); Margolin (1987; behavioral self-report); Beere (1990; gender roles); and Mangen, Bengtson, and Landry (1988; intergenerational self-report). Schumm (1990) provides a summary of the major reviews and compendia of marriage and family measures. (pp. 184-185)

The history of quantitative family measurement reflects the influences of many social science subdisciplines with their varying conceptual and methodological preferences influencing how the family measurement enterprise has been conducted over the years. (Bradbury & Fincham, 1990; Gottman, 1979; Grotevant & Carlson, 1989; Jacob, 1987). Some of the subdisciplines relied on survey and interview methods whereas the more hard-nosed behaviorists developed rigorous observational protocols to study relationships. Only in the most recent years have we seen the use of *multiple* measurement strategies to identify family-level constructs and to assess to some extent the biases of mono-method approaches. More on this below.

The previous sections have been a quick tour of the complex and burgeoning family assessment area. In one sense, there certainly appears to be much vitality to the enterprise—many studies, many measures, lots of publications—but how well are we doing? Not as well as the mini-history might indicate. Let us look at some of the problems in this area as I see them (and as seen by others as well!).

PROBLEMS IN FAMILY ASSESSMENT

When you examine the literature the first thing that strikes you is that much of family measurement research is still rather small-scale with investigators working in relative isolation from each other. Part of this is no surprise—the "engine" of family research is the graduate thesis or dissertation, done by people with limited means. This research is often never replicated nor the measure used again by other people. Generations of this kind of research has led to the greatest weakness in family assessment: *There are too many measures measuring too many constructs.* Any review of family measurement (e.g., Touliatos, Perlmutter, & Straus, 1990) will quickly reveal there are *hundreds* of family measures, most with limited reliability and barely adequate psychometric properties. Even the few measures that might possess decent psychometrics have been used in just a study or two. Indeed, Schumm (1990) cites the research of Straus (1969) that *80%* (!) of surveyed measures had never been used more than once. Schumm also cites Bonjean, Hill, and McLemore (1967) who report equally dismal findings: 28% of the measures had been used more than once and only 2.2% had been used as many as five times! Coupled with the above is the fact that many investigators seemed prone to develop new measures when they needed one to measure their favorite construct, or worse, adopt ones with unknown psychometric properties.

Closely allied to the problem of too many measures (and really a result of it) is the problem of *too many constructs being assessed by all these family instruments.* This problem of too many constructs reflects the fact that there is really no consensus on what are the most important constructs in assessing family relationships. If you look carefully at most constructs defined by the various assessment devices, it becomes apparent that many constructs with the same name may not be measuring the same underlying variable *and* there is *always* the possibility that constructs with very different labels may be capturing the same underlying variance (what my colleague Jack Block [personal communication, June, 1991] refers to as the "jingle-jangle" problem).

With the multitude of measures partially identifying many, many constructs *and* very little in the way of replicated findings, it is really quite impossible for most family researchers to identify potentially useful measures of family functioning. All these measures of unknown validity and reliability leads to a serious dilution of research efforts. Instead of systematic research on a small number of constructs identified by a manageable number of measures, we have instead example after example of *one or two studies that identify a construct with only one measure and then little or no follow-up, or replication.*

In an earlier chapter the utility of the theory of critical multiplism was noted (Wampler & Halverson, 1993):

> Recall the perspective of critical multiplism (Houts et al., 1986) cited earlier. A multiplist perspective asserts that no one measurement system is adequate to exhaust the meaning of any complex social science construct. In the family area we mostly deal with highly complex, abstract, "nonvisible" constructs that must be estimated from fallible and biased measurement systems. The bias is maximized when our constructs are estimated by one measure from one source with one method at one point in time (e.g., self-report questionnaire from wife on family cohesion). This typical case must be remedied by "building constructs" across methods, sources, different times, and contexts if we intend to have constructs general across such domains. The point is to "average out" the limitations and biases from any one single source and method and to aggregate the underlying construct variance across sources, methods, contexts, and time for a stable, well-defined construct that is not tied to any one source setting or method. We must devote both theory and empirical work to aggregation and construct building (cf., Patterson & Bank, 1989) that can include all sorts of measurement at all levels of quantitative sophistication from nominal data to ratio scales. (p. 189)

Let me give you a brief example from our own recent work. In her dissertation, Nancy Hollett (1992) discovered the value of aggregation of measures over *time* and *source* in predicting some peer-acceptance outcomes some 3 years after we had stopped collecting family data. Originally in our modeling of predictors of peer acceptance (measured in the classroom), we used data from the 4th-year observation of the parent-child interaction in our lab to predict peer acceptance. The predictions derived from these observational Q-sort ratings (of about 20 minutes of interaction) showed little convergence with other measures of parenting (self-report and interview ratings) and no predictability to our criterion measure. We could have at that point concluded that there was no predictability from our family data to peer data. We decided to instead aggregate the three sources of data over 4 years of observations, self-reports, and interview ratings to see if we could construct a more robust and reliable measure of competent parent-child interaction. Consistent with the lessons we have learned from our personality-researcher colleagues (see Epstein & O'Brien, 1985), such aggregate measures proved much more adequate than any single measure. Each measure contained theoretically relevant components that were not in the other measures such that aggregated 4-year observation Q-sorts became more reliable and converged with the other measures to form a latent construct with path coefficients of .40 and .47 to peer acceptance (for mother and father parenting style respectively). Obviously, the aggregate measures must show *convergent* validity in order to be useful in a prediction equation. In this case we built a construct with both relatively molar and molecular variables that came from three different sources that converged on a construct of competent parenting having real predictive potential.

This example leads me to yet another weakness in family assessment—the lack of studies where one can compare the usefulness and distinctiveness of various constructs included in the same study. In terms of the multiplist agenda, we have almost no work done on the *nomological net* of our constructs (Campbell & Fiske, 1959). In Campbell and Fiske's article on the multitrait-multimethod matrix, construct validity could be demonstrated when two or more methods were used to measure two or more traits in a nomological net. Multitrait-multimethod studies allow us to examine construct validity as well as to distinguish truly different traits from those with overlapping variance. Studies where this is possible are mostly missing from family research. It is difficult to find a study that includes three or four operationalizations (even if all self-report!) of some key family construct. This problem is especially serious in family data where most comparisons are *within* method (e.g., method variance is almost always confounded with construct variance). Indeed, the lack of convergence of measures from different or same sources is always ambiguous. We seem to be swimming in a *sea* of measures of unknown meaning most of the time!

One might think the solution to this problem could be solved by getting large *N*s and using a potful of family measures to see "what is related to what." I believe this strategy is a mistake. Along with Jacob Cohen (1990) I think *less is more*. Cohen convincingly demonstrates the folly of studies with "prodigious numbers of dependent variables...[and] far too many independent variables, or (heaven help us) both" (p. 1304). There is considerable muddle in relating, for example, 10 predictors to 6 outcome measures. A little thought reveals that the Type I error rate is very high—there are going to be many "significant" chance correlations (more with larger *N*s) and we really cannot tell which are the real associations.

Related to the weakness above is the unfortunate fact that many or most of the measures we have of the family are self-report. These instruments elicit information from *individuals* who report on their family's functioning. Almost without exception, instruments are developed, normed, and used as *individual* measures rather than as family measures—even when the content refers to families. Obviously, the reliance on single-source, single-method data as a proxy for family functioning produces many difficulties that cannot be solved by factoring a large number of instruments together (assuming we could get a huge sample to fill out 35 or 40 of these measures). Such studies might find a few, broad replicable "factors" (probably evaluation—good family—bad family). Reports of internal consistency, reliability, etc., could not erase the problem of method and source variance in the measures: These new clusters will always refer to single individual's perceptions of family, not to descriptions of the family based on multiple *sources, settings,* and *times!*

Another way to phrase this issue is by asking the question: Are family measures capturing unique variance about family relationships or are they just individual characteristics disguised as family measures? (Wampler & Halverson, 1993). The issue is most salient for self-report measures because they measure individual perceptions of relationships rather than actual quality of relationships (Christensen & Arrington, 1987). In our data, correlations are consistently high between self-report measures of family constructs such as cohesion and individual constructs such as depression, clearly an individual measure. Further, for many analyses, family-level constructs do not add significant variance in a step-wise multiple regression after we have first entered individual measures. In an earlier publication (Wampler & Halverson, 1993) we wrote:

> The individual difference issue is closely tied to the treatment of two or more different sources of information about a relationship (Fisher, Kokes, Ransom, Phillips, & Rudd, 1985; Schumm, Barnes, Bollman, Jurich, & Milliken, 1985). These discussions are often, however, in the context of how to combine scores rather than conceptualizing how different perceptions may be central to family process, a possibly far-reaching conceptual issue. If measures are simply individual scores, most information could be gained by leaving them separate. In contrast, if they are biased indicators of a construct, they should be combined. The point is that although we may combine individual perceptions of the family (and we have several proposed ways of doing it—see Schumm et al., 1985; Walters, Pittman, & Norrell, 1984), these combined scores then must be thought of as biased indicators of constructs to be combined with other methods and sources—*and that is almost never done!* (p. 187)

SAMPLING AND FAMILY MEASUREMENT

Finally, no discussion about the family measurement field could be complete without some discussion of the issues revolving around sampling. First, let me note that for the most part, family assessment measures have been developed on relatively small and restricted samples. One lesson we have not heeded from our psychometric mentors is that without large sample sizes, much of our data are unstable and therefore mostly uninterpretable. I have seen many, many instruments "developed" with nearly as many items as subjects; factor analyses done on small samples and results interpreted as stable and meaningful, etc. Obviously, this is part of the general validity problem. The constructs we measure are subtle and complex. The indicators of those constructs need to be very carefully crafted and tested, and that requires large samples and replication of factor structures before we can be sure of our indices. Samples of 100-200 with as many variables are unfortunately all too common!

A second issue related to sample size is the lack of normative data on most of the extant instruments in the family area. Because most measures have been developed on small or restricted samples, the interpretation of *mean level* scores remains moot. What is a high score on cohesion? On conflict? What is the norm? This issue often escapes us because we tend to deal in correlations, but the usefulness of family measures would be greatly enhanced if we could interpret mean level scores against a normative base. Let me give you an example from the child psychopathology area—namely the Child Behavior Checklist (CBCL; Achenbach & Edelbrock, 1988); Achenbach's group has normed his behavior problem checklist on large, national (and now international) samples by age, gender, social class, clinical status, etc. (Achenbach, McConaughy, & Howell, 1987). If I use the measure on my sample I can describe the sample relative to those norms (e.g., we have 21% of our children above the 90% percentile on behavior problems, Mavis Hetherington had 80% of her boys of divorced parents scoring above the clinical cutoff, etc.).

What do we know with most of our family measures? Not much. What is a high score? A "clinical" score? It is clear that demographic variables do affect family functioning and that family form (divorced, step, single parent, reconstituted, etc.) will make our assessment job more difficult. Do we study normal or distressed families with the same or different measures? More basically, how do we define family? Can we sample by living arrangements, setting, etc.? Large, diverse samples need to be used during construct development to allow us to begin to develop preliminary answers to these important questions. We simply do not know whether the same instruments will work for all family forms in most settings (allowing us to compare mean levels) or whether we need different kinds of measures for different groups. "For example, since wives generally indicate lower levels of marital satisfaction than husbands, does it make sense to use separate norms based on gender or is it preferable to use raw scores?" (Wampler & Halverson, 1993, p. 189). As long as we muddle along on small, convenience samples, we can never begin to address these questions of when, where, and for whom our measure applies, not to mention how we can interpret mean scores.

SUMMARY

So, whither the field of family measurement? Clearly, there are many things left undone in my opinion. My assessment of the maturity of the field is not positive at this time. We still have many measures of many theoretical constructs. Many of those measures have not only poor psychometric qualities, but they are also saturated with method variance and of unknown discriminant validity. I am sure many measures with different names tap mostly the same variance whereas others with the same name (e.g., cohesion) measure quite different things.

We also seem to lag far behind theory in places. I agree with Grotevant and Carlson (1989) that the "theoretically powerful transactional view of socialization processes has not yet been matched in terms of measurement technology" (p. 149). Further, we are still without tests and measures with known normative data and cross-replicated findings from different studies employing "benchmark" measures.

What is to be done? I believe that there most likely will be no nation-wide "rigorous, and programmatic efforts" to improve measurement technology (Jacob, Tennenbaum, & Krahn, 1987, p. 322). It is difficult to fund large-scale measurement studies where there is still much disagreement about the key constructs to be measured. More likely are the cross-laboratory replications of measures derived from programmatic research programs like Patterson's (1982) and Gottman's (1979).

For example, Patterson's (1982) ongoing research has always stressed the need to build constructs from multiple methods and sources. When those multiple-measured constructs are used by multiple investigators across the country, their replicated usefulness as well as the ever-growing nomological net (when these constructs are compared to new ones for predictive efficacy) will help us to know which are the best multiple-source/method constructs to use in our own work. These techniques, many based on new multivariate procedures like LISREL and confirmatory factor analysis, are just now beginning to have an impact on family measurement. In a sense, we have a very short history of solid, sophisticated measurement that is psychometrically sound and theoretically useful. I remain hopeful as we increasingly emphasize data collection from multiple sources and recognize the importance of replication, more agreement will emerge about the basic dimensions related to family functioning and the best ways to measure them.

REFERENCES

Achenbach, T. M., & Edelbrock, C. (1988). Child Behavior Checklist. Burlington, VT: Thomas M. Achenbach.

Achenbach, T. M., McConaughy, S. H., & Howell, C. T. (1987). Child/adolescent behavioral and emotional problems: Implications of cross-informant correlations for situational specificity. *Psychological Bulletin, 101,* 213-232.

Bales, R. F. (1950). *Interaction process analysis.* Cambridge, MA: Addison-Wesley.

Bank, L., Dishion, T., Skinner, M., & Patterson, G. R. (1990). Method variance in structural equation modeling: Living with "GLOP." In G. R. Patterson (Ed.), *Depression and aggression in family interaction* (pp. 247-249). Hillsdale, NJ: Lawrence Erlbaum Associates.

Beere, C. A. (1990). *Gender roles: A handbook of tests and measures.* Westport, CT: Greenwood.

Bell, R. Q. (1968). A reinterpretation of the direction of effects in studies of socialization. *Psychological Review, 75,* 81-95.

Bengtson, V. L. (1989). The problems of generations: Age group contrasts, continuities and social change. In V. L. Bengtson & K. W. Schaie (Eds.), *The course of later life: Research and reflections* (pp. 25-54). New York: Springer.

Block, J. H., Block, J., & Morrison, A. (1981). Parental agreement-disagreement on child-rearing orientations and gender-related personality correlates in children. *Child Development, 52,* 965-974.

Bonjean, C. M., Hill, R. J., & McLemore, S. D. (1967). *Sociological measurement: An inventory of scales and indices.* San Francisco: Chandler.

Bradbury, T. N., & Fincham, F. D. (1990). Dimensions of marital and family interaction. In J. Touliatos, B. F. Perlmutter, & M. A. Straus (Eds.), *Handbook of family measurement techniques* (pp. 37-60). Newbury Park, CA: Sage Publications.

Brody, G., & Stoneman, Z. (1990). Sibling relationships. In I. Sigel & G. Brody (Eds.), *Methods of family research* (vol. 1, pp. 189-212). Hillsdale, NJ: Lawrence Erlbaum Associates.

Burgess, E. W., & Cottrell, L. S. (1939). *Predicting success or failure in marriage.* New York: Prentice-Hall.

Campbell, D. T., & Fiske, D. W. (1959). Convergent and discriminant validation by the multitrait-multimethod matrix. *Psychological Bulletin, 56,* 81-105.

Christensen, A., & Arrington, A. (1987). Research issues and strategies. In T. Jacob (Ed.), *Family interaction and psychopathology: Theories, methods, and findings* (pp. 259-296). New York: Plenum Press.

Cohen, J. (1990). Things I have learned (so far). *American Psychologist, 45,* 1304-1312.

Draper, T. W., & Marcos, A. C. (Eds.). (1990). *Family variables: Conceptualization, measurement, and use.* Newbury Park, CA: Sage Publications.

Epstein, S., & O'Brien, E. J. (1985). The person-situation debate in historical and current perspective. *Psychological Bulletin, 98,* 513-537.

Filsinger, E. E. (Ed.) (1983b). *Marriage and family assessment.* Beverly Hills, CA: Sage Publications.

Filsinger, E. E., & Lewis, R. A. (Eds.). (1981). *Assessing marriage.* Beverly Hills: Sage Publications.

Fisher, L., Kokes, R. F., Ransom, D. C., Phillips, S. L., & Rudd, P. (1985). Alternative strategies for creating "relational" data. *Family Process, 24,* 213-224.

Forman, B. D., & Hagan, B. J. (1983). A comparative review of total family functioning measures. *The American Journal of Family Therapy, 11,* 25-40.

Forman, B. D., & Hagan, B. J. (1984). Measures for evaluating total family functioning. *Family Therapy, 11,* 1-35.

Fredman, N., & Sherman, R. (1987). *Handbook of measurements for marriage and family therapy.* New York: Brunner/Mazel.

Gilbert, R., & Christensen, A. (1985). Observational assessment of marital and family interaction: Methodological considerations. In L. L'Abate (Ed.), *The handbook of family psychology and therapy* (pp. 961-1005). Homewood, IL: The Dorsey Press.

Gjerde, P. F. (1986). The interpersonal structure of family interaction settings: Parent-adolescent relations in dyads and triads. *Developmental Psychology, 22,* 297-304.

Gottman, J. M. (1979). *Marital interaction: Experimental investigations.* New York: Academic Press.

Grotevant, H. D., & Carlson, C. I. (1989). *Family assessment: A guide to method and measures.* New York: The Guilford Press.

Halverson, C. F., & Wampler, K. S. (1993). The mutual influence of child externalizing behavior and family functioning: The impact of a mild congenital risk factor. In R. Cole, & D. Reiss (Eds.), *How do families cope with chronic illness?* (pp. 71-94) Hillsdale, NJ: Lawrence Erlbaum Associates.

Hollett, N. (1992). *Predictors of children's social acceptance: Building a systemic model.* Unpublished doctoral dissertation, The University of Georgia, Athens, GA.

Houts, A. C., Cook, T. D., & Shadish, W. R., Jr. (1986). The person-situation debate: A critical multiplist perspective. *Journal of Personality, 54,* 52-105.

Huston, T. L., & Robins, E. (1982). Conceptual and methodological issues in studying close relationships. *Journal of Marriage and the Family, 44,* 901-926.

Jacob, T. (1987). Family interaction and psychopathology: Historical overview. In T. Jacob (Ed.), *Family interaction and psychopathology: Theories, methods, and findings* (pp. 3-22). New York: Plenum Press.

Jacob, T., & Tennenbaum, D. L. (1988). *Family assessment: Rationale, methods and future directions.* New York: Plenum Press.

Jacob, T., Tennenbaum, D., & Krahn, G. (1987). Factors influencing the reliability and validity of observation data. In T. Jacob (Ed.), *Family interaction and psychopathology: Theories ,methods, and findings* (pp. 297-328). New York: Plenum Press.

Locke, H. J. (1951). *Predicting adjustment in marriage: A comparison of a divorced and happily married group.* New York: Henry Holt & Co.

Locke, H. J., & Williamson, R. C. (1958). Marital adjustment: A factor analysis study. *American Sociological Review, 23,* 562-569.

Mangen, D. J., Bengtson, V. L., & Landry, P. H. (Eds.). (1988). *Measurement of intergenerational relations.* Newbury Park, CA: Sage Publications.

Margolin, G. (1987). Participant observation procedures in marital and family assessment. In T. Jacob (Ed.), *Family interaction and psychopathology: Theories, methods, and findings* (pp. 391-426). New York: Plenum Press.

Markman, H. J., & Notarius, C. I. (1987). Coding marital and family interaction: Current status. In T. Jacob (Ed.), *Family interaction and psychopathology: Theories, methods, and findings* (pp. 329-341). New York: Plenum Press.

Moos, R. H., & Moos, B. S. (1984). *Family Environment Scale manual* (rev. ed.). Palo Alto, CA: Consulting Psychologists Press.

O'Leary, K. D. (Ed.). (1987). *Assessment of marital discord: An integration for research and clinical practice.* Hillsdale, NJ: Lawrence Erlbaum Associates.

Olson, D. H., McCubbin, H. I., Barnes, H., Larsen, A., Muxen, M., & Wilson, M. (1985). *Family inventories*. St. Paul, MN: University of Minnesota.

Olson, D. H., & Ryder, R. G. (1970). Inventory of marital conflict (IMC): An experimental interaction procedure. *Journal of Marriage and the Family*, *32*, 443-448.

Patterson, G. R. (1982). *A social learning approach: Vol. 3. Coercive family process*. Eugene, OR: Castalia.

Patterson, G. R., & Bank, L. (1989). Some amplifying mechanisms for pathologic processes in families. In M. R. Gunnar & E. Thelen (Eds.), *Systems and development: The Minnesota symposia on child psychology* (vol. 22, pp. 167-210). Hillsdale, NJ: Lawrence Erlbaum Associates.

Rausch, H. L., Barry, W. A., Hertel, R. K., & Swain, M. A. (1974). *Communication, conflict, and marriage*. San Francisco: Jossey-Bass.

Reiss, D., & Klein, D. (1987). Paradigm and pathogenesis: A family-centered approach to problems of etiology and treatment of psychiatric disorders. In T. Jacob (Ed.), *Family interaction and psychopathology: Theories, methods, and findings* (pp. 203-258). New York: Plenum Press.

Sabatelli, R. (1988). The assessment of marital relationships: A review and critique of contemporary measures. *Journal of Marriage and the Family*, *50*, 891-915.

Schumm, W. R. (1990). Evolution of the family field: Measurement principles and techniques. In J. Touliatos, B. F. Perlmutter, & M. A. Straus (Eds.), *Handbook of family measurement techniques* (pp. 23-36). Newbury Park, CA: Sage Publications.

Schumm, W. R., Barnes, H. L., Bollman, S. R., Jurich, A. P., & Milliken, G. A. (1985). Approaches to the statistical analysis of family data. *Home Economics Research Journal*, *14*, 112-122.

Sears, R. R., Maccoby, E., & Levin, H. (1957). *Patterns of childrearing*. Evanston, IL: Row Peterson & Co.

Skinner, H. A. (1987). Self-report instruments for family assessment. In T. Jacob (Ed.), *Family interaction and psychopathology: Theories, methods, and findings* (pp. 427-452). New York: Plenum Press.

Spanier, G. B. (1976). Measuring dyadic adjustment: New scales for assessing the quality of marriage and similar dyads. *Journal of Marriage and the Family*, *38*, 15-30.

Straus, M. A. (1969). *Family measurement techniques: Abstracts of published instruments, 1935-1965*. Minneapolis, MN: University of Minnesota Press.

Straus, M. A., & Tallman, I. (1971). SIMFAM: A technique for observational measurement and experimental study of families. In J. Aldous (Ed.), *Family problem solving: A symposium on theoretical, methodological, and substantive concerns* (pp. 380-438). Hinsdale, IL: Dryden.

Thompson, L., & Walker, A. J. (1982). The dyad as the unit of analysis: Conceptual and methodological issues. *Journal of Marriage and the Family, 44*, 889-900.

Touliatos, J., Perlmutter, B. F., & Straus, M. A. (Eds.). (1990). *Handbook of family measurement techniques.* Newbury Park, CA: Sage Publications.

Victor, J. B., Halverson, C. F., & Wampler, K. S. (1988). Family-school context: Parent and teacher agreement on child temperament. *Journal of Consulting and Clinical Psychology, 56*, 573-477.

Walters, L. H., Pittman, J. F., & Norrell, J. E. (1984). Development of a quantitative measure of a family from self reports by family members. *Journal of Family Issues, 5*, 37-48.

Wampler, K. S. & Halverson, C. F. (1993). Quantitative measurement in family research. In P. G. Boss, W. J. Doherty, R. LaRossa, W. R. Schumm, & S. K. Steinmetz (Eds.). *Sourcebook of family theories and methods: A contextual approach* (pp. 181-194). New York, NY: Plenum Press.

Weiss, R. L., Hops, H., & Patterson, G. R. (1973). A framework for conceptualizing marital conflict: A technology for altering it, some data for evaluating it. In F. W. Clark & L. A. Hammerlynck (Eds.), *Critical issues in research and practice: Proceedings of the fourth Banff conference on behavior modification* (pp. 111-120). Champaign, IL: Research Press.

Weiss, R. L., & Perry, B. A. (1983). The Spouse Observation Checklist: Development and clinical applications. In E. E. Filsinger (Ed.), *Marriage and family assessment* (pp. 65-85). Beverly Hills, CA: Sage Publications.

FAMILIES AS THE FOCUS OF ASSESSMENT: THEORETICAL AND PRACTICAL ISSUES

Cindy I. Carlson

University of Texas at Austin

The role of early and concurrent family relationships in the etiology of individual development and psychopathology has received increased attention in both research and practice within psychology in recent decades. Although the importance of family relationships in shaping personality has always been central in psychology, it was assumed with psychoanalytic theory that these forces were internalized within the individual such that intrapsychic dynamics were the dominant forces controlling behavior. Consistent with the premises of the dynamic model, *the individual* was the focus of assessment, treatment, and research within the discipline of psychology. Several converging developments in the 1950s led clinicians to break with the individualistic premises of psychology to view behavior as meaningfully related to the social system in which it was embedded. Systems theory was readily embraced by many clinicians disenchanted with the efficacy of individual treatment approaches for problems which had roots in dysfunctional relationships. The paradigmatic shift to a systems conceptualization of individual pathology generated the development of theoretical conceptualizations and treatments that were distinctive from those developed for the individual. The family was the obvious target for systemic intervention as the social context with the earliest, most continuous, and most affect-laden influence on individual behavior and development.

Conceptually, interventions with the family system are unique in that they emphasize human behavior as it occurs within the relationship matrix of an active social system and acknowledge and integrate multiple sources of psychological influence (individual, relationship, family, social) within a single treatment approach (Bednar, Burlingame, & Masters, 1988). As noted by these family scholars the conceptual distinctions are far from trivial:

> They suggest the wisdom, if not the absolute necessity, of having the family therapies based on psychological and treatment principles (a) that reflect multiple levels of psychological influence, (b) with variables that can be conceptually defined and empirically measured, (c) that capture the essence of personal, interpersonal, group, and systemic influences within any active social system, (d) at higher than usual levels of psychological immediacy and intensity, (e) that are derived from methods of measurememt and data analyses that can identify reciprocal influences among interacting variables, (f) that will eventually define and describe the principles that regulate human behavior in complex social systems....Even the most seasoned researcher and practitioner should feel overwhelmed by the complexity of the phenomena we are discussing. (Bednar, Burlingame, & Masters, 1988, pp. 408-409)

Despite the challenges presented by the systems perspective, it has had a dramatic influence on the conceptualization of models of family functioning and the related development of family assessment measures. A review of recent measures and methods of family assessment, for example, found all measures of the family unit to be considered by their authors to be consistent with the premises of systems theory (Grotevant & Carlson, 1989). The influence of systems theory has also been evident in recent research and conceptualization within developmental psychology (e.g., Ford & Lerner, 1992), suggesting a stronger impetus to construct measures and to determine analytic methods for evaluating the premises of systems theory.

This chapter on family assessment, although acknowledging the input from diverse theoretical perspectives, will emphasize the family systems perspective because this premise underlies the development of the majority of current clinical models of family functioning and the operationalization of their constructs in measures (see Grotevant & Carlson, 1989, and Touliatos, Perlmutter, & Straus, 1990, for reviews). As will be evident in subsequent discussion, one's theoretical orientation will strongly influence decisions about assessment of the family. The emphasis on systems theory as the underlying framework for family assessment in the present chapter is not intended to communicate that general systems theory is a valid, scientific theory of family relationships, or that it is the only valid theory. In fact, systems theory, which has provided such a useful paradigm for clinicians, has been criticized as overly holistic and antianalytic, with constructs that are difficult to operationalize, and a theory that is difficult to falsify (see Grotevant, 1989). Lending some validity to the antianalytic accusations, assessment has been viewed by many family clinicians with ambivalence. This has been due, in part, to the "action" orientation of family therapy which mediates against the systematic gathering of information to arrive at a diagnostic formulation (Karpel & Strauss, 1983). If one accepts the scientist-practitioner model of psychology, however, which emphasizes the reciprocal value of scientific inquiry to accountable practice and the importance of clinical results to theory building, then the field is faced with either the falsification of systems theory as a model of family process or the reconciliation of systems theory in family assessment.

Systems theory does, however, pose considerable challenge to family assessment. It is the purpose of this chapter to examine the theoretical and practical challenges inherent in assessment of the family *as a system*. The chapter will be organized commonly accepted steps of the assessment process:

1. Define the purpose, objective, or research question.
2. Make theory or assumptions explicit.
3. Inventory instruments or resources.
4. Perform the assessment.
5. Analyze and interpret the data.

Within the first step the differential goals of family assessment in research versus clinical practice will be discussed. In the second assessment step the links between theory and assessment will be discussed, and a brief review of the diverse theoretical influences on family assessment will be provided. An overview of methods of family assessment will next be provided (Step 3) followed by a discussion of the practical concerns in the selection and integration of family assessment measures and methods (Step 4). Finally, issues in the compilation and interpretation of family assessment data (Step 5) will be examined with particular attention to the use of statistical analytic techniques for resolving family assessment challenges.

STEP 1: DEFINE THE PURPOSE OF THE FAMILY ASSESSMENT

The choice of measures and methods for a family assessment should be consistent with the goals, objectives, or research questions that are to be answered by family assessment data. The importance of careful and specific measurement in the ordering and classifying of behavior, the prediction of behavior, and the modification of behavior is emphasized in the scientist-practitioner model (Hersen & Bellack, 1984). Family assessment as a means to systematically and empirically test theories and hypotheses regarding family behavior and attitudes is the central concern of the family-oriented social science researcher. Assessment of the family as a means by which to determine, guide, and evaluate treatment effectiveness should be a central concern of the family clinician. Thus, both family clinicians and researchers are concerned with the development of theoretically and psychometrically sound measures and methods of evaluating family process. Without minimizing this shared concern, it is realistic to also consider the distinctiveness of the goals of a family assessment conducted for purposes of research versus clinical practice. The following discussion of these differences is based on a previous articulation of this issue by the author (see Carlson, 1989).

The primary goal of a family assessment in research is to operationalize abstract concepts or constructs such that hypotheses derived from theory regarding the interrelations of the constructs can be tested. Assessment and measurement are interchangeable terms from the research perspective. Both imply identification of specific features of the phenomena and the creation and use of clear rules or procedures for quantification (Nunnally, 1978). The degree to which the identified abstract concepts have some rational and empirical correspondence with reality is the validity of the measure; the creation of good rules, that is, rules that can be repeatedly empirically tested is the measure's reliability. The psychometric quality of a family assessment measure is essential to the researcher.

It is acknowledged that theory development and empirical validation are progressive. The testing of theoretical hypotheses includes the multiple aims and strategies of description, correlation, prediction, and controlled experimentation. The methods and measures useful to these various stages of theory testing will vary. Moreover, as theories differ substantially from one another, so will the operationalization of their constructs in measures. Thus, research demands the continuous development of new measures or the adaptation of existing measures. The effects of the demands of the research context on family assessment can be seen, for example, in the development of family systems observation coding schemes (Grotevant & Carlson, 1987, 1989). These coding systems are all designed to capture the interactive processes of the whole family, yet each differs in the behavioral constructs that are examined, a reflection of the variations in theoretical perspectives and questions of the researchers. Moreover, few, if any, of these coding schemes were used in multiple studies or across research laboratories, providing replication of findings. In summary, a family assessment conducted for the purpose of research must be most concerned that the methods and measures selected reliably and validly measure the constructs to be operationalized such that hypotheses can be tested. The continuous creation and revision of family assessment measures limits determination of their clinical utility.

Assessment in the clinical context has been defined as the careful analysis of clients such that the appropriate strategy of helping them can be undertaken (Filsinger, 1983). A clinical assessment of the family serves two distinct purposes: (a) it can assist clinicians in understanding complex family patterns and (b) it can permit the more accurate assessment of an underlying state or pathology that is hard for the clinician to perceive directly (Reiss, 1983). Unlike assessment in the research context, where the primary function is the operationalization of theoretical constructs, a clinical assessment can be differentiated by various sequential functions. These functions may include: (a) screening and general disposition; (b) definition, which may include diagnosis, labelling, or quanitification of problem severity; (c) planning or matching treatment; (d) monitoring treatment progress; and (e) evaluation of treatment outcome (Hawkins, 1979). The criteria for an adequate family assessment method will vary depending upon the clinical function for which it is developed. The measurement issues related to each stage of clinical assessment have been articulated by Hawkins (1979) for behavioral assessment and intervention and adapted for family assessment by Carlson (1989). A summary follows.

Screening for family dysfunction requires a broad-band family assessment capable of detecting, but not necessarily specifying, the nature of a problem. Optimally a family measure used for screening would also provide guidance regarding the direction of further assessment for defining the problem. In addition screening instruments must be brief in terms of professional and family members' time. At the screening phase the adequacy of a family functioning measure will depend primarily on its cost-effectiveness and predictive validity.

At the diagnosis phase, family assessment must confirm hypotheses regarding the functioning of the family unit, quantify or measure the severity of dysfunction, and determine the primary locus of the problem. The value of a family assessment method or measure at the diagnostic phase would be determined primarily by its discriminative and differential predictive validity. Norm-referenced measures and validated clinical cutoff scores or profiles are particularly important for the diagnostic phase.

The goals of family assessment at the treatment planning phase are to specify objectives for change, analyze the contingencies maintaining the problematic behavior, identify family strengths and resources, and determine the intervention sequence and the level of change that is adequate for treatment to be terminated. The multiple goals of assessment at this phase may necessitate a multimethod approach.

Monitoring treatment progress requires a method of family measurement that is narrow in focus (targeted to the focus of change) and amenable to a repeated measures design. Family measurement techniques that are unresponsive to spurious influences, such as retesting effects or instrument decay, and that are sensitive to change and easily administered are important for this phase. In addition, the impact of the intervention on the subjective realities of family members may be as relevant to assess as changing family interaction patterns.

Evaluation of treatment outcome frequently requires a multimethod approach to assessment. The use of a pre-post treatment design is common, which would call for a repetition of relevant measures used in the diagnostic phase. Finally, in the follow-up of treatment, the goal of a family assessment would be to determine the durability and sufficiency of the behavioral and subjective changes that have resulted from treatment. A continuation of the family assessment method used in monitoring treatment progress, less frequently administered, may be an appropriate follow-up measure, as may be a repeat of selected measures used in the pre-post treatment design. In follow-up the criteria of breadth of coverage and economy are highlighted. Breadth is necessary to evaluate broader effects of treatment and economy is relevant as families are unlikely to be motivated to complete complex or time-consuming measures.

Thus, family assessment in the clinical context requires a consideration of a series of sequential decision-making functions demanded by treatment. A single measure or method may have multiphase utility; however, a measure may have excellent validity for one function and low validity for another. The multiple functions of assessment in the clinical context then may necessitate the selection or development of multiple, complementary family assessment methods, based upon a single theory regarding family process and change, and the subsequent psychometric evaluation of these measures as to their utility for the specific purposes and phases of treatment for which they were designed.

To summarize, a family assessment conducted for purposes of answering a research question may have different requirements than a family assessment completed to determine appropriate treatment and/or treatment effectiveness. As noted by Hayes, Nelson, and Jarrett (1987), classical psychometric theory determines the structural but not the functional adequacy of a measure. Structural adequacy (i.e., reliability and validity) is essential for substantiating theoretical premises. Functional adequacy refers to the treatment utility of a measure (i.e., the degree to which it can be shown that treatment outcome is positively influenced by the measure). It is possible, according to these authors, for a measure to have functional or treatment utility without demonstrating structural adequacy. Furthermore, these authors argue that the evaluation of the treatment utility of assessment measures sets the stage for important theoretical development because it points out important functional differences which then require theoretical explanation. A review of the family assessment field (Grotevant & Carlson, 1989) suggests that neither treatment utility or structural adequacy are well tested in existing measures; thus, researchers and clinicians should be mindful of their goals in conducting a family assessment and attentive to data on structural adequacy.

STEP TWO: MAKE THEORY OR ASSUMPTIONS EXPLICIT

It is a basic assumption of assessment activities that these should be explicitly guided by theory. Family assessment potentially encompasses a wide variety of techniques, domains to be measured, and numerous family members or subsystem levels. As noted by Grotevant (1989), theory should provide a guide for separating elements that are worthy of attention from those that are not. *Why* we measure, *what* we measure, and *how* we choose to measure should be guided by theory. Multiple disciplines and theories have influenced the development of current family assessment measures and methods. These will next be discussed within a historical perspective followed by further discussion of the linkages between theory and family assessment proposed by Grotevant (1989).

Theoretical Influences

The many theoretical orientations and methodological strategies in family studies have been addressed comprehensively in a recent publication, *Sourcebook of Family Theories and Methods: A Contextual*

Approach (Boss, Doherty, Larossa, Schum, & Steinmetz, 1993). The following brief description of theoretical influences on family assessment is based on this publication as well as others (Grotevant, 1989; Jacob, 1987; Carlson, 1991).

The founding decades: family sociology. The study of the family is considered to have its origins in sociology with the publication of Ernest Burgess's (1926, cited in Jacob, 1987) paper, "The Family As A Unit of Interacting Personalities." Burgess's ideas can be seen as important forerunners to current conceptualizing about the family. Specifically, Burgess (a) emphasized the process versus the content of family interaction, (b) conceptualized the family as the unit of study, and (c) analyzed the family in terms of family patterns and roles (Jacob, 1987).

Post World War II family theorists shifted from the prewar focus on the family as a "closed system of interacting personalities" to a view of the family as a "semi-closed system" in transaction with other systems in society (Hill & Rodger, 1964, p. 178, cited in Doherty, Boss, LaRossa, Schumm, & Steinmetz, 1993). Important theoretical developments included Duvall's (1957) conceptualization of the family developmental life cycle and Talcott Parsons's (Parson & Bales,1955) structural-functional model of family process. Structural-functional theory of the family viewed the family as a small group with clear roles differentiated by gender. It also emphasized the harmony of goals and functions between families and society. Structural-functionalism appears to have been influential in the development of clinical models of family functioning that emphasize the fit between role performance and family organization (e.g., the Family Process Model, Steinhauer, Santa-Barbara, & Skinner, 1984; the structural family therapy model, Minuchin, 1974).

Structural-functional theory came under attack in the 1960s for its political conservatism, sexism, and lack of empirical validation (Doherty et al., 1993). One alternative theoretical framework proposed was social exchange theory which viewed social interaction in terms of such concepts as rewards and costs. Social exchange theory represented the joining of behavioral psychology, with its emphasis on reinforcement contingencies with utilitarian economic theory, with its emphasis on cost-benefit ratios, and provided a set of theoretical propositions that could be quantitatively analyzed. Social exchange theory also refocused the analysis of the family from it interface with society to analysis of exchange processes in dyads or small groups. Nye (1982) is credited as the leading articulator of social exchange theory and family processes. His influence is evident in current family assessment measures in the measurement of domains related, for example, to role performance and task accomplishment.

In addition to these major theoretical streams, sociology contributed significantly to the methodology of family assessment. Parsons's and Bales's (1955) development of the Interaction Process Analysis observational coding scheme for analyzing small group process provided both the methodology and key variables for subsequent family process coding schemes (see Grotevant & Carlson, 1987). Strodtbeck's Revealed Difference Technique (Strodtbeck, 1951) continues to be the stimulus situation for many studies of family process and clinical evaluations of families.

In summary, sociology provided critical impetus to the family studies tradition and made a significant contribution to family assessment methodology, particularly with the development of observation coding schemes and marital questionnaires. Moreover, despite the diversity of theories within sociology, a consistent focus remained on the role of the family in adjustment. The hegemony of sociology in the family field, however, had clearly ended by the 1980s and has been replaced with more multidisciplinary, integrative theories (Doherty et al., 1993). The family studies field continues to influence the development of family assessment measures and methods; however, this is primarily within the academic or research domain. Clinical assessment of the family has been more strongly influenced by systems theory.

Systems/communications theory. Beginning in the 1950s, clinical researchers turned their attention to the role of the family in the etiology of severe adult psychopathology. Common to this research was a focus on family communication patterns, theoretical models that emphasized the primacy of the interactional context in understanding deviant behavior, and, over time, acceptance of the explanatory power of general systems theory (Bertalanffy, 1956).

At the core of a systems orientation is the concept that elements exist in a state of active communicative interrelatedness and interdependence within a bounded unit (e.g., the individual, the family, the classroom, the organization), such that the activities of one element cannot help but have a direct or indirect influence on the other elements of the system, resulting in a whole which is greater than the sum of the elements (Koman & Stechler, 1985). In addition to the concept of interrelatedness of elements, the concepts of organization and hierarchy are key within systems theory. All systems reflect an organization of parts and parts in relation to the whole. Hierarchy is frequently a characteristic of the organization of complex systems such that certain elements or subsystems are hierarchically superordinate to lower subsystems. The properties of any living system, (e.g., the quality of interrelatedness, hierarchy, organization), as well as the mechanisms that maintain any dysfunctional behavior, are evident in the repeated interactional or communication sequences between members (elements) of the system who are in a mutual and interdependent relationship with one another.

The systems/communication perspective has significant implications for the metholodogy required for family assessment. First, individual dysfunctional behavior is viewed as meaningless without a view to the systemic context in which it is embedded. Second, a systems orientation implies a relational versus individual focus to assessment. A relational focus demands techniques that measure the interactions of elements within systems and between systems in contrast with traditional techniques which focus on individual variability across systemic settings such as the home and school. Third, this orientation underscores the complexity of relationships that can exist within and between systems, and between an individual's dysfunctional behavior and their systemic contexts. Thus, this perspective encourages the utilization of family assessment procedures that go beyond single variables aimed at only one level of the family matrix (Jacob, 1987). In application, the premise of systems theory that the whole is greater than the sum of the parts has resulted in an emphasis on the development of measures that capture the "whole" of the family system.

Family Development. Family development theory provides an analytic understanding of the changing characteristics of families as they move through life cycle stages; more recently, the theory has been reconceptualized as a way to provide a longitudinal understanding of the interrelationships and processes among several levels of family analysis—individual, dyadic, group, and societal (Rodgers & White, 1993). Family development theory proposes that the family over time represents a set of mutually contingent individual developmental trajectories. With the passage of family members, and the family as a small group, through normative and paranormative developmental stages, roles, norms, and position transform. Family development theory is concerned with how families transform roles over time and the nature of the process of transformation. Concerns focus on both the process and content of normative role changes, changes in response to paranormative events (e.g., divorce, death of a family member), and transitional states. Family developmental theory has been criticized as lacking in empirical support and predictive power; however, recent reconceptualizations may prove promising (see Rodgers & White, 1993, for review). Family developmental theory has been applied to clinical work with families by Carter and McGoldrick (1989). These authors assert that an assessment of family functioning must consider the roles and structure appropriate for the developmental needs of family members.

Ecological psychology. Ecological psychology is concerned with the relationship between individual behavior and the total life space (Barker, 1968). Much of early ecological psychology research was concerned with the study of the inextricably linked behavior-environment interface such that behavior of participants and the surrounding environment formed a bounded unit, the behavior setting (Barker, 1968; Wicker, 1979). More recently, ecological theory has been integrated with developmental psychology (e.g., Bronfenbrenner, 1979), with home economics theories about the family (i.e., human ecology theory) (Bubolz & Sontag, 1993), and in clinical practice with systems theory (e.g., Jasnowski, 1984); however, the distinctions between the two perspectives are salient. Ecology is a broader construct that includes the concept of system; however, the concept of system does not necessarily include the concept of ecology (Mannino & Shore, 1984). With regard to family assessment, the system frequently refers to the family context, whereas ecology frequently refers to the embeddedness of the family system within a matrix of relationships with systems beyond the family (e.g., the school, church, neighborhood). Thus, the primary contribution of ecological psychology to assessment of the family has been to provide a theoretical framework for operationalization of constructs that assess the family-environment interface or to provide impetus to the development of measures of the family as a life space for individual members (e.g., the Family Environment Scale, Moos & Moos, 1986).

Social learning theory. Another major influence on family measurement has been behavioral psychology, and particularly, social learning theory. Although far from a homogeneous discipline, the research tradition of social learning can be characterized by the following: (a) a continuing view that behavior and its variation is a function of the reinforcement contingencies of the environment; (b) a concern with illuminating the reciprocal, bidirectional chains of interaction or social exchange that comprise the environment; (c) a preference for naturalistic observation as an assessment methodology; (d) a commitment to scientific, methodologically rigorous procedures and the clinical application of findings; (e) concern with the macro-environmental contingencies that impact on the family (Jacob, 1987). The social learning researchers concerned with child problems (e.g., Patterson, 1982) have made substantial methodological contributions to family assessment with the provision of valid and reliable observation and quasi-observation procedures, as well as excellent models of multimethod/multilevel studies of family process (see, for example, Patterson & Dishion, 1988).

Emerging theories in psychology. A final category of influence, expected to have a more significant impact on the future course of family assessment than the present as reflected in current measures of the family, derives from curent research that emphasizes two distinct sources of explanation for the behavior of individuals—relationships and biology. Three theoretical models, that have had as their goal the explication of the processes governing close social relationships, are viewed as having a potentially significant impact on family assessment measures and practice. These include the transactional model within developmental psychology and within social psychology, the close relationships model and the social relations model. In addition, research in behavioral genetics and more recently, the genetic influences on family processes, is proving to have significant implications for family assessment.

Within developmental psychology research on the parent-child relationship has shifted over the past decades from a "social mold" theoretical viewpoint, in which parent influences were viewed as unidirectional from the parent to the child, to a transactional view (see Sameroff, 1989), in which the parent and child are viewed as establishing organized, reciprocal patterns of interaction that characterize their relationship (Hartup, 1978). Moreover the origins of adult interactional style and self-organization are viewed as the direct outcome of these organized, reciprocal dyadic interaction patterns within the family (Sroufe & Fleeson, 1986). Research on the effect of the family on child development has emphasized the effect of relationships on relationships (see Hinde & Stevenson-Hinde, 1988). In contrast to the emphasis on assessment of the whole family that has been viewed by family psychologists as consistent with systems theory, developmental psychology researchers have emphasized assessment of the interrelatedness of dyadic relationships within the family. (An excellent collection of research studies using this approach can be found in Hinde & Stevenson-Hinde, 1988.) Hinde (1989) argues that exclusive measurement of the family as a unit is too wholistic to be meaningful. Consistent with systems theory, Hinde views the family as an organization composed of hierarchical, nested relationships; however, he argues that each relationship or nested level contains properties that may be shared but also may be irrelevant to the preceding one. Thus, developmental psychologists concerned with the effect of relationships on relationships within family processes may contribute significantly over time to the field of family assessment by enhancing our understanding of how the parts or sybsystems of the family relate to one another and how relationships or subsystems relate to the whole in contrast with the current focus of family psychology, which has been how the whole family system affects the individual.

A second potentially important theoretical influence on family assessment may emerge from the research of social psychologists on close relationships (see Kelly et al., 1983). Within this literature a relationship is defined as existing when two entities have an impact on each other or are interdependent. A relationship can be described as close if the two people are highly interdependent upon each other, where interdependence is revealed in four properties of their interconnected activities: (a) the individuals have frequent impact on each other; (b) the degree of impact is strong; (c) the impact is upon diverse kinds of activities for each person; (d) all of these properties characterize the causally interconnected activity series for a relatively long duration. (Kelly et al., 1983). The close relationships model has been extended by Berscheid (1986) to include the role of emotion, which would appear to have particular relevance for close relationships within the family.

The close relationships literature has provided a useful methodological distinction relevant to family assessment, that is, the differentiation of measurement of interpersonal events, subjective events, subjective conditions, and relationship properties (Huston & Robins, 1982). *Interpersonal events* or event sequences refer to the overt, observable behaviors of family members measured with formal and informal observation methods. *Subjective events* refer to the covert and momentary ideas, thoughts, and emotions of each family member. When a relationship endures over time, as characterizes family relationships, stable attributions, attitudes, and beliefs about family members, their relationships, and characteristics of the whole family unit emerge. These relatively stable emotions and cognitions are termed *subjective conditions* and are measurable primarily by self-report methods. Once subjective conditions are in place they can affect patterns of interpersonal and subjective events These recurrent patterns of interpersonal or subjective events reflect *relationship properties*. Relationship properties, by definition, must be observed or recorded as a repetition of behavior or subjective response over time. In summary, the close relationships model would argue for the assessment of subjective events, subjective conditions, and the observed recurrent behavioral or subjective patterns within the family.

A third model which appears promising for conceptual advances, primarily in the analysis of family assessment data, is the social relations model (Kenny & LaVoie, 1984). The social relations model was designed to address the complexities of social interaction research. The model proposes that the behavior of one member of the family toward another member is a function of multiple independent components: the family or group effect; the actor effect (e.g., the tendency of the person to behave similarly regardless of partner); the partner effect, (e.g., the general tendency of the partner to elicit the same response from others); the relationship effect, (e.g., the degree to which the actor and partner's behavior cannot be accounted for by their individual effects). The social relations model has been successfully applied to family data (Cook, Kenny, & Goldstein, 1991; Cook & Goldstein, in press). As noted by Cook et al. (1991), a special advantage of the social relations model is that is provides indices of reciprocal effects in family relationships.

Finally, the biological revolution in psychology is challenging existing methods and conceptualizations of the family (Bussell & Reiss, 1993). Investigations of the genetic influences on family process, both with twin and sibling studies, are essentially finding that the use of the term family environment may be a misnomer. Rather family environment is experienced by each member of the family differently, that is, it is nonshared environment. Behavioral geneticists have proposed at least four classes of sibling differential experience (Bussell & Reiss, 1993): (a) differential parenting; (b) differential experienes with one another; (c) differential experiences in peer groups; and (d) differential experiences exposure to life events. Currently little attention is paid to these processes in family assessment.

More portentous for family assessment, behavioral geneticists have begun to examine the role of genetics in family processes. Two sorts of mechanisms are proposed to influence family interaction patterns (Bussell & Reiss, 1993). Parents genes may shape, in part, their perceptions and reaction patterns in relations with other family members and/or the heritable characteristics of the child might elicit from parents differential parenting. Specifically related to family assessment, using a behavioral genetics approach to the analysis of family environment measures, 26% of the variance was explained by genetic differences. Moreover, genetics appears to be differentially implicated in dimensions of family environment. Cohesion, for example, has been found across studies to demonstrate a higher heritability component (as much as 50%), whereas family control shows much less genetic influence (Bussell & Reiss, 1993; Rowe, 1983).

The implications of these findings are significant for family assessment in clinical practice and research. Based on Bussell and Reiss (1993), implications for family assessment include: (a) the necessity of including more than one child within a family in the assessment, as environments are child-specific; (b) as genetics can mediate environmental effects, these must be considered in data analysis; (c) as the family environment is a multidimensional construct that includes common exposure but differential experience, it can only be understood with data capturing both observed and subjective processes.

Emerging trends in the family studies field. In addition to emerging research in psychology, emerging trends in the family studies field are expected to impact family assessment. As noted by Doherty et al. (1993), emerging trends in family studies focus on diversity with the new era of family studies expected to be influenced by the following issues: (a) the impact of feminist and ethnic minority theories and perspectives; (b) the realization that family forms have changed dramatically; (c) the trend toward more theoretical and methodological diversity; (d) the trend toward more concern with language and meaning; (e) the movement toward more constructivist and contextual approaches to knowledge generation; (f) an increased concern with ethics, values, and religion; (g) cross-disciplinary study of the family; (h) a breakdown of the dichotomy between family social science and family intervention. One implication of some of these issues for family assessment measures and practice would appear to be increased concern, caution, and research regarding the validity of existing measures and methods with diverse family structures and populations, as well as the development of more culturally sensitive measures if needed.

The context of family research methods. Just as multiple theoretical influences can be seen in the domains measured in current family assessment measures, the methods by which families are evaluated are varied and have developed historically (see Doherty et al., 1993). The early study of the family in the 1920s and 1930s was characterized by both qualitative and quantitative methods. From the 1940s to the 1970s, quantitative methodology, especially the use of questionnaires and standardized interviews, was and continues to be the standard. Experimental studies of family interaction, using observational coding schemes, characterized the studies of the family as a small group in the 1950s and 1960s. Although based in other theoretical paradigms, observational studies of family process continue to be impor-

tant (e.g., Patterson, 1982). Observation studies have been greatly
enhanced by video technology, which has allowed the preservation of
family interactive processes for repeated analyses. The technology of
computers has provided social scientists with unprecedented ability
to conduct complex multivariate analyses of data. Thus, the current
decade is witness to the application of sophisticated statistical analytic
procedures to the analysis of family data, regardless of family assessment method, (e.g., Cook et al., 1991; Cole & McPherson, 1993). In
addition to the emphasis on increasingly sophisticated quantitative
methods for capturing the complexity of families, there is also re-
newed interest in qualitative methods of family research (e.g., Gilgun,
Daly, & Handel, 1992). This would appear consistent with the
emerging trend in family studies toward constructivist and contextual
approaches to understanding the family.

Linking Theory with Family Assessment

Evident in the above discussion, multiple theoretical perspectives
have influenced and continue to influence the development of family
assessment methods and measures. Each theoretical perspective and
research tradition has distinct assumptions and thus, places a somewhat different emphasis on how and what to measure in the family.
Grotevant (1989) notes the following linkages between theory and
family assessment to be appropriate:

1. Theory should specify the domain of family functioning
   that is being investigated so that the full relevant domain
   can be sampled.
2. Theory should lead to clear definitions of constructs and
   variables.
3. Theory should drive decisions about assessment strategies.
4. Theory should provide guidance for the 'levels of analysis'
   dilemma.
5. An interactive relationship should be established between
   theory and assessment.

In his evaluation of the current status of theory development and
family assessment, Grotevant (1989) noted that numerous theories in
the middle range have been developed for family functioning; however, no unifying theory has gained acceptance. Thus, current measures of the family as a unit suffer from a lack of construct validity, as
evidenced in the lack of convergence across measures. In addition, a
theory of the family has not yet provided an answer as to how the
various parts of the family system relate to the whole and in what

ways the parts are similar and distinctive from the whole. The recent work of Broderick (1993) represents an effort within systems theory to integrate theoretically the diverse levels of family process. This work, however, is too recent to have been operationalized with measures and tested empirically. Recent trends in family studies suggest that rather than simplification greater diversity and plurality of theories, measures, and methods will be characteristic of the field. It is therefore expected that family assessment measures and methods will continue to proliferate. Given the diversity of methods and measures, we turn to an examination of diverse family assessment methods.

STEP 3: INVENTORY INSTRUMENTS

The third step in the assessment process is to decide upon methods and measures to be used. As noted above, one's theory and assumptions, as well as the goals of assessment, should guide this choice. In addition, practical considerations, such as intrusiveness, the resources required for various assessment procedures, and fit with the setting, are likely to influence the choice of family assessment methods and measures. A variety of methods have been utilized to evaluate the family context. These include self-report questionnaires, interviews, formal and informal observation procedures, behavior ratings of self or others, projective methods, and structured tasks. It is beyond the scope of this chapter to review or recommend existing measures. Reviews of family assessment measures include *Marriage and Family Assessment* (Filsinger, 1983), *Family Assessment: A Guide for Clinicians and Researchers* (Grotevant & Carlson, 1989), and *Handbook of Family Measurement Techniques* (Touliatos, Perlmutter, & Straus, 1990). Reviews of family measures are also included in the *Mental Measurements Yearbooks* (e.g., Kramer & Conoley, 1992). In this section several key distinctions among methods of family assessment will be noted followed by a discussion of the most commonly used methods: observation and self-report questionnaires.

One key distinction among family assessment methods is the degree to which the data derived can be considered objective, that is, the data are numerical, and precisely and systematically describe the relationship or family. In contrast, data considered subjective are expected to be influenced by the attitudes, values, and beliefs of the family members and/or the researchers/clinicians. Subjectivity, in the form of beliefs and cognitions, is considered a legitimate topic for family assessment and research. The methodology of the social sciences, however, has remained focused on precision, and thus, the objective measurement of subjective conditions (Becvar & Becvar,

1993). Regarding observation methods, coding schemes, clinical rating scales, and participant observation reports, respectively, provide greater to less objectivity. Standardized self-report questionnaires provide the most objective index of family members' subjective reality. Although there is increasing interest in qualitative methodologies related to the study of the family (e.g., Gilgun, Daly, & Handel, 1992), in general, family assessments conducted for purposes of research have required a methodology that provides numerical data for analysis. For an extended discussion of the tension between the logical positivistic tradition of the social sciences, with its demands for objective measurement, and the systemic-cybernetic paradigm of family therapy, the interested reader is referred to Becvar and Becvar (1993).

A second distinction that can be made among the various methods of family assessment involves differentiating procedures based upon reports of family members from procedures based upon the direct observation of the interactions of family members. This distinction has often been characterized as the "insider" versus the "outsider" perspective in family relationships, that is, how viewpoints of members within the family system differ from the views of members outside the system (Olson, 1977; Gurman & Kniskern, 1981). Methods that utilize the outsider frame of reference include all measurement strategies that capture the observed behavior of the individual family members. Insider methods, which measure family members' subjective conditions, include self-report questionnaires, projective tests, and the family members' reports of their viewpoints in an interview. The insider and outsider perspectives have been found to tap distinct realities of family relationships, and to have a low correspondence with one another (Olson, 1977). For example, a family's perception of their level of closeness or cohesion may be only weakly correlated with a clinician's rating of the same dimension. Although the low correlation between insider and outsider viewpoints of the family has been attenuated when the methods are both derived from the same family functioning model (Hampson, Beavers, & Hulgus, 1989), the unique dimensions of family relationships captured by each method has led to the recommendation to family researchers and clinicians that both an insider and outsider perspective should be gathered in a family assessment.

In the remainder of this section, the two broad categories of family assessment methods—the observation methods of the outsider and the self-report questionnaires of the insider, will be discussed. The discussion is based on previous articulation of the distinctions in these methods by the author (Carlson, 1991; Carlson & Grotevant, 1987a, 1987b; Grotevant & Carlson, 1987, 1989).

OBSERVATIONAL METHODS

Observational methods permit the direct assessment of family interaction patterns. Appreciation for the value of observational methods has increased in recent decades due to a variety of factors: (a) the emphasis of many current theories of family therapy on here-and-now interactions versus history, (b) the questionable validity of self-report as a measure of actual behavior, and (c) technological and psychometric advances that improved the feasibility of collecting and analyzing observational data. Observational methods of family assessment range on a continuum from informal to formal, nonstandardized to standardized, clinical to scientific, unreliable to reliable. Specifically, along this continuum from subjective to objective lie several observation methods including interview procedures, clinical rating scales, and coding schemes.

Observation methods can vary also in degree of observer participation with the family. Participant observation refers to observation procedures in which the observer is clearly visible to the family or family members being observed. The observer may maintain a passive, noninteractive role, such as when trained coders observe interactions within the home setting, or observers may be involved in interaction with the family, such as during a clinical interview with the family (Margolin, 1987). Participant observation also refers to directives to the family or to family members to monitor or observe the behaviors of others within the family. Because the observer's objectivity is recognized to be influenced by participation in the interaction with the family and by the history of the association between the observer and the observed, several techniques have been developed to aid in the validity and reliability of these data (see Margolin, 1987). Participant observation within the home is frequently used by behavioral theorists. The focus of these observations, however, is seldom on the family as interacting unit, but rather on individuals or dyads within the family. With regard to assessment of the family unit, participant observation is most likely to occur within a clinical interview.

Interview procedures. Participant observation of family members during a clinical interview is the most common family assessment method of clinicians who are guided by theoretical perspectives that focus diagnosis on transactional patterns which occur in the here-and-now. A clinician engaged in observation of the family might direct attention to family transactions that reflect the quality of boundaries, hierarchy, emotional closeness, and clarity of communication among family members. In order to assure that transactions between family members which are of theoretical or clinical interest are likely to occur, family treatment models have developed interview procedures to aid in informal clinical evaluation (e.g., Weber, McKeever, & McDaniel, 1985), and several family functioning models have developed interview procedures to be used in conjunction with clinical rating scales, (e.g., the Beavers Systems Model, Circumplex Model of Marital and Family Systems, the McMaster Model) (for review, see Walsh, 1993). The interview procedure is also useful for eliciting and evaluating family members' subjective beliefs, such as attitudes and attributions regarding the family, family relationships, or a particular family member or problem. Procedures focusing on the cognitions of family members within a family interview are most well developed by cognitive-behavioral family therapists (see Epstein, Schlesinger, & Dryden, 1988).

Informal observation of family functioning during an interview with the family has distinct advantages and disadvantages. One advantage is cost. Informal observation during a family interview is relatively easily incorporated into one's clinical practice. The primary disadvantage of informal observation, of course, is the lack of objectivity, validity, and reliability of data that derive from the clinical judgment of the observer, albeit well trained, who is participating in the system being observed. Thus, informal participant observation is unlikely to be useful as a research methodology without the use of some means by which observations can be recorded, quantified, and completed by a second observer such that interrater reliability can be determined. Clinical rating scales of family functioning have been developed for such a purpose.

Clinical rating scales. Clinical rating scales are a family assessment measurement technique designed to permit a summary judgment on the part the rater/observer with regard to placement of an individual, dyad, or whole family on some psychological dimension. Family clinical rating scales are useful following a family interview as a means by which impressions can be recorded in a more standardized fashion or in a nonparticipant observation of the family in interaction, for example, from behind a one-way mirror or from video recordings. The advantages of clinical rating scales include cost efficiency, generation of quantitative data which can be evaluated for reliability and validity, and communication with other professionals.

The usefulness of clinical rating scales is largely constrained by two factors, rater competence and psychometric quality of the rating scale. Rating scales utilize the complex information-processing capabilities of humans in the ascription of a summary judgment regarding the family on particular dimensions; however, this very capacity of humans to integrate diverse information has contributed to the lack of reliability of rating methodology. Thus, for the clinical rating method to be useful in family assessment the following assumptions must hold (Cairns & Green, 1979): (a) raters share with the scale author, and with other raters, a theoretical concept of the quality or attribute to be rated; (b) raters share a concept of which behaviors reflect that quality or attribute; (c) raters are able to detect information relevant to the attribute in the stream of behavior; (d) raters share the same underlying psychometric "scale" (e.g., normal distribution), on which the attribute will be judged; and (e) raters have sufficient knowledge about the comparison or reference group to place observed behavior on a distribution. These rater assumptions are enhanced, of course, with rater training as well as with careful construction of the rating scale. Rating scales with clearly defined and behaviorally defined anchor points, equal psychological distance between anchor points, and an adequate number of anchor points, increase the likelihood that ratings will be reliable. A review of family clinical rating scales found evidence of validity to be emerging but incomplete, primarily as a function of the recency with which these measures have been developed (Carlson & Grotevant, 1987a). For additional discussion of clinical rating scales of family functioning, the reader is referred to Carlson and Grotevant (1987a) and Grotevant and Carlson (1989).

Coding schemes. The most objective and scientific observation method in family assessment involves the use of a family interaction coding scheme. Coding schemes refer to the precise recording of the precise actions of individuals in a group, the analysis of which is essential for understanding processes of interaction (Grotevant & Carlson, 1989). There are many research advantages to the use of family interaction coding schemes. Observational procedures require fewer inferences, are less susceptible to confounding influences, have greater face validity and generalizability, preserve the actions of family members for multiple analyses, are flexible in providing quantitative indices, are usable by nonprofessionals, and have enhanced reliability. In short, observation codes provide the most "objective" view of the family, and research aimed at determining the contingent patterns of interaction within families typically requires formal observation as the primary method of data collection.

Many of the characteristics of family interaction coding schemes that enhance the objectivity of this form of family assessment also create limitations. The recording of precise actions of family members in an interaction with one another is typically more costly than other family assessment or observation methods, even with the availability of advanced technology. For example, on a recent project by the author the recording, transcribing, and coding of a 20-minute family interaction required approximately 100 hours per family. The higher cost of using coding schemes frequently limits observation of the family to a single session, which may be unrepresentative of the family's behavior. Another limitation of observation coding schemes is their microanalytic perspective on the family. The precise recording of actions and reactions among family members requires a limited number and scope of behavioral codes. Every decision to limit the scope of behavior to be coded is likely to enhance reliability, and to afford greater power in data analysis, but at the cost of comprehensiveness. Analysis of data derived from coding schemes, particularly if sequential analytic or log linear methods are used, can require a large number of events, thus limiting the complexity of coding schemes and between family member analyses.

Additional threats to the validity of coding family interaction behaviors are related to the setting, task, reactivity, and recording method of the observation. To enhance reliability of the coding and comparability across families, codings of family interaction usually require consistency of task, setting, number, and role of family members. All of these controls for purposes of reliability may alter the pattern of family interaction that is desired by the researcher. Laboratory settings, for example, may constrain negative interactions among family members. Similarly, if the focus of the research is family conflict, it will be essential to develop a procedure and task that elicit conflict. The presence of the observer as well as the intrusiveness of the recording procedure are also likely to affect the family's interaction. Thus, the family researcher has numerous decisions to consider in coding family interaction.

In sum, family observation coding schemes are a method well suited to the investigation of well-focused, theoretically based research for which the goal is describing and analyzing the contingent behaviors of individuals within family relationships. Coding schemes have typically posed greater challenge to researchers attempting to capture molar qualities of the family system. Generally the use of systematic observation coding schemes is too costly for use in family assessment for clinical practice. For additional information on reliability and validity issues with family interaction coding schemes the interested reader is referred to Grotevant and Carlson (1987, 1989).

Self-Report Methods

In contrast with observation methods of family assessment, which are considered to provide an "outsider" perspective of the family (Olson, 1977), self-report methods provide the "insider" view of family functioning. Self-report measures are defined as standardized questionnaires which provide information about individual family members' subjective reality or experience, including perceptions of self and of other family members, attitudes regarding family (roles, values, etc.), and satisfaction with family relationships (Huston & Robins, 1982). Self-report measures of family relationships have numerous advantages including reliability, and ease of administration and scoring, as well as the demonstrated link between individuals' subjective reality and their behavioral interaction patterns (e.g., Gottman, 1979). In addition, self-report measures yield quantitative data useful for both research and clinical goals. Most importantly, family members, by virtue of their participation in the system, have access to a unique body of information that is unavailable to the clinician. Because family members see each other behave in a variety of situations, they may be able to differentiate cross-situational stabilities from situational effects on each others' behavior. Family members also observe one another over an extended period of time and, therefore, have the opportunity to differentiate temporally stable from temporally unstable behaviors. Finally, family members observe behaviors that are not displayed in public and not available to outside observers. Self-report measures of family functioning, therefore, are often the assessment method of choice for research or treatment evaluations involving families.

Issues in the use of family self-report instruments center on psychometric quality and clarity regarding the measurement goal. Regarding psychometric quality, Grotevant and Carlson (1989) concluded that researchers and clinicians must be judicious in their use of measures as the stability and validity of many measures is not yet well determined. Another issue in the use of self-report measures of the family is the discrepancy between the unit of perception, that is, the subjective evaluation of an individual family member, and the unit of inquiry, the whole family unit. The extent to which an individual respondent can provide useful information about systems variables is an important consideration in using this method in family research. Self-report measures are the method of choice only when the research question concerns the attitudes and comparisons of different family members' points of view; these measures cannot be used as a

true indicator of whole family characteristics without statistical manipulation, as will be discussed later (see Step 5) in this chapter.

In summary, self-report measures of family functioning are a
useful method for the assessment of individual members' subjective
evaluations of their family and family relationships. Although these
measures purport to be measures of the whole family unit, and utilize
constructs that are, in fact, consistent with characteristics of the whole
family, self-report questionnaire scores represent the perceptions of
individuals.

Multiple Method Approaches

Faced with multiple choices of measures and methods, the re-
searcher/clinician may seek a "battery" approach to family assessment. Several models of family functioning have been empirically
derived and include multiple methods of family assessment, which,
when used together, form a family assessment battery. The objective
of these models, for the most part, has been the assessment and
classification of family functioning on a variety of dimensions, which
may include, but are not limited to, the ideals proposed by the various
schools of family treatment (Becvar & Becvar, 1993). Although
multiple conceptual models of family functioning have been eluci-
dated, only a limited number have been operationalized in measures.
Models which have developed family assessment measures useful to
the clinician as well as the family researcher include the following:
Beavers Systems Model (Beavers & Hampson, 1993), Circumplex
Model of Marital and Family Systems (Olson, 1993); McMaster Model
(Epstein, Bishop, Ryan, Miller, & Keitner, 1993), and Process Model of
Family Functioning (Steinhauer, Santa-Barbara, & Skinner, 1984).
Each of these models includes a self-report measure of whole family
functioning as well as a clinical rating scale to be completed by
clinicians based on their observations of the family in interaction. In
addition, several of the models have developed interview protocols
and/or interaction tasks designed to capture data on the dimensions
of interest in the model. Although not yet adequately developed to
provide a comprehensive assessment of the family, these models of
family functioning with their related measures provide the beginnings of useful batteries for conducting a family assessment.

STEP 4: PERFORMING THE ASSESSMENT

Evident in the previous discussion are the numerous choices
available to the family researcher and clinician in methods of family
assessment and measures or techniques within each methodological

group. Each method has noteworthy strengths and limitations. Limited empirical data exist to support the predictive differential validity of particular measures or methods of evaluating family functioning (Grotevant & Carlson, 1989). Nor does there currently exist a theoretical consensus regarding the salient characteristics of the family to be assessed that predict or relate systematically to psychopathology (Grotevant, 1989). Given the state of the science, a multisystem-multimethod (MS-MM) approach to family assessment has been proposed as a solution, compatible with the hierarchical nature of the family organization, by which to minimize error that may occur with the use of a single measure (Cromwell & Peterson, 1983; Peterson & Cromwell, 1983). An MS-MM family assessment would include the use of multiple family evaluation methods across multiple family system levels. In a multisystem-multimethod assessment of the family context, Cromwell and Peterson (1983) indicate that the following steps are appropriate:

1. Conceptualize the family in terms of hierarchical levels.
2. Identify the system level(s) hypothesized to be most involved in the problem behavior.
3. Identify methods that correspond with the system level to be evaluated.

Given the lack of correspondence between insider and outsider perspectives on the family (Olson, 1977), it would also seem appropriate to include measures that capture both perspectives.

In a multisystem-multimethod analysis, data from each system level and method are juxtaposed and examined both within and across system levels for convergence and divergence of data. Assessment data examined across methods of collecting information about the marital subsystem, for example, might show a convergence of data regarding marital strain but a divergence of opinion between spouses about either the source or degree of strain. Self-report data, for example, might reveal that the husband evaluates his wife moderately negatively on task accomplishment whereas the wife is extremely dissatisfied with the level of affective involvement in the relationship. Observations of interaction might converge with self-report data finding the marital couple distant, guarded, or argumentative. Data examined across the levels of the family system reveal information about concerns, as well as strengths, that cut across relationships, as well as assist in focusing on specific subsystem dysfunction. For example, if the marital conflict were being detoured through a child, data might reveal a reported lack of cohesion across all levels of the family system but indicate that conflict is reported only in the father-adolescent relationship. The consistencies and discrepancies in data collected across multiple methods and system levels, interpreted in relation to the presenting problem, can suggest diagnostic hypotheses and treatment goals.

An example of the MS-MM approach within a single theoretical framework can be seen in the development of the *Family Assessment Measure* (FAM-III; Skinner, Steinhauer, & Santa-Barbara, 1983, 1984). The self-report measure developed by these family researchers assesses the multiple system levels of the family by creating three versions of the measure: a whole family scale, a dyadic scale, and an individual [within the family] scale. All three scales contain the same constructs regarding family functioning based on the Process Model of Family Functioning (Steinhauer, Santa-Barbara, & Skinner, 1984; Steinhauer, 1987). Items that comprise the subscales are also similar across the three versions with wording altered to reflect the unique perspective of each level (e.g., the individual, dyadic relationship, and whole unit). The *Family Assessment Measure Clinical Rating Scale* (FAM-CRS; Skinner & Steinhauer, 1986), to be used in conjunction with the self-report measure, provides an outsider method of evaluation. The FAM-CRS is dimensionally consistent with the self-report measure and intended to be used with a structured clinical interview based on the Process Model (see Grotevant & Carlson, 1989, p. 264). Thus, within a single theoretical framework three methods of family assessment have been developed, which tap both the insider and outsider perspectives of family functioning and cross the hierarchical family levels of individual, dyad, and whole system.

Olson (1988) has built on Cromwell's multisystem family assessment model and extended it to the measurement of treatment effectiveness. As such the assessment process is focused on capturing family change. Consistent with Cromwell and Peterson (1983), Olson recommends conceptualizing the family as a hierarchical system that includes the individual, marital, parent-child relationship, the family system, and the community level. In addition, he proposes three major categories of therapeutic domains that should be measured in an evaluation of treatment effectiveness: (a) symptoms and presenting problems, (b) mediating goals or first-order change, and (c) ultimate goals or second-order change (see Table 1).

As a measure of symptoms and presenting problems, Olson (1988) recommends the use of checklists of issues or problems. Goal Attainment Scaling is recommended as a method of measuring mediating goals, that is, therapist-specific goals for each family system level. It is expected that mediating goals will be unique to each family

Table I. Baseline and Outcome Variables for Family Therapy Studies

	Behaviors and Problems of Concern	Intermediate: First-Order Change	Long-Range: Second Order Change
Person	Psychiatric Disorders	Treatment goals developed in consultation with family	Alleviation of presenting problems/symptoms
Marriage	Relationship issues	Couples identify strengths and weaknesses of relationship	Reorganization of the marital system
Parenting	Parent-child issue	Parent and child skills needs are identified	Facilitation of parent-child system that enhances the child
Family Systems	Family subsystems and immediate environment	Goal attainment scaling (GAS) could be used to specify goals.	Family system boundaries become clear
Social Systems	Social supports and networks	An ecomap is used to display available social support	Links to support change experience of family

Note. Based on "Capturing Family Change: Multi-System Level Assessment" by D. H. Olson, 1988, in L. C. Wynne (Ed.), *The State of the Art in Family Therapy Research: Controversies and Recommendations.* New York: Family Process Press.

and therapeutic modality, and therefore, the use of a standardized measurement is not appropriate. Olson defines ultimate goals as the desired outcomes of treatment that would relate to changes in the underlying dynamics of the family system. Ultimate goals, according to Olson, could appropriately be measured with an existing "common battery." Several recommendations for family assessment are highlighted by Olson's model. These include the importance of the following: (a) measuring the complexity of the family system; (b) including all relevant members of the family system in the assessments; (c) using both behavioral and self-report methods; and (d) including multiple assessments during the treatment process as well as the traditional pre-post assessment design.

Building on the work of Cromwell and Peterson (1983) and Olson (1988), Carlson (1991) proposed a multisystem-multimethod clinical framework for assessing the family when the presenting problem concerns a child. Consistent with the frameworks discussed, the family is conceptualized hierarchically and both observational and self-report methods are used. Five principal areas of family functioning are viewed as relevant to assess: (a) family transactional patterns; (b) family developmental stage; (c) family stress and coping; (d) family members' subjective conditions; and (e) the presenting problem/symptoms. In addition, these domains of family functioning are evaluated within both the intergenerational and current sociocultural context. The methods used to assess these five areas and the family system level to which they are targeted are described in Table 2.

Information about each domain is obtained from multiple methods. For example, family members' subjective reality is obtained both through self-report measures, interviews, and interaction task procedures. Family members' evaluation of relationships may be consistent or inconsistent across these methods. In families where conflict is avoided, for example, data derived from self-report measures may give a more distressed evaluation than behavioral data. It is also

Table 2. Sample Multisystem/Multimethod Approach to Family
          Assessment with Children

	Family	Marital Dyad	Parent-Child Dyad	Individual Member
Outsider Perspective: observation methods	Family Interaction Tasks & Clinical Rating Scale			
Insider Perspective: self-report methods				
adolescents & adults	FAM-Global	FAM-Dyadic	FAM-Dyadic PSI	CBCL
children under 11 yrs.	FAT		PPI	
Insider/Outsider	Initial Family Interview & Goal Attainment Scale			

Note. FAM = Family Assessment Measure; CBCL = Child Behavior Checklist; PSI = Parenting Stress Index; FAT = Family Apperception Test; PPI = Parenting Perception Inventory.

assumed that functioning in one domain is interrelated with functioning in another domain, and measures are likely to provide information about more than one domain. For example, the Child Behavior Checklist (Achenbach & Edelbrock, 1983) is a measure of individual child symptomatology but also a measure of parent(s) subjective reality.

The process of conducting the assessment described involves two sessions with the whole family, one 2-hour assessment session and a second hour-long initial interview session. Parents complete background questionnaires on individual and family history prior to the assessment sessions. Within the initial session, the family completes as a group the genogram (to assess transgenerational patterns) (McGoldrick & Gerson, 1985) and the ecomap (to assess stress and coping in the family's interface with its community) (Holman, 1983). Family members are next separated to complete individually self-report measures appropriate to their age, role, and the family's unique organization (see Table 2). Finally, family members complete a series of five 5-minute interaction tasks derived from the assessment procedures of Beavers (Beavers, n.d.). In a second session, an initial interview focused on the presenting problem is conducted with the family. Both the interaction tasks and the initial interview are videotaped and rated by two clinicians using a clinical rating scale. Assessment data are collected before, during and after treatment. Pre and post data are analyzed, as described above, with a view to the consistency and inconsistency of patterns and themes across methods and system levels. Data are integrated into a pretreatment and posttreatment report. The goal of the integration in the pretreatment report is creation of hypotheses regarding symptomatology that will form the basis for treatment. The goal of integration of data in the posttreatment report is to measure change in the system as well as to develop further treatment recommendations. Ongoing therapy is evaluated with goal attainment scaling as described by Olson (1988).

A final step in performing the family assessment is the provision of feedback to the family regarding the assessment results. Interestingly, this step in the assessment process has been almost completely ignored within the family field. As noted in previous discussion, this may reflect the ambivalence with which assessment is viewed by family clinicians and its perceived incompatibility with many family treatment models. Additionally, many popular family therapy models (e.g., structural, strategic) are based on the careful manipulation of feedback to the family system such that change can be maximized and resistence minimized. Thus, a search for guidelines in the communication of assessment data to families yielded only one publication which carefully addressed this topic (see chapter 3 in Sanders & Dadds, 1993); it is based theoretically in behavioral family intervention. Although embedded within a behavioral paradigm, the communication process outlined by Sanders and Dadds (1993) appears useful to the communication of family assessment data regardless of theory base.

Sanders and Dadds (1993) recommend sharing assessment findings with family members to increase treatment compliance, treatment commitment, and generalization of learning. As noted, " This process of sharing hypotheses and inferences with clients promotes better, more open, informed participation and collaborative problem solving" (Sanders & Dadds, 1993, p. 94). Regarding guidelines for sharing assessment data, these authors note that the information shared should be based on valid and reliable measures, not only on a clinical interview. They further recommend several steps in the preparation of data for communication. The first is the integration of all available assessment information into a coherent, empirically derived formulation (set of propositions or hypotheses) about the nature of the problem and its causes. This formulation should also include hypotheses of family members regarding the nature and cause of the problem. Next, this clinical formulation must be translated into language that is comprehensible to the family, including children, when appropriate. Finally, the therapist must be sensitive to the possible emotional impact of the data and use the data to introduce treatment goals and procedures. Sanders and Dadds (1993) present a step-by-step one-session process, which they term "a guided participation model of information giving," as a means by which to accomplish their noted goals.

In summary, several variations of the multisystem-multimethod assessment of the family have been presented. Although the MS-MM approach resolves some of the challenges of family assessment, it is not without it critics. Reiss (1983) has argued that the integration of such diverse data as in a multisystem-multimethod matrix requires specific theories to relate, for example, social processes in families to processes in marriage, to processes in the parental subsystem, and both of those to processes in the parent-child relationship, sibling relationship, and individual child and adult functioning. This lack of theory development seriously limits current family assessment practice. Of the existing family assessment measures, those developed in conjunction with The Process Model of Family Functioning (i.e., the Family Assessment Measure-III and the Family Assessment Measure Clinical Rating) come closest to operationalizing the interface between the multiple system levels of the family. According to Steinhauer (1987), "The process model....emphasizes understanding each parameter [of the family] as a separate entity and also stresses the effects of ongoing interaction at the interfaces between contiguous parameters and subsystems" (p. 86). The process model, however, can be criticized because dimensions of process across family system levels are shared, as reflected in the use of identical constructs across measures of subsystems, possibly at the expense of important distinctions in subsystem processes. In fact, the lower reliability of the self in family scale (see Skinner et al., 1984) may provide some support to this argument.

Another concern for clinicians or researchers attempting to follow the MS-MM model is the lack of adequate measures within a single theoretical framework to complete an assessment of the family. As noted above, only one family functioning model has developed measures applicable across family subsystems. This dilemma is particularly acute for the family with young children as no family functioning models have developed measures for elementary-school-aged children. Thus, a comprehensive evaluation of the family using the MS-MM model requires mixing measures developed from distinct (albeit frequently systems based) theoretical models. As noted earlier, low correspondence across family measures for identical constructs has been common (see Grotevant & Carlson, 1989, for discussion). A comparison across family relationships then must consider that differences obtained may be a reflection of the distinctiveness of the measures.

In summary, several issues in the analysis and interpretation of data using the MS-MM framework have been discussed. These include concerns regarding the comparability of data collected across system levels that are derived from measures that are not theoretically compatible, the lack of an accepted theoretical model for the effect of relationships on relationships within the family, and the lack of adequate measures for certain subsystems. These all reflect current limitations of available family assessment measures. In addition to the limitations of existing family assessment measures, however, there are challenges inherent in the analysis of family assessment data, even when the measure used is psychometrically adequate. Central to this issue is the coordination in data analysis of the multiple perspectives of family members. Proposed resolutions of this challenge will next be discussed.

STEP 5: ANALYZING FAMILY ASSESSMENT DATA

Several methodological problems are inherent in the analysis of family assessment data, and the failure to resolve these problems has been noted to confound studies relating family processes and individual pathology. Clearly summarized by Cole and McPherson (1993), the methodological problems include: (a) the uncritical use of global family constructs; (b) the overreliance on a single informant in research; and (c) the underutilization of statistical techniques that enable the researcher to control for unwanted sources of shared method variance. The uncritical use of global constructs refers to the traditional practice of combining individual ratings of family characteristics into a family unit score. The overreliance on single informants in research raises the question of whether any single family member can be representative of a family shared perspective. Finally, these authors argue for the use of statistical techniques that tease apart shared and nonshared variance in the reports of family members as a proposed solution to the first two methodological problems.

The first concern posed by Cole and McPherson (1993) is the use of global as opposed to specific family constructs. As has been noted throughout this chapter, the emphasis of systems theory on the premise that the whole is greater than the sum of the parts has resulted in the development of numerous self-report measures designed to measure characteristics of the whole family. When data are collected from more than one member on aspects of the family, however, the researcher will inevitably get a somewhat distinctive report from each person. The essence of the dilemma is whether to regard a family member's report about the family system to be the unique and subjective perspective of an *individual* or whether it might reflect objective traits and processes of the family as a *system* that could be confirmed by other knowledgeable informants such as outside observers.

The traditional solution to the dilemma of creating a family construct from multiple individual family member perspectives on self-report data has been the creation of a family score by aggregating individual scores. Some researchers pool and average scores across the individual family members to create a family unit score. This strategy has serious limitations. It rests on the assumption that all members perceptions are equally valid and can distort important deviations on the part of a single family member(s) from others in the family (Larsen & Olson, 1990). Other proposed solutions to the problem of multiple perceptions, therefore, are the derivation of discrepancy scores or ratio scores; however, these solutions continue to leave unresolved the possibility that the perspective of a particular member is more related to the individual pathology than the discrepancy between members and do not allow an assessment of the reliability of the individual perspectives.

The theoretical rationale for aggregation is the operationalization of a family variable. The methodological rationale for aggregating over multiple raters is that systematic variance due to the shared perceptions of the raters will cumulate when reports from different raters are combined, whereas the random effects of errors in measurement will not cumulate (Kenny & Berman, 1980). It is expected that, compared to the report of a single rater, the ratio of true-score variance to error variance (i.e., reliability) will improve with aggregation across multiple raters, and, in fact, aggregating over multiple family members' reports has been found to result in improved precision of measurement (Schwartz, Barton-Henry, & Pruzinsky, 1985).

The degree to which individual family members share perspectives on the family environment, and/or the degree to which one family member's perspective is more valid than another, has become of central concern to family researchers. Recent studies of nonclinical families consistently find that family members hold distinctive viewpoints regarding their family milieu and family relationships (Carlson, Cooper, & Spradling, 1991; Feldman, Wentzel, & Gehring, 1989; Hampson & Beavers, 1987; Hampson, Beavers, & Hulgus, 1989; Noller & Callan, 1986). Furthermore, in conflict with the clinical viewpoint that disagreement among family members regarding their family milieu signifies stress and dysfunction, (Moos & Moos, 1986; Olson, McCubbin, Barnes, Larsen, Muxen, & Wilson, 1983), low intermember agreement about family relationships has been reported to be typical of families rated by clinicians as the most, not least, healthy (Hampson, Beavers, & Hulgus, 1989). Thus, the distinctiveness of family member's perceptions regarding their family may be a critical dynamic to measure in relation to outcome variables.

These findings support the second concern noted by Cole and McPherson (1993), the overreliance on a single informant in family research. As noted by these authors, implicit in this strategy is the assumption that the informant's view of the family converges with that of other members and that the informant is unbiased in his or her view of the family. Because convergence of perspectives among family members is uncharacteristic, it cannot be assumed that any one perspective represents an unbiased view of the family. In short, it would only appear appropriate to collapse the scores of individual family members into a single family construct when little or no information about the individual (or subsystem) is lost (Cole & McPherson, 1993). This is a decision that requires a statistical solution.

The third principal concern of family assessment expressed by Cole and McPherson (1993) was the underutilization of statistical techniques that enable the researcher to control for unwanted sources of shared method variance. A recent solution to the problem is the use of structural equations analysis to distinguish variance attributable to individual members of the family, the family as a system, and to error (Cook, Kenny, & Goldstein, 1991; Cole & Jordan, 1989; Cole & McPherson, 1993; Kenny & LaVoie, 1985). The following discussion of structural equations analysis is based on a previous articulation of this topic by the author (Carlson, Cook, & Cooper, 1995).

Structural equations analysis permits the separation of individual and shared perspectives on family functioning such that the presence of systematic individual respondent effects can be determined. In order to distinguish variance due to the unique perspective of family members from variance due to the common or group effects in family self-report data, one must first specify what is meant by a group effect. In the present context, a group effect is the degree to which the reports of multiple family members are in agreement. Another way to express this is to say that the family member's reports are all measures of the same family construct, although their reliabilities and validities might vary. This type of agreement can be operationalized within a structural equations analysis by specifying that all the ratings of a particular construct load on a common factor. By way of contrast, variance unique to the individual is indicated by the extent to which a family members' rating is not a function of the common underlying factor. The path model in Figure 1 presents these ideas graphically.

In the model the shared or family unit perspectives, indicated by the large circles, are unobserved or latent variables. The individual perspectives or reports of mothers, fathers, and adolescents (indicated by squares) are specified as imperfect indicators of the shared perspective on family conflict and control. The single-headed arrows directed from the latent variables of family conflict and family control to the observed scores (i.e., individual reports) reflect the hypothesis that family members' scores are caused by the family's actual levels of conflict and control (i.e., the intersubjective reality). The estimated value of these effects are factor loadings. In the completely standardized model, the factor loadings can be interpreted as reliability estimates. In other words, the extent to which a rater is a reliable judge of the family's conflict or control is estimated by the extent to which his or her rating is predicted by the underlying factor. The residuals (E1 through E6) represent the extent to which the individual reports are not predicted by the common perspective. Conceptually, the residuals represent sources of variability that are unique to the individual family member. These sources may include errors of measure-

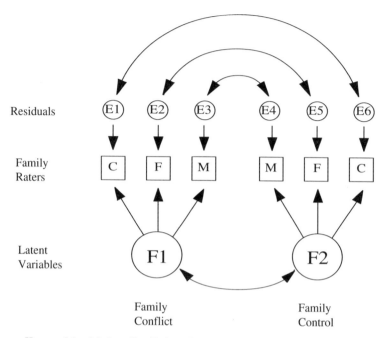

Residuals

Family
Raters

Latent
Variables

Family
Conflict

Family
Control

Key: M = Mother, F = Father, C = Child.
Curved lines with double arrows are correlations.
Straight lines with single arrows are structural paths.

Figure 1.

ment and method variance (i.e., social desirability and acquiescence response sets), as well as variance due to the unique perspective of the rater. If a family member's rating of the family on a particular domain were perfectly predicted by the latent variable, there would be no residual variance, which would imply both the absence of a unique perspective on the particular construct for that rater and the absence of errors of measurement.

In addition to providing a means to separate individual effects from group effects, structural equations analysis allows one to investigate and control for systematic rater effects. Systematic rater effects are represented in Figure 1 by the correlations between those residuals that are common to a particular individual family member. For example, the correlation between E3 and E4 measures the extent to which the individual effects in mother's ratings of family conflict are associated with her individual effects in rating family control.

In summary, structural equations modelling permits the separation of individual from group or family effects. The latent variables provide an indicator of the family's shared perspective and thus the operationalization of a family variable. The residuals provide a measure of the variance due in part to the unique perspective of the individual family member. Correlations between residuals permit the assessment of systematic rater effects in the data. Systematic rater effects, that is, the tendency of a particular family member to respond consistently regardless of dimension, unless examined, can result in spurious correlations between aggregate family unit variables (Kenny & Berman, 1980).

Structural equation modeling was used with self-report data by Cole and McPherson (1993) to separate individual and subsystem (not family unit) effects in an assessment of the family environment as it relates to adolescent depression. Using this method of data analysis these researchers were able to ascertain that mothers were the most valid reporters of the family environment and adolescents least valid. They also found significant differences between all family subsystems in their perceptions of family variables underscoring the distinctiveness of subsystems and measurement of that distinctiveness. Finally, characteristics of specific subsystems were found to differentially relate to the adolescent's depression. Moreover, these researchers suggest, based on results of their analyses, that family researchers consider examining family subsystem structure differently depending on the phenomenon under investigation. For example, family subsystems were found to correlate highly on the dimension of interpersonal conflict; however, they diverged considerably on perceptions of cohesion. These data certainly suggest that within this sample some constructs could more appropriately be viewed as relational or subsystem constructs where scores could perhaps be aggregated, whereas others clearly reflected individual perspectives and aggregation would create spurious correlations between variables.

Structural equations modelling was used by the author (Carlson, Cook, & Cooper, 1995) to separate individual and whole family unit effects in an assessment of the family environment as it related to teacher ratings of adolescent school competence. Results indicated that both a unique and a consensus or a shared family perspective on several family variables could be identified. In addition, the shared perspective of control in the family was significantly related to teacher ratings of the adolescents behavior in school. Although a latent family variable was confirmed for key characteristics, systematic rater bias on the part of the adolescents was also supported by the data, with adolescent's responding differently from parents, regardless of the family characteristic to be measured.

Taken together these two studies provide an illustration of the usefulness of the structural equations approach to the analysis of family self-report data Structural equations modelling has several advantages. It provides a valid method for the integration of individual data into a family variable. It permits examination of systematic rater effects, that is, the consistent discrepancy of one family member from the others. It can be used to determine the correct level of analysis regarding an outcome variable. Because structural equations analysis corrects for attenuation due to measurement error, it provides more adequate control for the effects of third variables. In addition, the structural equations approach, although used with self-report data in the current examples, is applicable to a broad range of family research questions and designs (see, for example, Cook & Goldstein, 1993; Kenny & Berman, 1980). There is, however, a significant disadvantage to structural equations analysis, that is, the necessity of a large sample size. A sample of 100, for example, is considered small. Thus, structural equations modelling is more relevant to family assessment for purposes of research than clinical practice.

Conclusion

It has been the purpose of this chapter to examine the theoretical and practical issues related to family assessment in research and clinical practice with particular attention paid to the challenges inherent in evaluating the family as a systemic whole. Illustrated throughout the chapter, the family researcher/clinician has numerous choices and few clear guidelines at each step in the assessment process. At Step 1, the importance of being clear about the goals of family assessment was underscored, as these may differ somewhat in the research versus clinical setting. In Step 2, clarity regarding one's theoretical perspective was emphasized, because when to assess, how to assess, and what methods will be used in family assessment are strongly influenced by theoretical orientation. Moreover, multiple theoretical perspectives have in the past, and continue in the present, to influence the development of family assessment measures. Without a commonly accepted theory of family process and functioning, theoretical clarity for both the researcher and clinician becomes essential to the communication and comparability of family assessment results across samples. In Step 3, selecting measures, the choices in methods of family assessment were presented with an emphasis on the two broad categories of observation and self-report methods. Advantages and limitations of all methods were noted and must be considered in selection. In Step 4, performing the family assessment, the multisystem/multimethod of family assessment was recommended for clinicians operating within the systems framework as a way to capture processes at multiple levels and from multiple perspectives (insider and outsider) of the family system. This is viewed as the "best possible" solution given the current state of family assessment development. As noted, the relationships between family levels and perspectives have not been adequately explained theoretically nor has a battery of measures been developed that permits a multisystem/multimethod evaluation within a single family functioning model. The multisystem/multimethod approach, which emphasizes a comprehensive evaluation of the family, was not uniformly recommended for family assessments conducted in research as the research questions may not necessitate such a broad assessment. Finally, in Step 5 of the assessment process, analysis and interpretation of the data, the use of the structural equations approach was discussed as an analytic method that permits the separation of individual from subsystem or individual from whole family system effects. The ability to differentiate the variance attributable to the parts versus the whole of the family system greatly enhances the validity of research findings regarding the linkages between family processes and individual outcomes.

This is an exciting, but also unruly, period in family theory and its related domain of family assessment. Despite the optimism of the early family studies researchers that a unified theory of the family would be forthcoming, none has gained acceptance. Family systems theory has perhaps been the most unifying theory, clearly providing a useful framework for clinicians; however, it remains challenging to researchers who attempt to operationalize systemic constructs and test systemic premises. Furthermore, greater, not less, diversity appears to be on the horizon for the field of family psychology. Diversity in family assessment can be expected as researchers attempt to explain processes in nontraditional family forms and within a multicultural social milieu. Diversity in family assessment is also anticipated as social scientists focus their lense on the interrelatedness of the parts of the family systems, that is, the linkages between individual family members and the whole, members and subsystems, and subsystems with the whole. Finally, the biological revolution in psychology is challenging existing methods and conceptualizations of the family (Bussell & Reiss, 1993). Family assessment in clinical practice and research can no longer exclude consideration of genetic effects in measurement and must assume differential experience of the family by different members. Each of the theoretical advances noted challenges conceptualizations of the family as a system to become more precise. Although this is most welcome to the field of family studies and will likely result over time in much improved measurement of family processes, in the interim it would appear that the metaphor of the hydra from Greek mythology, noted by Grotevant and Carlson (1989) in their review of the domain of family assessment, continues to be relevant. As will be recalled, the hydra was a nine-headed monster, and when one head was severed, two new heads grew in its place. Within family psychology researchers have managed to develop psychometrically reliable and valid measures for use in family assessment and thus, one head of the hydra has been severed. In its place, however, emerge significant challenges to the adequacy of existing measures and analytic strategies designed to measure the family as a system.

REFERENCES

Achenbach, T. M., & Edelbrock, C. S. (1983). *Manual for the Child Behavior Checklist and Revised Child Behavior Profile*. Burlington, VT: University of Vermont Department of Psychiatry.

Barker, R. G. (1968). *Ecological psychology: Concepts and methods for studying the environment of human behavior*. Stanford, CA: Stanford University Press.

Beavers, W. R. (n.d.). *Beavers-Timberlawn Family Evaluation Scale and Family Style Evaluation Manual*. (Available from the Southwest Family Institute, 12532 Nuestra, Dallas, TX 75230).

Beavers, W. R., & Hampson, R. B. (1993). Measuring family competence: The Beavers Systems Model. In N. Walsh (Ed.), *Normal family processes* (2nd ed.; pp. 73-103). New York: Guilford.

Becvar, D. S., & Becvar, R. J. (1993). *Family therapy: A systemic integration* (2nd ed.). New York: Allyn & Bacon.

Bednar, R. L., Burlingame, G. M., & Masters, K. S. (1988). Systems of family treatment: Substance or semantics. *Annual Review of Psychology, 39*, 401-434.

Berscheid, E. (1986). Emotional experience in close relationships: Some implications for child development. In W. W. Hartup (Ed.), *Relationships and development* (pp. 135-166). Hillsdale, NJ: Lawrence Erlbaum Associates.

Bertalanffy, L. von (1956). General systems theory. *General Systems Yearbook, 1*, 1-10.

Boss, P. G., Doherty, . J., LaRossa, R., Schumm, W. R., & Steinmetz, S. K. (Eds.). (1993). *Sourcebook of family theories and methods: A contextual approach.* New York: Plenum.

Broderick, C. B. (1993). *Understanding family process.* Newbury Park, CA: Sage.

Bronfenbrenner, U. (1979). *The ecology of human development: Experiments by nature and design.* Cambridge, MA: Harvard University Press.

Bubolz, M. M., & Sontag, M. S. (1993). Human ecology theory. In P. G. Boss, W. J. Doherty, R. LaRossa, W. R. Schumm, & S. K. Steinmetz (Eds.), *Sourcebook of family theories and methods: A contextual approach* (pp. 419-447). New York: Plenum.

Bussell, D. A., & Reiss, D. (1993). Genetic influences on family process: The emergence of a new framework for family research. In F. Walsh (Ed.), *Normal family processes* (2nd ed.; pp. 161-184). New York: Guilford.

Cairns, R. B., & Green, J.A. (1979). How to assess personality and social patterns: Observations or ratings? In R. B. Cairns (Ed.), *The analysis of social interactions: Methods, issues, and illustrations* (pp. 209-226). Hillsdale, NJ: Lawrence Erlbaum Associates.

Carlson, C. I. (1989). Criteria for family asessment in research and intervention contexts. *Journal of Family Psychology, 3*(2), 158-176.

Carlson, C. I. (1991). Assessing the family context. In R. Kampaus & C. R. Reynolds (Eds.), *Handbook of psychological and educational assessment of children. Vol. II: Personality, behavior, and context* (pp. 546-575). New York: Guilford.

Carlson, C. I., Cook, W. L., & Cooper, C. R. (1995). *Separating individual and group effects in self-report family assessment data using structural equations analysis.* Manuscript submitted for publication.

Carlson, C. I., Cooper, C. R., & Spradling, V. Y. (1991). Developmental implications of shared versus distinct perceptions of the family in early adolescence. *New Directions in Child Development, 51,* 13-32.

Carlson, C. I., & Grotevant, H. D. (1987a). A comparative review of family rating scales: Guidelines for clinicians and researchers. *Journal of Family Psychology, 1*(1), 23-47.

Carlson, C. I. & Grotevant, H. D. (1987b). Rejoinder: The challenges of reconciling family theory with method. *Journal of Family Psychology, 1*(1), 62-65.

Carter, E. A., & McGoldrick, M. (1989). *The changing family life cycle: A framework for family therapy* (2nd ed.). New York: Gardner.

Cole, D. A., & Jordan, A. E. (1989). Assessment of cohesion and adaptability in component family dyads: A question of convergent and discriminant validity. *Journal of Counseling Psychology, 36,* 456-463.

Cole, D. A., & McPherson, A. E. (1993). Relation of family subsystems to adolescent depression: Implementing a new family assessment strategy. *Family Psychology, 7*(1), 119-133.

Cook, W. L., & Goldstein, M. J. (1993). Multiple perspectives on family relationships: A latent variables model. *Child Development, 64,* 1377-1388.

Cook, W. L., Kenny, D. A., & Goldstein, M. J. (1991). Parental affective style risk and the family system: A social relations model analysis. *Journal of Abnormal Psychology, 100,* 492-501.

Cromwell, R. E., & Peterson, G. W. (1983). Multisystem-multimethod family assessment in clinical contexts. *Family Process, 22,* 147-171.

Doherty, W. J., Boss, P. G., LaRossa, R., Schumm, W. R., & Steinmetz, S. K. (1993). Family theories and methods: A contextual approach. In P. G. Boss, W. J. Doherty, R. LaRossa, W. R. Schumm, & S. K. Steinmetz (Eds.), *Sourcebook of family theories and methods: A contextual approach* (pp. 1-30). New York: Plenum.

Duvall, E. M. (1957). *Family development.* Philadelphia: Lippincott.

Epstein, N. B., Bishop, D. S., Ryan, C., Miller, I., & Keitner, G. (1993). The McMaster Model: View of healthy family functioning. In N. Walsh (Ed.), *Normal family processes* (2nd ed.; pp. 138-160). New York: Guilford.

Epstein, N., Schlesinger, S. E., & Dryden, W. (Eds.). (1988). *Cognitive-behavioral therapy with families.* New York: Brunner/Mazel.

Feldman, S. S., Wentzel, K. R., & Gehring, T. M. (1989). A comparison of views about family cohesion and power. *Journal of Family Psychology, 3,* 39-60.

Filsinger, E. E. (Ed.). (1983). *Marriage and family assessment.* Beverly Hills, CA: Sage.

Ford, D. H., & Lerner, R. M. (1992). *Developmental systems theory.* Newbury Park, CA: Sage.

Gilgun, J. F., Daly, K., & Handel, G. (Eds.). (1992). *Qualitative methods in family research.* Newbury Park, CA: Sage.

Gottman, J. (1979). *Marital interaction: Experimental investigations.* New York: Academic Press.

Grotevant, H. D. (1989). The role of theory in guiding family assessment. *Journal of Family Psychology, 3,* 104-117.

Grotevant, H. D., & Carlson, C. I. (1987). Family interaction coding schemes: A descriptive review. *Family Process, 26* (1), 49-74.

Grotevant, H. D., & Carlson, C. I. (1989). *Handbook of family assessment.* Guilford Press.

Gurman, A.S., & Kniskern, D.P. (1981). Family therapy outcome research: Knowns and unknowns. *Handbook of family therapy* (pp. 742-776). New York: Bruner-Mazel.

Hampson, R. B., & Beavers, W. B. (1987). Comparing male's and female's perspectives through family self-report. *Psychiatry, 55,* 24-30.

Hampson, R. B., Beavers, W. B., & Hulgus, Y. F. (1989). Insiders and outsiders' views of family. *Journal of Family Psychology, 3,* 118-136.

Hartup, W.W. (1978). Perspectives on child and family interaction: Past, present, and future. In R. M. Lerner & G. B. Spanier (Eds.), *Child influences on marital and family interaction: A life-span perspective* (pp. 23-46). New York: Academic Press.

Hawkins, R. P. (1979). The functions of assessment: Implications for selection and development of devices for assessing repertoires in clincial, educational, and other settings. *Journal of Applied Behavior Analysis, 12,* 501-516.

Hayes, S. C., Nelson, R. O., & Jarrett, R. B. (1987). The treatment utility of assessment: A functional approach to evaluating assessment quality. *American Psychologist, 42,* 963-974.

Hersen, M., & Bellack, A. S. (1984). Research in clinical psychology. In A. S. Bellack & M. Hersen (Eds.), *Research methods in clinical psychology* (pp. 1-23). New York: Pergamon.

Hinde, R. A. (1989). Reconciling the family systems and relationships approaches to child development. In K. Kreppner & R. M. Lerner (Eds.), *Family systems and life-span development* (pp. 149-164). Hillsdale, NJ: Lawrence Erlbaum Associates.

Hinde, R. A., & Stevenson-Hinde, J. (Eds.). (1988). *Relationships within families: Mutual influences.* Oxford, England: Clarendon Press.

Holman, A. M. (1983). *Family assessment: Tools for understanding and intervention.* Beverly Hills, CA: Sage.

Huston, T. L., & Robins, E. (1982). Conceptual and methodological issues in studying close relationships. *Journal of Marriage and the Family, 44*(4), 901-925.

Jacob, T. (Ed.) (1987). *Family interaction and psychopathology.* New York: Plenum.

Jasnowski, M. L. (1984). The ecosystemic perspective in clinical assessment and intervention. In W. A. O'Connor and B. Lubin (Eds.), *Ecological approaches to clinical and community psychology* (pp. 41-56). New York: Wiley.

Karpel, M. A., & Strauss, E. S. (1983). *Family evaluation.* New York: Gardner.

Kelly, H. H., Berscheid, E., Christensen, A., Harvey, J. H., Huston,T. L., Levinger, G. McClintock, E., Peplau, L. A., & Peterson, D. R. (1983). *Close relationships.* San Francisco: Freeman.

Kenny, D. A., & Berman, J. (1980). Statistical approaches to the correlation of correlation bias. *Psychological Bulletin, 88,* 288-295.

Kenny, D. A., & LaVoie, L. (1984). The social relations model. In L. Merkowitz (Ed.), *Advances in experimental social psychology* (vol. 18; pp. 142-182). Orlando, FL: Academic.

Kenny, D. A., & LaVoie, L. (1985). Separating individual and group effects. *Journal of Personality and Social Psychology, 48,* 339-348.

Koman, S.L., & Stechler, G. (1985). Making the jump to systems. In M. P. Mirkin & S.L. Koman (Eds.), *Handbook of adolescents and family therapy* (pp. 1-20). New York: Gardner.

Kramer, J. J., & Conoley, J. C. (Eds.). (1992). *The eleventh mental measurements yearbook.* Lincoln, NE: Buros Institute of Mental Measurements.

Larsen, A. & Olson, D. H. (1990). Capturing the complexity of family systems: Integrating family theory, family scores, and family analysis. In T. W. Draper & A. C. Marcos (Eds.), *Family variables: Conceptualization, measurement, and use* (pp. 19-47). Newbury Park, CA: Sage.

Mannino, F. V., & Shore, M. F. (1984). An ecological perspective on family intervention. In W. A. O'Connor & B. Lubin (Eds.), *Ecological approaches to clinical and community psychology* (pp. 75-93). New York: Wiley.

Margolin, G. (1987). Participant observation procedures in marital and family assessment. In T. Jacobs (Ed.), *Family interaction and psychopathology* (pp. 391-426). New York: Plenum.

McGoldrick, M., & Gerson, R. (1985). *Genograms in family assessment.* New York: Norton.

Minuchin, S. (1974). *Families and family therapy.* Cambridge, MA: Harvard University Press.

Moos, R. H., & Moos, B. S. (1986). *Family Environment Scale manual* (rev. ed.). Palo Alto, CA: Consulting Psychologists Press.

Noller, P., & Callan, V. J. (1986). Adolescent and parent perceptions of family cohesion and adaptability. *Journal of Adolescence, 9,* 97-106.

Nunnally, J. C. (1978). *Psychometric theory* (2nd ed.). New York: McGraw-Hill.

Nye, F. I. (1982).The basic theory. In F. I. Nye (Ed.), *Family relationships: Rewards and costs* (pp. 13-32). Beverly Hills, CA: Sage.

Olson, D. H. (1977). Insiders' and outsiders' views of relationships: Research studies. In G. Levinger & H. Rausch (Eds.), *Close relationships: Perspectives on the meaning of intimacy.* Amherst, MA: University of Massachusetts.

Olson, D. H. (1988). Capturing family change: Multi-system level assessment. In L. Wynne (Ed.), *The state of the art in family therapy research: Controversies and recommendations* (pp. 75-80). New York: Family Process Press.

Olson, D. H. (1993). Circumplex Model of Marital and Family Systems: Assessing family functioning. In F. Walsh (Ed.), *Normal family processes* (2nd ed.; pp. 104-138). New York: Guilford.

Olson, D.H., McCubbin, H.I., Barnes, H.L., Larsen, A.S., Muxen, M. J., & Wilson, M.A. (1983). *Families: What makes them work.* Newbury Park, CA: Sage.

Parsons, T., & Bales, R. F. (1955). *Family, socialization and interaction process.* New York: Free Press.

Patterson, G. R. (1982). *A social learning approach to family intervention: Vol. 3. Coercive family process.* Eugene, OR: Castalia.

Patterson, G. R., & Dishion, T. J. (1988). Multilevel family process models: traits, interactions, and relationships. In R. Hinde & J. Stevenson-Hinde (Eds.), *Relationships within families: Mutual influences* (pp. 283-310). Oxford, England: Clarendon Press.

Peterson, G. W., & Cromwell, R. E. (1983). A clarification of multisystem-multimethod assessment: Reductionism versus wholism. *Family Process, 22,* 173-178.

Reiss, D. (1983). Sensory extenders versus meters and predictors: Clarifying strategies for the use of objective tests in family therapy. *Family Process, 22,* 165-172.

Rodgers, R. H., & White, J. M. (1993). Family development theory. In P. G. Boss, W. J. Doherty, R. LaRossa, W. R. Schumm, & S. K. Steinmetz (Eds.), *Sourcebook of family theories and methods: A contextual approach* (pp. 225-257), New York: Plenum. .

Rowe, D. C. (1983). A biometrical analyis of perceptions of family environment: A study of twin and singleton siblings. *Child Development, 54,* 416-423.

Sameroff, A. J. (1989). Principles of development and psychopathology. In A. J. Sameroff & R. N. Emde (Eds.), *Relationship disturbances in early childhood* (pp. 17-32). New York: Basic Books.

Sanders, M. R., & Dadds, M. R. (1993). *Behavioral family intervention.* New York: Allyn & Bacon.

Schwartz, J.C., Barton-Henry, M. L., & Pruzinsky, T. (1985). Assessing childrearing behaviors with the CRPBI: A comparison of ratings by mother, father, student, and sibling. *Child Development, 56,* 462-479.

Skinner, H.A., Steinhauer, P.D., & Santa-Barbara, J. (1983). The Family Assessment Measure. *Canadian Journal of Community Mental Health, 2,* 91-105.

Skinner, H.A., Steinhauer, P.D., & Santa-Barbara, J. (1984). *The Family Assessment Measure: Administration and interpretation guide.* (Available from Addiction Research Foundation, 33 Russell St., Toronto, Ontario, Canada M5S 2S1).

Skinner, H. A., & Steinhauer, P. D. (1986). *Family Assessment Measure Clinical Rating Scale.* Toronto: Addictions Research Foundation.

Sroufe, L. A., & Fleeson, J. (1986). Attachment and the construction of relationships. In W. W. Hartup & Z. Rubin (Eds.), *Relationships and development* (pp. 51-72). Hillsdale, NJ: Lawrence Erlbaum.

Steinhauer, P. D. (1987). The family as a small group: The Process Model of Family Functioning. In T. Jacob (Ed.), *Family interaction and psychopathology* (pp. 67-115). New York: Plenum.

Steinhauer, P. D., Santa-Barbara, J., & Skinner, H. (1984). The process model of family functioning. *Canadian Journal of Psychiatry, 29,* 77-88.

Strodtbeck, F. L. (1951). Husband-wife interaction over revealed differences. *American Sociological Review, 16,* 468-473.

Touliatos, J., Perlmutter, B. F., & Straus, M. A. (Eds.). (1990). *Handbook of family measurement techniques.* Newbury Park, CA: Sage.

Walsh, F. (Ed.). (1993). *Normal family processes* (2nd ed.). New York: Guilford.

Weber, T., McKeever, J. E., & McDaniel, S. H. (1985). A beginner's guide to the problem-oriented first family interview. *Family Process,* 24(3). 356-364.

Wicker, A. W. (1979). *An introduction to ecological psychology.* Monterey, CA: Brooks/Cole.

Section Two

Investigation of Critical Elements
of Family Dynamics

This section presents information on the assessment of family constructs that are of interest to most families. Dr. James Bray tackles an area of family issues in which some confusion reigns. Bray addresses the dilemma of the multiple processes and constructs involved with family health with definitions of the most salient features of family functioning. These include communication, conflict, problem solving, emotional bonding, affect, roles, differentiation and individuation, triangulation, intimacy, personal authority in the family system, and family stress. Bray identifies valid and reliable self-report measures available to assess each construct and future research directions for the study of family health and distress. He advocates a multi-level approach to family assessment, consideration of cultural and ethnic influences, and precision in the measurement of factors associated with family functioning.

Dr. Jane Close Conoley and Lorrie E. Bryant expand upon Bray's call for a consideration of cultural and ethnic influences by posing the hypothesis that most assessment approaches are based on constructs identified as important in majority culture families. There are no commercially available instruments that were developed with American ethnic minorities or recent immigrants to the United States and none that contain sufficient minority families in the norm groups to allow for clearly valid interpretations. Conoley and Bryant urge clinicians to consider client behaviors in light of cultural expectations for family life, how different groups understand psychological distress, belief systems used by various ethnic groups regarding the etiology of psychological disorders and family dysfunction, acceptable interpersonal and interactional styles to families of color, and the level of acculturation that characterizes the family.

There is a growing interest in assessing the experience of siblings in a family. The role sibling relationships play in child and adult development and in family life is under intense scrutiny in current research literature. It is an area not well investigated by clinicians, but clearly of clinical importance. Michelle Schicke offers a review of methods and procedures used for the purpose of assessing sibling relationships including observation, interview, and rating scales. She addresses some of the problems inherent in current assessment practices and considerations involved in the planning of assessment of sibling relationships and compares the methods with an emphasis on the practical applications of measurement.

Marital quality is analyzed by Dr. David Johnson. He evaluates a number of approaches ranging from subjective reports of marital well-being to those that include both evaluative and behavioral components to those that differentiate between well-adjusting and failing marriages and those suitable for use with cohabiting couples. Johnson concludes his chapter by making five recommendations to scientists in the field regarding the future direction for further study of marital quality in terms of conceptualization, assessment, analysis, and research.

3

ASSESSING FAMILY HEALTH AND DISTRESS: AN INTERGENERATIONAL-SYSTEMIC PERSPECTIVE

James H. Bray

Baylor College of Medicine

In the past several decades there has been a proliferation of interest and development of family systems theories. A unique aspect of a systems perspective is that human problems develop in and because of social interactions usually within the family, rather than solely from some internal process within an individual. A second innovation is the view that human behavior always occurs in a context, and that understanding the context is essential for understanding problem development and resolution. The empirical evaluation and validation of these perspectives has lagged behind theoretical and therapeutic developments. Further, research in this area has been hampered by a lack of reliable and valid measures of constructs of interest. During the 1980s there were significant developments concerning measurement issues and instrument development that facilitate the assessment of family relationships. This chapter will review and discuss issues and methods for assessing family health and distress.

Preparation of this paper was partially supported by Grant RO1 HD22642 from the National Institute of Child Health and Human Development to James H. Bray.

THEORETICAL AND PRAGMATIC ISSUES IN ASSESSING FAMILY HEALTH AND DISTRESS

What is a Healthy Family?

There are as many definitions of healthy and dysfunctional families as there are theories of family functioning and family relationships (Gurman & Kniskern, 1981; Walsh, 1982). Although many of these theories overlap in their perspectives, there are unique aspects that are important to consider in describing healthy family processes. A complete review of theories of healthy families is beyond the scope of this chapter. However, a brief discussion of common aspects of systems approaches to families and family health is provided to orient the reader to basic assumptions of this approach.

A systems perspective to families views each family member as part of an interdependent interactional system that mutually influences other aspects of the family system. Change within one aspect of the system is believed to produce change in other parts of the family through a process of reciprocal feedback and shared meanings between family members. This is referred to as *circular causality* because the focus is on patterns of interactions rather than linear explanations of causality. The *nonsummativity* principle views the entire family as greater than the sum of the parts. It is essential to examine the pattern of relationships rather than just the pieces. Thus, assessing components or subsystems of the family system will not provide a picture of the whole family. All behavior within the family is considered *communication* that transmits interpersonal messages. Communication includes both the content of the messages and the process or how the messages are transmitted (Watzlawick, Beavin, & Jackson, 1967). *Homeostasis* refers to the mechanism by which the family maintains a steady state and equilibrium. Homeostasis is maintained through deviation-reducing feedback loops within the family, similar to how a thermostat regulates the temperature within a room. *Morphogenesis* is the process by which families change and adapt to internal and external demands. Positive feedback loops within the family that are deviation amplifying contribute to system change. *Equifinality* refers to the belief that systems may start at the same beginning, but may end with different outcomes because of system organization and response to the social and environmental context. *Multifinality* is the same principle in reverse; families can start with divergent beginnings and end with the same outcomes. Some systems approaches to families also view family functioning in a multigenerational perspective, with at least three generations considered (Bowen, 1978; Boszormenyi-Nagy & Ulrich, 1981; Kerr, 1981; Williamson & Bray, 1988). Learned patterns of relating, attitudes, unresolved emotional issues, and loyalties are presumed to be passed down through the generations and directly affect current family functioning.

Healthy families promote the well-being and functioning of each individual family member through the maintenance of clear and effective communication, mutually beneficial interactional patterns, clear boundaries between the generations and between family subsystems, and expectations that change over time to the internal demands of family members and external demands of the environment. A balance is maintained between the needs for family stability and change that promotes the health of individual family members. All families have problems as they go through transitions across the life cycle, and dysfunctional families have an inability to make these transitions without experiencing problems (Watzlawick, Weakland, & Fisch, 1974). "An ordinary family; that is, the couple has many problems of relating to one another, bringing up children, dealing with in-laws, and coping with the outside world. Like all normal families, they are constantly struggling with these problems and negotiating the compromises that make a life in common possible" (Minuchin, 1974, p. 6).

Individual pathology or dysfunction is considered to be the result of family dysfunction or the adjustment of an individual to a "crazy" situation (Haley, 1976). The symptoms of the individual may serve to stabilize the family through homeostatic processes (Minuchin, 1974) or because of positive feedback that escalates problematic family interactions (Watzlawick et al., 1974). Psychopathology is an interactional process that is the result of problematic relationships within a family or relevant social context. Unless the family system changes, individual dysfunction will be maintained or alternatively the dysfunction will move to other family members.

Although it is argued that family assessment should flow from solid family theory, a major problem in the family assessment area is the lack of a unified theory of family functioning (Grotevant, 1989). There is no agreed upon family diagnostic system, as with the DSM-IV for individual psychopathology, and there are many disagreements in the field about the constructs or processes that are essential to assess. Some family-oriented theorists argue that formal assessment is unnecessary for clinical practice. Although family assessment is alive and vital, the field is still in the early stages of development.

Assessment of Family Health

Given the different and multiple perspectives on family systems it is not surprising that researchers have struggled to develop reliable and valid measures of concepts from these disparate theoretical formulations. Although there is overlap in definitions of healthy family functioning, there is also diversity in these points of view. Froma Walsh (1982) provides an organizational structure for family theories and discusses four basic perspectives for defining family normality and health:

1. *Asymptomatic family functioning.* If there are no family or individual symptoms, then the family is considered normal or healthy. This comes from the medical-psychiatric perspective that defines normality as the absence of pathology. In this perspective there is no affirmative or positive definition of normal family functioning. Thus, terms such as "nonclinical" or "nonsymptomatic" are used to describe such families.

2. *Optimal family functioning.* This approach defines healthy family functioning in terms of positive or ideal characteristics. Optimally functioning families are at one end of the spectrum with average or asymptomatic families in the middle and dysfunctional families at the other end of the continuum. Specific values and models are proposed to describe healthy families. The models may define specific family structures and/or processes within families. These models and values may or may not be linked to empirical evidence on family functioning.

3. *Average family functioning.* Families are considered healthy and normal if they fit the typical pattern for families at a given time. This point of view comes from a social science perspective with definitions based on statistical norms. For example, in the 1950s divorced families were "abnormal" because they were relatively uncommon, whereas in the 1990s first-marriage families with fathers solely employed are "abnormal" because they are less common. This perspective also differentiates the concepts of health, normality, and absence of symptoms, as a normal family may have problems and symptoms if it fits within the normative group.

4. *Transactional family processes.* Universal processes are conceptualized that characterize all family systems. These basic processes promote the maintenance and growth of families for individual members and in relation to social systems. Normality and health are defined by social contexts that require adaptation over the life cycle.

In addition to these perspectives there are other issues that are important to consider in defining normal family functioning. Similar to individuals, families undergo a series of developmental changes that are referred to as the family life cycle. The family life cycle posits that families undergo predictable and unpredictable changes over time and that families face common issues throughout the life cycle stages (Carter & McGoldrick, 1980). Further, it is apparent that family relations are embedded within cultural and ethnic contexts which may impact the specific family life cycle stages and processes of certain groups of families (McGoldrick, 1982).

Building on previous work in family assessment, categories of family relationships were created to evaluate aspects of family functioning (Fisher, 1976; Grotevant, 1989). These categories provide a means to organize the multitude of concepts and factors related to family functioning.

1. *Family Status*: This includes the makeup of the family (e.g., nuclear family, divorced family, stepfamily) and membership (e.g., couple only, couple with children, single-parent family). Family status has major implications for other aspects of family functioning.

2. *Family Process*: This includes actions, behaviors, and interactions that characterize family relationships. These processes include factors such as differentiation, communication, problem solving, conflict, and control.

3. *Family Affect*: This includes emotional expression and responses among family members. Affect often sets the "tone" for other family processes and has an impact on how family members experience communications.

4. *Family Organization*: This refers to roles and rules within the family and expectations for behavior that contribute to family functioning. Aspects such as boundaries and hierarchy are included as examples of family organization.

MEASUREMENT ISSUES IN ASSESSING FAMILY HEALTH AND DISTRESS

A common problem with family assessment is determining the appropriate unit of analysis for study. A large portion of the research conducted on families is based on data from individual family members, rather than data from multiple sources or direct study of families (Carlson, 1989; Fisher, 1982; Fisher, Kokes, Ransom, Phillips, & Rudd, 1985; Grotevant, 1989). Are self-report measures of family functioning from individual family members representative of the "whole" family or do they simply represent the perceptions of that individual? Is it necessary to have "whole" family assessments to evaluate family health and distress or is it sufficient to have individual perspectives? The answer to these questions depends on the purpose for the assessment and the type of data that need to be collected.

Fisher et al. (1985) provide a classification scheme of family assessment and make suggestions for methods of developing "relational" and "whole" family data. They argue that data from a single person about family relationships occur at the "individual" level of assessment and may not reflect the functioning of the entire family system. In some cases, as in the assessment of marital satisfaction or differentiation from the family of origin, this level of data is appropriate for evaluating certain aspects of the family system. However, it is not truly "family" data as such information is restricted to a single individual's perceptions. Most surveys rely on these types of data, yet the researchers often conclude that the data represent a valid assessment of family functioning. A problem with this approach is illustrated by research on marital satisfaction and marital disruption. As frequently noted, there is often such a discrepancy between spouses that researchers have noted that there are "his and hers" marriages and divorces (Barnard, 1972; Hetherington, Cox, & Cox, 1982).

The second category of data are "relational" assessments. Individual data are collected from two or more family members and the data are then "related" to each through some methodology. These types of data represent descriptive information *about* the family. Individual family responses may be combined to form some composite family assessment or discrepancies between family members' data may be used to assess agreement or satisfaction (Fisher et al., 1985). There are many new sophisticated statistical methodologies for developing relational data, such as multivariate analyses, confirmatory factor analysis, structural equation modeling, and hierarchical linear modeling (Bray, Maxwell, & Cole, 1995; Bray & Maxwell, 1985; Bryk & Raudenbush, 1987; Jöreskog & Sorbom, 1986). Data from these first two categories usually represent "insider's" data, because they include the internal perceptions of individual family members of family functioning (Olson, 1977).

The third category of family assessment is "transactional" data. These types of data reflect an assessment of the entire family unit through some type of observation or structured interaction. It represents system interaction, rather than a sum or combination of the individual parts. These types of data represent assessments of the family as a whole or subsystems within the family. In most cases such information also represents an "outsider's" view of the family, as some observer or rater makes judgments about family interactions. Transactional data can be combined with relational assessments to provide multimethod, multisource measures of family functioning using multivariate statistical methods (see Hetherington & Clingempeel, 1992 for an excellent example).

Another relevant question concerns the necessity of assessing the "whole" family to determine family health (Carlson, 1989). Is it the case that certain dyads or triads within the family may provide better data for this assessment rather than an evaluation of the whole family? Family research from developmental psychology perspectives argues that various family dyads, such as parent-child interactions, may be more useful than examining the family as a whole (Cowan, 1987). The argument is that these approaches provide more valid and more powerful prediction of individual family member's adjustment and development.

Currently, there is no definitive answer to these issues and much more research is needed to evaluate the "best" methods for assessing family health. From a systems perspective, there will probably never be "one" best method, because it is often necessary to evaluate multiple aspects of the family system. In addition, family evaluation also depends on the context, purpose, and specific aspect of family functioning being evaluated. Thus, in some cases it may be more important to evaluate individual family members' perceptions of family process, whereas in other situations it may be necessary to evaluate the family as a unit to understand the multiple family interactions and functioning.

FAMILY FACTORS AFFECTING FAMILY HEALTH AND DISTRESS

There is no "gold standard" measure of family health and distress, such as the Minnesota Multiphasic Personality Inventory (MMPI) for psychological assessments. Given the proliferation of family theories and methodologies for evaluating families, it is not surprising that one single measure has not been developed. Some measures are based on specific family theory, whereas others are empirically developed, and still other measures are a hodge podge of constructs with no clear theoretical basis. However, research on families is beginning to identify key processes that are important to assess for family health and distress. This section discusses these factors and reviews self-report instruments that are available for assessing these processes. A problem within the field is that researchers have given different processes and constructs similar labels or names (Grotevant & Carlson, 1989). Thus, it is sometimes difficult to understand the meaning of particular scales, which may explain why researchers may find different results when supposedly assessing similar constructs. The review of the instruments is not comprehensive and includes those instruments that have acceptable levels of reliability and validity. For more comprehensive reviews of instruments readers are referred to Grotevant and Carlson (1989) and Touliatos, Perlmutter, and Straus (1990).

Communication

Communication within families refers to how verbal and nonverbal information is exchanged among family members (Watzlawick et al., 1967). Communication entails the ability of family members to explain and clarify their needs, wants, and desires (Hetherington, Clingempeel, Eisenberg, Hagan, Vuchinich, & Chase-Landsdale, 1986). This also includes the ability to listen to others so that responses can be appropriate, and further involves solicitation of others' views to clarify their positions. Healthy communication comprises appropriate focus of attention between family members, development of shared and common meanings, and clear and direct verbal exchanges (Epstein & Bishop, 1981; Wynne, Jones, & Al-Khayyal, 1982). Dysfunctional communication is characterized by disturbances in attention between family members, lack of shared meanings, and indirect and masked verbal exchanges. Communication deviance (CD) has been associated with severe forms of psychopathology, such as schizophrenia and personality disorders (Wynne et al., 1982). Less severe forms of communication problems contribute to family conflict and ineffective problem solving, whereas good communication contributes to effective problem solving, emotional bonding, and intimacy between family members.

Measures. Several measures assess communication skills and patterns in families. These measures include assessments of dyadic and whole family communication patterns. The Family Assessment Device (FAD; Epstein, Baldwin, & Bishop, 1983) includes a Communication scale that assesses the whole family. The Parent-Adolescent Communication Scale (PAC; Barnes & Olson, 1982) provides a measure for both adults and adolescents to rate their communication between parent and child, and the Communication scale from the Parent-Adolescent Relationship Questionnaire (PARQ; Robin, Koepke, & Moye, 1990) provides a similar measure. Other scales include the Communication scale from the Family Environment Scale (FES; Moos & Moos, 1974), the Family Communication scale from the Self-Report Family Inventory (SFI; Beavers, Hampson, & Hulgus, 1985), and the Communication scale from the Family Assessment Measure-III (FAM-III; Skinner, Steinhauer, & Santa-Barbara, 1984).

Conflict

Conflict in families ranges from mild forms of disagreement and criticism to physical altercations with significant negative affect and verbal assaults. Conflict is an interactional process that requires at least two family members engaging in a disagreement (Hetherington et al., 1986). Conflict increases as the intensity and reciprocation of the negative interactions increase; conflict tends to decrease when one or both parties attempt to de-escalate the conflict. Alexander (1973) described the escalation and de-escalation of conflict in terms of defensive and supportive communication patterns. When one member of a family makes a statement that is perceived by another member as critical, individuals tend to respond by defending themselves. This defensive response tends to be perceived as a critical statement to the original speaker and tends to invoke another defensive response from the previous speaker. As this cycle of defensive statements continues, the conflict escalates. Alexander found that when a family member responded to a perceived criticism with a supportive statement, the original speaker was more likely to respond with a non-critical, neutral, or supportive statement and conflict did not ensue. Conflict is also related to other individual and family processes, such as family stress, depression and anxiety, poor communication, and poor problem-solving skills.

Early research on family process viewed conflict as always negative and reflective of dysfunctional family relationships. However, recent research by Gottman and colleagues (Buehlman, Gottman, & Katz, 1992; Gottman & Krokoff, 1989) suggests that couples who engage in conflict and resolve the conflicts are more likely to have higher marital satisfaction in the long run than couples who avoid or "stone-wall" against conflict. This process may generalize to other family relationships as well. Conflict is associated with increased psychological and health problems in family members (Doherty & Campbell, 1988). In addition, interparental conflict is strongly predictive of children's behavior problems (Emery, 1982; Hetherington et al., 1982).

Measures. The Conflict Tactics Scale (CTS; Straus, 1979) is a widely used measure of family conflict. The scale measures both verbal conflict and aggression and physical violence. The FES includes a useful family conflict scale that measures verbal aspects of conflict. Other measures of family conflict include the Conflict scale from the Colorado Self-Report Measure of Family Functioning (Bloom, 1985), the Family Conflict Avoidance/ Expression scale of the Structural Family Interaction Scale (SFIS; Perosa, Hansen, & Perosa, 1981), the School Conflict and Sibling Conflict scales from the PARQ, and the Conflict scale from the SFI.

Problem Solving

Effective problem-solving skills include the ability to accurately identify issues, discuss or communicate about those issues, and develop alternative solutions that resolve or help family members cope with these problems. Problem-solving skills and styles are essential for problem resolution within families. Problem solving is a family's ability to resolve difficulties and problems in a manner that maintains effective family functioning (Epstein & Bishop, 1981). Family problems include system maintenance issues, such as money management or rules for relating, and family emotional issues, such as how families handle feelings. Effective problem solving is related to good communication and negotiating skills. Research indicates that all families encounter problems and healthy families do not necessarily have fewer problems than dysfunctional families (Epstein & Bishop, 1981), rather healthy families are better able to resolve the conflict and problems.

Measures. The FAD includes a Problem Solving scale that assesses this dimension. Other scales include the Problem Solving scale from the PARQ, the Task Accomplishment scale from the FAM-III, and the Problem Solving scale from the Family Functioning Index (FFI; Pless & Satterwhite, 1973). The FACES-II Adaptability scale assesses aspects of problem solving and the ability of families to cope with change.

Emotional Bonding

Emotional bonding and cohesion refers to the degree to which family members view themselves as emotionally close or distant from each other (Olson, McCubbin, Barnes, Larsen, Muxen, & Wilson, 1982). This dimension usually ranges from over-involvement or enmeshed to disengagement or disconnection. This factor also includes aspects of family support, involvement, and shared interests and friends. Families that are enmeshed are believed to have diffuse family boundaries, excessive emotional responsiveness, and poorly differentiated family relationships (Minuchin, 1974). Families that are disengaged tend to have rigid family boundaries, a lack of emotional responsiveness, and lack of communication between family subsystems.

Measures. There are several instruments that include scales measuring emotional bonding. The most popular measure is the Cohesion scale from the Family Adaptability and Cohesion Evaluation Scales (FACES; Olson, Bell, & Portner, 1983). The latest version of this instrument is FACES-III. Other measures include the FAD Affective Involvement scale, Family Cohesion scale of the SFI, the Cohesion scale of the FES, the Cohesion scale from the PARQ, the Cohesion scale of the Colorado Self-Report Measure of Family Functioning, and the Parent-Child Cohesion/Estrangement and Enmeshment/Disengagement scales of the SFIS.

Affect

Family affect includes the expression of affection and reactions to affection between family members. It is similar to emotional bonding; however, it also includes affect expression and regulation, rather than just emotional connectedness (Epstein & Bishop, 1981). Family affection is also indicated by the mood or emotional tone of the family. This dimension is usually bipolar from positive to negative mood and may vary in intensity. In addition, the emotional tone may include highly expressive to overly controlled expression of affect within the family. Affect frequently changes the perceived meaning of statements and may override the verbal communication.

Strong negative emotions in families, called "expressed emotion" (EE) have been associated with relapse in families with schizophrenic and depressed patients (Brown, Birley, & Wing, 1972; Vaughn & Leff, 1976; Wynne et al., 1982). EE is critical statements, hostility, and emotional overinvolvement with an identified patient that includes significant negative affect in tone. Emotional statements are also predictive of functional and dysfunctional couple relationships. The work of Gottman and colleagues (Buehlman et al., 1992; Gottman & Krokoff, 1989) indicates that negative emotional statements carry much more weight and have stronger influence on family interactions than positive affect.

Measures. The FAD includes the Affective Responsiveness scale that taps these dimensions. Other scales include the FES Expressiveness scale, the Inventory of Family Feelings (Lowman, 1973), the Affective Expression and Affective Involvement scales from the Family Assessment Measure-III (Skinner et al., 1984), and the Expressiveness scale of the Colorado Self-Report Measure of Family Functioning (Bloom, 1985). Shields, Franks, Harp, McDaniel, and Campbell (1992) recently developed the Family Emotional Involvement and Criticism Scale (FEICS), a self-report measure of expressed emotion.

Roles

Roles are expectations and repetitive patterns of interactions that fulfill family functions and needs (Epstein & Bishop, 1981). Most families have multiple roles to accommodate family needs and expectations. Epstein and colleagues (Epstein & Bishop, 1981; Epstein et al., 1983) describe five groups of roles for families. These include roles for provision of resources (e.g., food, shelter, clothing), roles for nurturance and support (e.g., emotional support, comfort), roles for life skills development (e.g., aspects that promote development and success), roles for maintenance and management of family systems (e.g., leadership, decision-making, or finances), and roles for sexual gratification of marital partners. Healthy family roles include the meeting of all family functions and needs. Dysfunctional family roles might include rigidly defined roles or unmet needs and family functions.

Measures. The FAD Roles scale provides a measure of family roles. The Adult-Adolescent Parenting Inventory (AAPI; Bavolek, 1984) provides a measure of role-reversal in parent-child relations.

Differentiation and Individuation

Individuation or differentiation of self is defined as the person's ability to function in an autonomous manner without feeling unduly responsible for or being impaired by significant others. In addition, differentiation includes the ability to distinguish and control emotional reactions with one's intellectual and cognitive capacities (Bowen, 1978). *Emotional fusion* is at the opposite end of the continuum with individuation. Individuation is a process by which a person differentiates within their relational contexts (Bowen, 1978; Karpel, 1976). The major relational contexts are the family of origin and nuclear family. Emotional fusion represents diminished autonomous functioning in relationships and more emotional reactivity in interactions. Further, it is the tendency to take undue responsibility for others or to avoid taking responsibility for oneself. Emotional fusion is believed to be due to unresolved emotional attachments to the family of origin (Bowen, 1978).

Differentiation of self is a broad construct that encompasses a number of other family processes. Differentiation implies clear and effective communication, appropriate assertiveness, and control of affective moods and responsiveness. In addition, differentiated families have more effective problem-solving skills and can negotiate resolutions to conflictual situations. Families with significant emotional fusion are likely to be emotionally responsive and engage in unresolved conflicts because of poor communication and problem-solving abilities.

Measures. The Personal Authority in the Family System Questionnaire (PAFS-Q; Bray, 1991; Bray, Williamson, & Malone, 1984) provides two scales that measure individuation. The Intergenerational Individuation/ Fusion scale measures individuation with parents, whereas the Spousal Individuation/Fusion scale measures individuation in the marital or adult dyadic relationship. The Differentiation in the Family System Scale (DIFS; Anderson & Sabatelli, 1992) provides another measure of differentiation from the family of origin. In addition, the Differentiation of Self Scale (DOSS; Kear, 1978) provides a measure of differentiation in the current family.

Triangulation

Triangulation is a process of dealing with anxiety and emotional fusion between two people by involving a third person to diffuse tension in the dyad via diversion, collusion, or scapegoating of the third person. Triangulation and fusion both reflect a lack of differentiation of self, although they are different processes (Bray et al., 1984). Triangulation involves three people, whereas emotional fusion occurs between two people. Although the effects of being in an emotionally fused relationship can be detrimental to an individual's functioning (e.g., increased emotional and/or physical problems), fusion is often experienced as positive. In contrast, the triangled person is generally stressed as he/she is pulled between two others. The other two members of the triangle usually experience a decrease in anxiety and tension by the process of triangulation. Bowen (1978) views triangulation as a normal process that is used to cope with emotional fusion, whereas other family systems theorists view triangulation as a pathological process (Haley, 1976; Minuchin, 1974)

Measures. The PAFS-Q provides two measures of triangulation— Intergenerational Triangulation, which measures triangled relationships between an adult-child and parents, and Nuclear Family

Triangulation, which measures triangulation between a married couple and their children. In addition, the SFIS has a scale on Parent Coalition/Cross-Generational Triads and the PARQ includes the Coalitions scale and the Triangulation scale.

Intimacy

Intimacy is a dyadic process that includes voluntary closeness while maintaining distinct boundaries to the self (Bray et al., 1984; Williamson, 1981, 1982). Attachment and involvement in which the individuals lose their unique boundaries, is experienced as involuntary and reflects emotional fusion rather than intimacy. Intimacy includes several components including trust, love-fondness, self-disclosure, and commitment (Larzelere & Huston, 1980; Peplau, 1982). Intimate relationships embody mutual respect and freely initiated self-disclosure while individuation of the participants is maintained. At the other end of the continuum of intimacy is *isolation*. Intergenerational intimacy within the family of origin and intimacy with peers, particularly with one's spouse or significant other are components of relational intimacy. Intimacy is obviously related to emotional bonding and affective expression in families. Yet, this construct measures distinct aspects of family relationships (Bray et al., 1984).

Measures.   The PAFS-Q has two intimacy scales—the Intergenerational Intimacy scale, which measures intimacy between and adult-child and parents, and a Spousal Intimacy scale, which measures marital intimacy. On the Young Adult Version of the PAFS-Q there is a Peer Intimacy scale which measures intimacy between the person and their significant other.

Personal Authority in the Family System (PAFS)

PAFS is a synthesizing construct that represents the inherent tension between differentiation and intimacy within the family of origin and other important personal relationships (Williamson, 1981; Williamson & Bray, 1988). The PAFS continuum includes personal authority at one end and *intergenerational intimidation* at the other. PAFS is reflected by being a differentiated person, through which increased control is exercised over an individual's life course, personal health, and well-being (Bowen, 1978; Karpel, 1976; Kerr, 1981; Williamson, 1982).   PAFS includes reconnection and intimacy with members of the family of origin, while simultaneously maintaining a differentiated stance *within* the family of origin.   This process requires termination of the intergenerational hierarchical boundary which enables a person to relate to all human beings, including one's parents, as peers in the basic human experience (Williamson, 1981, 1982).

Intergenerational intimidation reflects the presence of the intergenerational hierarchy between parents and their offspring and a lack of intimacy and individuation between the adults. Intergenerational intimidation develops from the dependency that children have on their parents. Intergenerational intimidation is reflected by family processes such as triangulation (Bowen, 1978) and covert loyalties (Boszormenyi-Nagy & Ulrich, 1981). Boszormenyi-Nagy and Ulrich argue that children have both conscious and unconscious loyalties to their parents that are expressed through perceived expectations and parental mandates. Children also may protect their parents by finding ways to absolve them of transgressions or failures, for example, by not embarrassing or showing them up in their life functioning (Harvey & Bray, 1991). Therefore, intergenerational intimidation constitutes an obstacle to the adult offspring's development of autonomous and effective functioning through the life course.

Measures. The PAFS-Q has two scales, the Personal Authority in the Family System scale and the Intergenerational Intimidation scale that measure these concepts.

Family Stress

Stress is both a family process and product related to internal family functioning and the family's transactions with the larger social context. Stress is defined as the experience of undesirable, negative life events and everyday hassles (Kanner, Coyne, Schaefer, & Lazarus, 1981; Sarason, Johnson, & Siegel, 1978). Stress is a multi-system construct that ranges from social/family interactions through physiological responses within individuals (Doherty & Campbell, 1988; Dohrenwend & Dohrenwend, 1974). Stress is generated by other family processes, such as conflict and negative emotional expressions. At the same time stress is likely to interact with other family dynamics, such as level of differentiation to produce symptomatic behaviors in family members. In addition, significant stress may interfere with family functions such as communication and emotional bonding.

Measures. Overall family stress is assessed by the Family Inventory of Life Events and Changes (FILE; McCubbin, & Patterson, 1987). The Parenting Stress Index (PSI; Abidin, 1985) measures adult's stress due to parenting; the Life Events Survey (Sarason et al., 1978) measures an individual's perceived life stress; and the Hassles Scale (Kanner et al., 1981) measures daily hassles and disruptions in peoples' lives.

FAMILY IMPACT ON MENTAL AND PHYSICAL HEALTH OF FAMILY MEMBERS

The impact of family status, process, affect, and organization on the health of family members is of increasing concern to researchers, clinicians, and policy makers (Doherty & Campbell, 1988). Researchers investigating illness-behavior interactions have begun to emphasize the role of the family and social relationships in the etiology and maintenance of an individual's physical and emotional health (Doherty & Campbell, 1988; Henao & Grose, 1985).

Family Status

Researchers have found marital and family status are strongly related to the incidence of health problems and response to health and illness (Berkman & Syme, 1979; Bloom, Asher, & White, 1978; Chandra, Szklo, Goldberg, & Tonascia, 1983; Kiecolt-Glaser, Kennedy, Malkoff, Fisher, Speicher, & Glaser, 1988; Tcheng-Laroche & Prince, 1983). The relationship between marriage and health has been supported by a large body of research that investigated both mental and physical health outcomes, which include mortality, health care utilization, physical symptoms and overall health, immune response, psychological symptoms and distress, and suicide (Berkman & Syme, 1979; Bloom et al., 1978; Chandra et al., 1983; Gersten, Friis, & Langer, 1976; Kiecolt-Glaser et al., 1988; Weiss & Aved, 1978; Wertlieb, Budman, Demby, & Randall, 1984). The majority of evidence suggests that marriage is associated with greater health and well-being and that marital separation is a risk factor for both mental and physical health (Bloom et al., 1978; Burman & Margolin, 1992; Ross, Mirowsky, & Goldsteen, 1990).

Marital status is positively related to post-myocardial infarction survival time for men and women (Chandra et al., 1983), and husbands' marital satisfaction was found to predict their health at a 5-year follow-up (Gersten et al., 1976). Poorer marital adjustment in married women has been associated with more ill health and less satisfaction with health (Sheldon & Hooper, 1969). Marital satisfaction was a more powerful predictor of mental health than age, race (black, white, Spanish-speaking), education, income, and adverse childhood circumstances (Gove, Hughes, & Style, 1983). Related to these findings is the equally compelling evidence from the literature on divorce and separation and health status.

Separation and Divorce. Bloom et al. (1978), in their literature review, presented evidence linking separation and divorce to a variety of physical and emotional problems. Research has continued to demonstrate significant increases in medical utilization in the 6 months before and 12 months after separation as compared to a married control group (Wertlieb et al., 1984), and significantly more illness in separated and divorced persons than the married control group (Tcheng-Laroche & Prince, 1983). Kiecolt-Glaser et al. (1988) found that relative to a married control group, separated and divorced men have depressed immune functions on several functional indices of immunity. Decreased immune function is associated with greater morbidity and health problems.

Separated/divorced men were found to be more distressed and lonelier and divorced women reported significantly less life satisfaction, parenting satisfaction, and significantly more use of professional therapists than married controls (Bloom et al., 1978; Hetherington & Camara, 1984; Tcheng-Laroche & Prince, 1983). In a study of various types of marital disruption, the lowest levels of satisfaction and happiness were reported by widowed men and divorced women (Gove et al., 1983). The negative impact of divorce has been shown to be greater among older persons than younger people (Chiriboga, 1982).

Remarriage and Stepfamilies. Parental remarriage is associated with increased stress for adults and children that may persist for many years (Bray, 1988; Bray & Berger, 1994; Hetherington, 1993). In addition, children who experience a parental remarriage are at risk for developing behavioral problems, typically externalizing problems, and lowered social competency (Bray & Berger, 1993; Hetherington & Clingempeel, 1992). This places children and adolescents at risk for developing other types of psychopathology, school and learning difficulties, and other health problems (Zill & Schoenborn, 1990). Family processes within stepfamilies are also related to adult and child adjustment. However, it has been argued that there are different norms for stepfamily relationships due to the lack of accepted societal norms and expectations for stepparents (Bray & Berger, 1993).

Family Process and Affect

Family processes are also important predictors of individual health. Better parental health and better relationships between parents and their adult children and grandchildren are related to less anxiety and depression, better psychological adjustment, marital/intimate relationships, and less life stress for the adult children and grandchildren (Bray, Harvey, & Williamson, 1987; Fine, 1988; Harvey & Bray, 1991; Harvey, Curry, & Bray, 1991; Rakowski, Barber, & Seelbach, 1983). Markides and Krause (1985) found that life satisfaction of Mexican-American grandparents was positively related to affection with grandchildren. Lack of closeness to parents has been identified consistently with risk for development of lung cancer (Kissen, 1969; LeShan, 1959; LeShan & Worthington, 1956), and related to suicide, mental illness, hypertension, coronary heart disease, and malignant tumor (Thomas & Duszynski, 1974).

In families with residential children, parents' patterns of illness behavior and health care utilization influence how children experience and respond to illness (Apley, 1967) and use health care resources (Schor, Starfield, Stidley, & Hankin, 1987). In one study 5% of families were found to account for over 12% of health care utilization (Schor et al., 1987). These relationships suggest that it is important to assess intergenerational family patterns of health and illness to better understand the functioning of families and individuals.

Stress and Social Support. There is considerable evidence converging from different sources that stress enhances vulnerability to certain diseases (Cohen & Syme, 1985; Dohrenwend & Dohrenwend, 1974). Stress appears to affect the immunosuppressive process. This evidence comes from animal studies, in vitro human studies, and studies of immune responses in populations (Dorian & Garfinkel, 1987; Kiecolt-Glaser et al., 1988). This same research also suggests that social support plays a moderating role, possibly via enhanced adaptation, buffering, mastery, or coping (Cohen & Syme, 1985; Cohen & Wills, 1985; Dorian & Garfinkel, 1987; Norbeck & Tilden, 1983). The large epidemiological study by Berkman & Syme (1979) found that for both men and women, the overall level of social support predicted risk of mortality over and above baseline physical health status, education, income, and health practices such as smoking and alcohol consumption. Marriage and family relationships are major sources of social support, and family disruption is a major source of stress (Berkman & Syme, 1979; Cohen & Wills, 1985; Hetherington & Camara, 1984).

Stress and family relationships interact to impact health and illness. Boyce et al. (1977) noted that the combination of high stress and high family routines was directly related to the severity of children's respiratory illnesses but these factors were not independently related to severity of illness. Fergusson, Horwood, Gretton, and Shannon (1985) observed that stressful events were associated with child behavioral problems and maternal depression, but when maternal depression was controlled, there was no correlation between stressful events and behavioral problems. In addition, several studies have found that family relationships, family process such as cohesion and adaptability, and stress predict adjustment to diabetes and diabetic control (Anderson, Miller, Auslander, & Santiago, 1981; Cedarblad, Helgesson, Larsson, & Ludvigsson, 1982; Grey, Genel, & Tamborlane, 1980; Mengel et al., 1992), and over time high stressful events are related to deterioration from good to poor diabetic control in adolescents (Koski & Kumento, 1977).

However, there is a "dark side" to social support and family interaction that may negatively impact family members' health (Coyne & Bolger, 1990; Rook, 1984). Negative family and social relationships may actually impede well-being through social strain and increased negativity in the relationship. Thus, it is important to distinguish between the positive and negative aspects of social support and its impact on health functioning.

Family Organization

A common factor in family organization is role satisfaction and validation of role performance from the environment. Googins and Burden (1987) found that workplace versus family strain was strongly associated with decreased physical and emotional well-being. The relationship cannot be explained simply by inadequate time for role demands, as women with several roles are healthier than those with fewer roles (Froberg & Gjerdingen, 1986). In one study of role burdens and physical health, dissatisfaction with roles and feelings of very great or very little time pressure were associated with poor health (Verbrugge, 1986). In the case of employed women and homemakers, better health is associated with desired, positive roles, such as marriage and married parenthood (Muller, 1986). Poorer health is associated with unwelcome role expansions such as single-parenthood, child disability, having a sick spouse, and marital dissolution. Roles change significantly after divorce and remarriage (Hetherington & Camara, 1984) and there is considerable role ambiguity for stepparents which may add to their stress and ability to adjust (Bray, 1988; Bray & Berger, 1993).

Variations Due to Family Status Differences. There are important interactions between family status, family process, and individual functioning. Hypothesized relationships among these factors may not hold in different family structures, such as families following a divorce or remarriage. Bray (1988) found that in newly remarried stepfamilies children's externalizing behavior problems were related to mothers' reports of less cohesion, emotional bonding, and affective responsiveness, whereas for stepfathers' *more* cohesion, affective responsiveness, and overinvolvement in family matters were associated with more behavior problems for children.

Variations Due to Ethnic and Racial Differences. Most of the models of family relationships are based on White, middle-class families and do not necessarily include variations that may occur for families from different cultural and ethnic backgrounds. In addition, most of the family measures are based on these models and have not been validated with families from diverse ethnic backgrounds. Morris (1990) found that the Family Assessment Device appeared to make appropriate assessments of Hawaiian-American families, while providing inappropriate assessments of Japanese-American families. Hampson, Beavers, and Hulgus (1990) found no differences in global competence or family style between Anglo, African-American, and Mexican-American families. However, specific family style differences between the ethnic groups were noted in ratings that were consistent with theoretical and cultural expectations. This is clearly an area that needs further study and researchers and clinicians are cautioned in using measures and instruments developed on one ethnic group to assess the health and dysfunction of families from other ethnic and cultural backgrounds.

INTERGENERATIONAL SYSTEMS MODEL OF FAMILY HEALTH AND DISTRESS

How does family structure, process, and organization impact the health of individual family members? Our research has drawn on intergenerational family systems theories (Bowen, 1978; Kerr, 1981; Williamson & Bray, 1985, 1988) to explain the relationships between family functioning and individual health and distress. The family of origin is viewed as the major social group that impacts individuals' development. This influence is presumed to persist whether or not the person continues to interact with the family (Boszormenyi-Nagy & Ulrich, 1981; Bowen, 1978; Williamson, 1981). The influence is constituted by the individual's current perceptions of his/her family relationships (Williamson & Bray, 1988). The important family processes considered by intergenerational family systems theory include intimacy, individuation, triangulation, personal authority, and intimidation. As previously noted, other family processes, such as communication and problem solving, are subsumed in these broader concepts. We have conducted a series of studies to evaluate the relationship between intergenerational family relationships and individual psychological and physical health and adjustment.

Bray, Harvey, and Williamson (1987) conducted two studies that investigated intergenerational family processes, as measured by the PAFS-Q, and their relationship to life stress and health distress. In the first study, self-reports of relationships in the family of origin and current nuclear family were used to predict health/illness in an adult clinical sample. Over half (53%) of the variance in health distress was accounted for by family process variables. Family of origin relationships continued to predict health distress, even after controlling for nuclear family relationships. In the second study, self-reports of family of origin and peer relationships and life stress were used to predict health/illness in a nonclinical college-aged sample. Family processes were significant predictors of health distress over and above life stress.

Based on the previous studies and a re-examination of intergenerational family theory, a more complex model was developed that includes explicit causal relationships among multigenerational family relationships. Intergenerational family theory hypothesizes that relational patterns are transmitted and reproduced from generation to generation (Bowen, 1978). We speculate that these patterns are transmitted via social learning with parents and grandparents (Williamson & Bray, 1988) and maintained out of loyalty to the previous generations (Boszormenyi-Nagy & Ulrich, 1981). Thus, it is expected that patterns of differentiation and individuation in intimate relationships with peers (e.g., spouses, significant others) are similar to patterns with the parents. This hypothesis is specified in Figure 1 as the influences of intergenerational intimacy/individuation and intergenerational intimidation/fusion on peer intimacy/individuation. Circles enclose the theoretical constructs and unidirectional arrows indicate the hypothesized causal directions. The model represents only interfactor causal relationships; the causal influences of each factor on the same factor at a different time period are also included in the model but are not shown.

Bowen (1978) hypothesizes that experiencing stress or anxiety stimulates emotional fusion between family members which increases the probability of symptom development in one or more family members. The symptoms may be expressed as marital conflict, dysfunction (physical, psychological, and/or social) within self or a significant other, and/or dysfunction within children in the family.

Figure 1. Intergenerational (ITGL) Family Model Predicting Health and Psychological Adjustment (From Harvey & Bray, *Journal of Family Psychology*, 4, 298-325, copyright 1991 by the American Psychological Association. Reprinted by permission.)

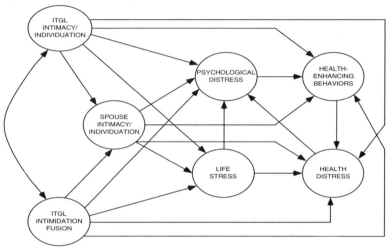

More individuated people are less likely to develop symptoms during stressful periods and recover more quickly following the period of stress.

Bowen (1978) and Williamson and Bray (1985) proposed that a person's level of individuation and personal authority in the family of origin are directly related to that person's psychological and physical health. Individuals who experience more individuation in their family and peer relationships are more likely to take personal responsibility for their well-being, engage in health-enhancing behaviors, cope effectively with life's difficulties, and less likely to experience negative reactions due to stress (Harvey & Bray, 1991). Positive family relationships and social support are expected to contribute to positive expectations and self-statements, perceiving fewer negative situations, and experiencing enhanced self-competency. In contrast, psychological distress is expected to be caused by emotional fusion and intergenerational intimidation created through emotional reactivity, unresolved emotional attachments to family members, and diminished levels of social support for individuals. Thus, higher levels of health-enhancing behaviors and lower levels of psychological distress, life stress, and health distress are expected to relate to intergenerational intimacy/ individuation and peer intimacy/ individuation. Individuation and personal authority are reflected by increasing freedom of choice regarding parental expectations, with an associated enhancement of coping and self-esteem (Harvey & Bray, 1991). Thus, psychological distress, life stress, and health distress are expected to relate to more intergenerational intimidation/fusion.

Reciprocal influences between health, stress, and individuation are expected. However, this model predicts that the current levels of intimacy/individuation and intergenerational intimidation/fusion are the principal and prominent influences on an individual's ability to cope with stresses and changes encountered throughout the life cycle (Williamson & Bray, 1985, 1988). Current perceptions of relational patterns are considered central influences on stress, illness, and distress, rather than historical perceptions and events (Williamson & Bray, 1988). The intergenerational perspective considers both the current interactional patterns of family relationships and the construction of the meanings of these relational patterns by individual family members (Harvey & Bray, 1991).

Tests of the Model

An evaluation of this causal model was conducted by Harvey and Bray (1991) in a short-term, two-wave, longitudinal study of young adults (see Figure 2). Results for the first administration indicated that the degree of individuation/intimacy in intergenerational and peer relationships directly influenced subjects' health-related behaviors. These factors accounted for 30% of the variance in health-enhancing behaviors. Intergenerational intimidation/fusion directly influenced the level of health distress and the complete model accounted for 35% of the variance in health distress. The degree of intimacy/individuation in peer relationships was found to directly influence subjects' level of psychological distress. The intergenerational family factors were found to directly influence life stress, but these factors had separate direct effects on health distress over and above life stress. The complete model accounted for 73% of the variance in psychological distress.

In a third paper, Harvey et al. (1991) extended and replicated the findings of the previous studies by simultaneously evaluating this theory using structural equation analysis in a sample of middle-aged adults and their college-aged offspring. This study directly examined intergenerational relationships and the transmission hypothesis between two generations of family members. Differences in family relationship patterns were noted between mothers and their children and fathers and their children (see Figures 3 and 4). For both mothers

Figure 2. Time 1 Intergenerational (ITGL) Family Model Results (From Harvey & Bray, Journal of Family Psychology, 4, 298-325, Copyright 1991 by the American Psychological Association. Reprinted by permission.)

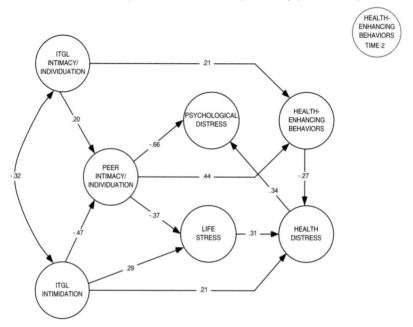

and fathers, levels of individuation and intimacy were significant predictors of their own health distress and psychological distress. Parents' patterns of individuation and intimacy directly and indirectly influenced their offsprings' family relationship patterns of individuation and intimidation providing partial support for the intergenerational transmission of family patterns. Fathers' intergenerational patterns operated through nuclear and marital relationships to influence their college-aged children's family patterns, whereas mothers' patterns had both direct and indirect influences on their college-aged children's family patterns, via nuclear family relationships. Overall, mothers' intergenerational and nuclear family relationships had stronger influences on their children's relationships and adjustment than did fathers' relationships.

Taken together these studies provide empirical support for an intergenerational family systems model and its influence on health and dysfunction. These studies highlight the importance of assessing family relationships in multiple generations to understand the impact of stress and social/family influences on health and well-being.

Figure 3. Intergenerational (ITGL) Model of Mothers and Children (From Harvey, Curry, & Bray, *Journal of Family Psychology, 5,* 204-236, Copyright 1991 by the American Psychological Association. Reprinted by permission.)

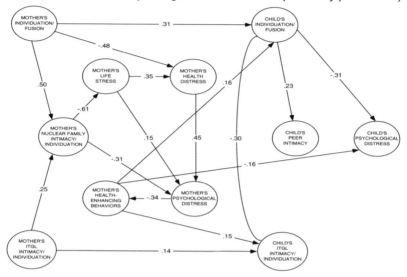

Figure 4. Intergenerational (ITGL) Model of Fathers and Children (From Harvey, Curry, & Bray, *Journal of Family Psychology, 5,* 204-236, Copyright 1991 by the American Psychological Association. Reprinted by permission.)

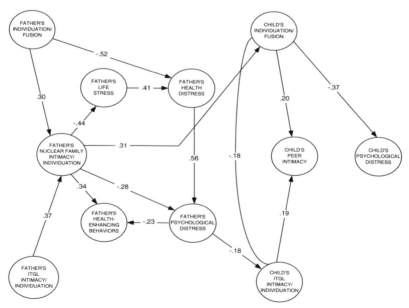

Family Health Influences on Individual Health [1]

A central question raised by this line of research is how do social interactions impact physiological and cellular functioning and dysfunction? Although a complete review of these relationships is beyond the scope of this chapter, a brief discussion addresses this relatively new and quickly developing area of science. Family systems theorists view the family as an emotional unit that not only develops relational patterns that foster adaptation, but also regulates emotional and affective responsiveness of its members (Bowen, 1978; Kerr, 1981; Epstein & Bishop, 1981; Mengel et al., 1992; Minuchin, Rosman, & Baker, 1978; Ramsey, 1989). Recent developments in our understanding of physiology-behavior relationships provide answers to how family interaction and behavior relates to individual physiological responsiveness and functioning (Mengel et al., 1992). There is considerable evidence that interactions within the family system have reciprocal influences with the nervous system, immune system, and endocrine system that result in physiologic functioning and play an important role in health and illness (Ramsey, 1989). Within the nervous system the limbic system is believed to have control of emotions and also originates signals that manifest as stress responses (Asterita, 1985). Thus, emotional states may cause stress responses, which in turn impact other physiologic responses. Therefore, emotional and affective responses in the family can be transmitted to an individual's body via the limbic system and impact the health and well-being of that individual (Smith & DeVito, 1984; Stebbens & Smith, 1964). Further, other emotional reactions generated by family interactions and process are also related to the nervous system and endocrine system. Depression is related to activation of the pituitary and adrenal cortical system, whereas anger, hostility, and active coping are related to activation of the sympathetic adrenomedulary system (Eckman, 1984; Henry & Stephens, 1977). As discussed previously, stress created by changes in family status, family relationships, and other environmental changes are also related to decreased immune functioning which is related to increased risk for illness (Kiecolt-Glaser et al., 1984, 1988). A recent study found that increased stress was directly related to susceptibility to viral infections, such as the common cold, and the ability of the immune system to destroy viral infections (Cohen, Tyrrell, & Smith, 1991). Thus, family

---

[1] I wish to acknowledge the consultation of Mark B. Mengel, M.D. for his help in preparation of this section.

systems functioning can impact an individual's emotional responsiveness and stress and can impact the body and influence the development of disease states.

FUTURE DIRECTIONS

It is clear that we have made significant progress in the development of family assessment tools and towards understanding family health and distress; however, there continues to be much to learn. Research is needed to further identify key family processes that contribute to family health and well-being and to clearly specify how to measure them. In addition, we need to increase our understanding of how family interaction and process contributes to individual family members' physical and mental health. Although overall measures of family functioning are useful, they do not capture the multiple levels of systems within systems that are considered in performing a family assessment. As Gottman (1989) poignantly stated, "The hallmark of this work is and must be precision. Global measures of family functioning are limited in that one does not really know what is being measured" (p. 213). Cultural and ethnic variations also must be considered, as well as the social context in which the changing American family resides. Most of our models of the family, and therefore our assessment instruments, do not consider these structural, cultural, and ethnic variations in families, or the massive and evolving changes in family demographics.

REFERENCES

Abidin, R. (1985). *The Parenting Stress Index*. Charlottesville, VA: Pediatric Psychology Press.

Alexander, J. F. (1973). Defensive and supportive communication in normal and deviant families. *Journal of Consulting and Clinical Psychology, 40*, 223-231.

Anderson, B. J., Miller, J. P., Auslander, W. F., & Santiago, J. V. (1981). Family characteristics of diabetic adolescents: Relationship to metabolic control. *Diabetes Care, 4*, 586-594.

Anderson, S. A., & Sabatelli, R. M. (1992). The Differentiation in the Family System Scale (DIFS). *The American Journal of Family Therapy, 20*, 77-89.

Apley, J. (1967). The child with recurrent abdominal pain. *Pediatric Clinics of North America, 14*, 63-72.

Asterita, M. F. (1985). *The physiology of stress*. New York: Human Sciences Press.

Barnard, J. (1972). *The future of marriage*. New York: Bantam.

Barnes, H., & Olson, D. H. (1982). The Parent-Adolescent Communication Scale. In D. H. Olson, *Family inventories* (pp. 33-48). St. Paul, MN: University of Minnesota, Department of Family Social Sciences.

Bavolek, S. J. (1984). Adult-Adolescent Parenting Inventory. Eau Claire, WI: Family Development Resources.

Beavers, W. R., Hampson, R. B., & Hulgus, Y. (1985). Commentary: The Beavers Systems approach to family assessment. *Family Process, 24*, 398-405.

Berkman, L. F., & Syme, L. S. (1979). Social networks, host resistance, and mortality: A nine-year follow-up study of Alameda County residents. *American Journal of Epidemiology, 109*, 186-204.

Bloom, B. J. (1985). A factor analysis of self-report measures of family functioning. *Family Process, 24*, 225-239.

Bloom, B. J., Asher, S., & White, S. (1978). Marital disruption as a stressor: A review and analysis. *Psychological Bulletin, 85*, 867-894.

Boszormenyi-Nagy, I., & Ulrich, D. (1981). Contextual family therapy. In A. S. Gurman & D. Kniskern (Eds.) *Handbook of family therapy* (pp. 159-186). New York: Brunner/Mazel.

Bowen, M. (1978). *Family therapy in clinical practice*. New York: Aronson.

Boyce, W. T., Jensen, E. W., Cassel, J. C., Collier, A. M., Smith, A. H., Ramey, C. T. (1977). Influence of life events and family routines on childhood respiratory illness. *Pediatrics, 60*, 609-615.

Bray, J. H. (1988). Children's development in early remarriage. In E. M. Hetherington & J. D. Arasteh (Eds.), *The impact of divorce, single-parenting and step-parenting on children* (pp. 279-298). Hillsdale, NJ: Lawrence Earlbaum Associates.

Bray, J. H. (1991). The Personal Authority in the Family System Questionnaire: Assessment of intergenerational family relationships. In D. S. Williamson (Ed.), *The intimacy paradox: Personal authority in the family system* (pp. 273-286). New York: Guilford Press.

Bray, J. H., & Berger, S. H. (1993). Developmental issues in stepfamilies research project: Family relationships and parent-child interactions. *Journal of Family Psychology, 7*, 76-90.

Bray, J. H., & Berger, S. H. (1994). *Length of remarriage, conflict, stress, and children's adjustment in stepfather families and nuclear families.* Manuscript submitted for publication.

Bray, J. H., Harvey, D. M., & Williamson, D. S. (1987). Intergenerational family relationships: An evaluation of theory and measurement. *Psychotherapy, 24*, 516-528.

Bray, J. H., & Maxwell, S. E. (1985). *Multivariate analysis of variance.* Beverly Hills: Sage Publications.

Bray, J. H., Maxwell, S. E., & Cole, D. (1995). Complex family systems require complex analyses: Multivariate statistics for family psychology research. *Journal of Family Psychology, 9,* in press.

Bray, J. H., Williamson, D. S., & Malone, P. E. (1984). Personal authority in the family system: Development of a questionnaire to measure personal authority in intergenerational family processes. *Journal of Marital and Family Therapy, 10,* 167-178.

Brown, G. W., Birley, J. L. T., & Wing, J. K. (1972). Influence of family life on the course of schizophrenic disorders: A replication. *British Journal of Psychiatry, 121,* 241-258.

Bryk, A. S., & Raudenbush, S. W. (1987). Application of hierarchical linear models to assessing change. *Psychological Bulletin, 101,* 147-158.

Buehlman, K. T., Gottman, J. M., & Katz, L. F. (1992). How a couple views their past predicts their future: Predicting divorce from an oral history interview. *Journal of Family Psychology, 5,* 295-318.

Burman, B., & Margolin, G. (1992). Analysis of the association between marital relationships and health problems: An interactional perspective. *Psychological Bulletin, 112,* 39-63.

Carlson, C. I. (1989). Criteria for family assessment in research and intervention contexts. *Journal of Family Psychology, 3,* 158-176.

Carter, E. A., & McGoldrick, M. (Eds.), (1980). *The family life cycle: A framework for family therapy.* New York: Gardner Press.

Cedarblad, M., Helgesson, M., Larsson, Y., & Ludvigsson, J. (1982). Family structure and diabetes in children. *Pediatric and Adolescent Endocrinology, 10,* 94-98.

Chandra, V., Szklo, M., Goldberg, R., & Tonascia, J. (1983). The impact of marital status on survival after an acute myocardial infarction: A population based study. *American Journal of Gerontology, 117,* 320-325.

Chiriboga, D. A. (1982). Adaptation to marital separation on later and earlier life. *Journal of Gerontology, 37,* 109-114.

Cohen, S., & Syme, S. L. (Eds.). (1985). *Social support and health.* San Francisco: Academic Press.

Cohen, S., Tyrrell, D. A. J., & Smith, A. (1991). Psychological stress and susceptibility to the common cold. *New England Journal of Medicine, 325,* 606-612.

Cohen, S., & Wills, T. A. (1985). Stress, social support, and the buffering hypothesis. *Psychological Bulletin, 98,* 310-357.

Cowan, P. A. (1987). The need for theoretical and methodological integrations in family research. *Journal of Family Psychology, 1*, 48-50.

Coyne, J. C., & Bolger, N. (1990). Doing without social support as an explanatory concept. *Journal of Social and Clinical Psychology, 9*, 148-158.

Doherty, W. J., & Campbell, T. L. (1988). *Families and health.* Newbury Park, CA: SAGE Publications.

Dohrenwend, B. S., & Dohrenwend B. P. (1974). *Stressful life events: Their nature and effects.* New York: Wiley.

Dorian, B., & Garfinkel, P. E. (1987). Stress, immunity and illness—a review. *Psychological Medicine, 17*, 393-407.

Eckman, P. (1984). Expression and the nature of emotion. In K. R. Scherer & P. Eckman (Eds.), *Approaches to emotion* (pp.   ). Hillsdale, NJ: Lawrence Erlbaum and Associates.

Emery, R. E. (1982). Interparental conflict and the children of discord and divorce. *Psychological Bulletin, 91*, 310-330.

Epstein, N. B., Baldwin, L. M., & Bishop, D. S. (1983). The McMaster family assessment device. *Journal of Marital and Family Therapy, 9*, 171-180.

Epstein, N. B., & Bishop, D. S. (1981). Problem-centered systems therapy of the family. In A. Gurman & D. Kniskern (Eds.), *Handbook of family therapy* (pp. 444-482). New York: Brunner/Mazel.

Fergusson, D. M., Horwood, J. J., Gretton, M. E., & Shannon, F. T. (1985). Family life events, maternal depression, and maternal and teacher descriptions of child behavior. *Pediatrics, 75*, 30-35.

Fine, M. (1988). The relationship of perceived health in the family of origin to levels of state and trait anxiety. *Family Therapy, 15*, 51-57.

Fisher, L. (1976). Dimensions of family assessment: A critical review. *Journal of Marriage and Family Counseling, 2*, 367-382.

Fisher, L. (1982). Transactional theories but individual assessment: A frequent discrepancy in family research. *Family Process, 21*, 313-320.

Fisher, L., Kokes, R. F., Ransom, D. C., Phillips, S. L., & Rudd, P. (1985). Alternative strategies for creating "relational" family data. *Family Process, 24*, 213-224.

Froberg, D., & Gjerdingen, D. (1986). Multiple roles and women's mental and physical health. *Women & Health, 11*, 79-96.

Gersten, J. C., Friis, R., & Langer, T. (1976). Life dissatisfaction and illness of married men over time. *American Journal of Epidemiology, 103*, 333-341.

Googins, B. & Burden, D. (1987). Vulnerability of working parents. *Social Work, 32*, 295-300.

Gottman, J. M. (1989). Toward programmatic research in family psychology. *Journal of Family Psychology, 3,* 211-214.

Gottman, J. M., & Krokoff, L. J. (1989). Marital interaction and satisfaction: A longitudinal view. *Journal of Consulting and Clinical Psychology, 57,* 47-52.

Gove, W. R., Hughes, M., & Style, C. B. (1983). Does marriage have positive effects on the psychosocial well-being of the individual? *Journal of Health and Social Behavior, 24,* 122-131.

Grey, M. J., Genel, M., & Tamborlane, W. V. (1980). Psychosocial adjustment of latency-age diabetics. *Pediatrics, 65,* 69-73.

Grotevant, H. D., & Carlson, C. I. (1989). *Family assessment: A guide to methods and measures.* New York: Guilford Press.

Grotevant, H. D. (1989). The role of theory in guiding family assessment. *Journal of Family Psychology, 3,* 104-117.

Gurman, A. S., & Kniskern, D. (Eds.). (1981). *Handbook of family therapy.* New York: Brunner/Mazel.

Haley, J. (1976). *Problem-solving therapy.* San Francisco: Jossey-Bass.

Hampson, R. B., Beavers, W. R., & Hulgus, Y. (1990). Cross-ethnic family differences: Interactional assessment of White, Black, and Mexican-American families. *Journal of Marital and Family Therapy, 16,* 307-319.

Harvey, D. M., & Bray, J. H. (1991). An evaluation of an intergenerational theory of personal development: Family process determinants of psychological and health distress. *Journal of Family Psychology, 4,* 42-69.

Harvey, D. M., Curry, C. J., & Bray, J. H. (1991). Individuation and intimacy in intergenerational relationships and health: Patterns across two generations. *Journal of Family Psychology, 5,* 204-236.

Henry, J. P., & Stephens, P. M. (1977). *Stress, health, and the social environment.* New York: Springer-Verlag.

Henoa, S., & Grose, N. (Eds.) (1985). *Principles of family systems in family medicine.* New York: Brunner/Mazel.

Hetherington, E. M. (1993). An overview of the Virginia longitudinal study of divorce and remarriage. *Journal of Family Psychology, 7,* 39-56.

Hetherington, E. M., & Camara, K. (1984). Families in transition: The process of dissolution and reconstitution. In R. D. Parke (Ed.), *Review of child development research Vol. 7: The family* (pp. 398-439). Chicago: University of Chicago Press.

Hetherington, E. M., & Clingempeel, W. G. (1992). Coping with marital transitions: A family systems perspective. *Monographs of the Society for Research in Child Development, 57,* Nos. 2-3, Serial No. 227.

Hetherington, E. M., Clingempeel, W. G., Eisenberg, M., Hagan, M. S., Vuchinich, R., & Chase-Landsdale, L. (1986). *Manual for the Family Interaction Coding System.* Charlottesville, VA: University of Virginia, Department of Psychology.

Hetherington, E. M., Cox, M., & Cox, R. (1982). The effects of divorce on parents and children. In M. Lamb (Ed.), *Nontraditional families* (pp. 233-288). Hillsdale, NJ: Lawrence Earlbaum Associates.

Jöreskog, K. G., & Sorbom, D. (1986). *LISREL: Analysis of linear structural relationships by the method of maximum likelihood.* Mooresville, IN: Scientific Software.

Kanner, A. D., Coyne, J. C., Schaefer, C., & Lazarus, R. S. (1981). Comparison of two modes of stress management: Daily hassles versus major life events. *Journal of Behavior Medicine, 4,* 1-39.

Karpel, M. (1976). Individuation: From fusion to dialogue. *Family Process, 15,* 65-82.

Kear, J. S. (1978). Marital attraction and satisfaction as a function of differentiation of self. *Dissertation Abstracts International, 39B,* 2505B. (University Microfilms No. 78-19, 970)

Kerr, M. E. (1981). Family systems theory and therapy. In A. Gurman & D. Kniskern (Eds.) *Handbook of family therapy* (pp. 226-266). New York: Brunner/Mazel.

Kiecolt-Glaser, J. K., Garner, W., Speicher, C., Penn, G. M., Holliday, J., & Glaser, R. (1984). Psychosocial modifiers of immuno-competence in medical students. *Psychosomatic Medicine, 46,* 7-14.

Kiecolt-Glaser, J. K., Kennedy, S., Malkoff, S., Fisher, L., Speicher, C.E., & Glaser, R. (1988). Marital discord and immunity in males. *Psychosomatic Medicine, 50,* 213-229.

Kissen, D. M. (1969). Present status of psychosomatic cancer research. *Geriatrics, 24,* 129-137.

Koski, M. L., & Kumento, A. (1977). The interrelationship between diabetic control and family life. *Pediatric and Adolescent Endocrinology, 3,* 41-45.

Larzelere, R. E., & Huston, T. L. (1980). The Dyadic Trust Scale: Toward understanding interpersonal trust in close relationships. *Journal of Marriage and the Family, 42,* 595-604.

LeShan, L. (1959). Psychological states as factors in the development of malignant disease. *Journal of National Cancer Institute, 22,* 1-18.

LeShan, L. L., & Worthington, R. E. (1956). Personality as factor in the pathogenesis of cancer. *British Journal of Medical Psychology, 29,* 49-56.

Lowman, J. C. (1973). *Inventory of Family Feelings*. Chapel Hill, NC: University of North Carolina.

Markides, K. S., & Krause, N. (1985). Intergenerational solidarity and psychology well-being among older Mexican-Americans: A three-generation study. *Journal of Gerontology, 40*, 390-392.

McCubbin, H. I., & Patterson, J. M. (1987). FILE: Family Inventory of Life Events and Changes. In H. I. McCubbin & A. I. Thompson (Eds.), *Family assessment inventories for research and practice* (pp. 81-98). Madison: University of Wisconsin-Madison, Family Stress, Coping and Health Project.

McGoldrick, M. (1982). Normal families: An ethnic perspective. In F. Walsh (Ed.), *Normal family processes* (pp. 399-424). New York: Guilford Press.

Mengel, M. B., Blackett, P. R., Lawler, M. K., Volk, R. J., Viviani, N. J., Stamps, G. S., Dees, M. S., Davis, A. B., & Lovallo, W. R. (1992). Cardiovascular and neuroendocrine responsiveness in diabetic adolescents within a family context: Association with poor diabetic control and dysfunctional family dynamics. *Family Systems Medicine, 10*, 5-33.

Minuchin, S. (1974). *Families and family therapy*. Cambridge: Harvard University Press.

Minuchin S., Rosman, G. L., & Baker, L. (1978). *Psychosomatic families: Anorexia nervosa in context*. Cambridge: Harvard University Press.

Moos, R., & Moos, B. (1974). *The Family Environment Scale*. Palo Alto, CA: Consulting Psychologists Press.

Morris, T. M. (1990). Culturally sensitive family assessment: An evaluation of the Family Assessment Device used with Hawaiian-American and Japanese-American families. *Family Process, 29*, 105-116.

Muller, C. (1986). Health and health care of employed women and homemakers. *Women & Health, 11*, 7-26.

Norbeck, J. S., & Tilden, V. P. (1983). Life stress, social support, and emotional disequilibrium in complications in pregnancy: A prospective, multivariate study. *Journal of Health and Social Behavior, 24*, 30-36.

Olson, D. H. (1977). Insiders' and outsiders' view of relationships: Research and strategies. In G. Levinger & H. Raush (Eds.), *Close relationships* (pp   ). Amherst: University of Massachusetts Press.

Olson, D. H., Bell, R., & Portner, J. (1983). *FACES-II manual*. St. Paul, MN: University of Minnesota, Department of Family Social Sciences.

Olson, D. H., McCubbin, H. I., Barnes, H., Larsen, A., Muxen, M., & Wilson, M. (1982). *Family inventories*. St. Paul, MN: University of Minnesota, Department of Family Social Sciences.

Peplau, L. A. (1982). Interpersonal attraction. In D. Sherrod (Ed.), *Social psychology* . New York: Random House.

Perosa, L. M., Hansen, J., & Perosa, S. (1981). Development of the Structural Family Interaction Scale. *Family Therapy, 8*, 77-91.

Pless, I. B., & Satterwhite, B. (1973). A measure of family functioning and its application. *Social Science and Medicine, 7*, 613-621.

Rakowski, W., Barber, C. E., & Seelbach, W. C. (1983). Perceptions of parental health status and attitudes toward aging. *Family Relations, 32*, 93-99.

Ramsey, C. N. (1989). The science of family medicine. In C. N. Ramsey (Ed.), *Family systems in medicine* (pp. 3-17). New York: Guilford Press.

Robin, A. L., Koepke, T., & Moye, A. (1990). Multidimensional assessment of parent-adolescent relations. *Psychological Assessment, 2*, 451-459.

Rook, K. S. (1984). The negative side of social interaction: Impact on psychological well-being. *Journal of Personality and Social Psychology, 46*, 1097-1108.

Ross, C. E., Mirowsky, J., & Goldsteen, K. (1990). The impact of the family on health: The decade in review. *Journal of Marriage and the Family, 52*, 1059-1078.

Sarason, I., Johnson, J., & Siegel, J. (1978). Assessing the impact of life changes: Development of the Life Experiences Survey. *Journal of Consulting and Clinical Psychology, 46*, 932-946.

Schor, E., Starfield, B., Stidley C., & Hankin, J. (1987). Family health: Utilization and effects of family membership. *Medical Care, 25*, 616-626.

Sheldon, A., & Hooper, D. (1969). An inquiry into health and ill-health and adjustment in early marriage. *Journal of Psychosomatic Research, 13*, 95-101.

Shields, C. G., Franks, P., Harp, J. J., McDaniel, S. H., & Campbell, T. L. (1992). Development of the Family Emotional Involvement and Criticism Scale (FEICS): A self-report scale to measure expressed emotion. *Journal of Marital and Family Therapy, 18*, 395-407.

Skinner, H. A., Steinhauer, P. D., & Santa-Barbara, J. (1984). *Family Assessment Measure (FAM-III)*. Toronto, Canada: Addiction Research Foundation.

Smith, O. A., & DeVito, J. L. (1984). Central neural integration for the control of autonomic responses associated with emotion. *Annual Review of Neurosciences, 7*, 43-65.

Stebbens, W. C., & Smith, O. A. (1964). Cardiovascular concomitants of the conditioned emotional response in the monkey. *Science, 144*, 881-883.

Straus, M. A. (1979). Measuring intrafamily conflict and violence: The Conflict Tactics (C. T.) Scales. *Journal of Marriage and the Family, 41,* 75-88.

Tcheng-Laroche, F., & Prince, R. (1983). Separated and divorced women compared with married controls. *Social Science and Medicine, 17,* 95-105.

Thomas, C. B., & Duszynski, K. R. (1974). Closeness to parents and the family constellation in a prospective study of five states. *Johns Hopkins Medical Journal, 134,* 251-270.

Touliatos, J., Perlmutter, B. F., & Straus, M. A. (Eds.). (1990). *Handbook of family measurement techniques.* Newbury Park, CA: SAGE Publications.

Vaughn, C. E., & Leff, J. P. (1976). The influences of family and social factors on the course of psychiatric illness: A comparison of schizophrenic and depressed neurotic patients. *British Journal of Psychiatry, 129,* 125-137.

Verbrugge, L. M. (1986). Role burdens and physical health of women and men. *Women & Health, 11,* 47-77.

Walsh, F. (1982). Conceptualizations of normal family functioning. In F. Walsh (Ed.), *Normal family processes* (pp. 3-44). New York: Guilford Press.

Watzlawick, P., Beavin, J., & Jackson, D. (1967). *Pragmatics of human communication.* New York: Norton.

Watzlawick, P., Weakland, J., & Fisch, R. (1974). *Change: Principles of problem formation and problem resolution.* New York: Norton.

Weiss, R. L., & Aved, B. M. (1978). Marital satisfaction and depression as predictors of physical health status. *Journal of Consulting and Clinical Psychology, 46,* 1379-1384.

Wertlieb, D., Budman S., Demby, A., & Randall, M. (1984). Marital separation and health: Stress and intervention. *Journal of Human Stress, 10,* 18-26.

Williamson, D. S. (1981). Personal authority via termination of the intergenerational hierarchical boundary: A "new" stage in the family life cycle. *Journal of Marital and Family Therapy, 7,* 441-452.

Williamson, D. S. (1982). Personal authority in family experience via termination of the intergenerational hierarchical boundary. Part III: Personal authority defined and the power of play in the change-process. *Journal of Marital and Family Therapy, 8,* 309-323.

Williamson, D. S., & Bray, J. H. (1985). The intergenerational point of view. In S. Henao & N. Grose (Eds.), *Principles of family systems in family medicine* (pp. 90-110). New York: Brunner/Mazel.

Williamson, D. S., & Bray, J. H. (1988). Family development and change across the generations: An intergenerational perspective. In C. J. Falicov (Ed.), *Family transitions: Continuity and change over the life cycle* (pp. 357-384). New York: Guilford.

Wynne, L. C., Jones, J. E., & Al-Khayyal, M. (1982). Healthy family communication patterns: Observations in families "at risk" for psychopathology. In F. Walsh (Ed.), *Normal family processes* (pp. 142-166). New York: Guilford Press.

Zill, N., & Schoenborn, C. A. (1990). Developmental, learning, and emotional problems: Health of our Nation's children, United States, 1988. *Advance data from vital and health statistics; No. 190.* Hyattsville, MD: National Center for Health Statistics.

MULTICULTURAL FAMILY ASSESSMENT

Jane Close Conoley

Lorrie E. Bryant

University of Nebraska-Lincoln

Assessing individuals who are members of minority or recent immigrant groups creates special and critical challenges for psychologists committed to equitable practices (Dana, 1993). As previous chapters in this volume have shown, the goal of accomplishing valid family assessments is daunting in its own right. Culturally sensitive procedures of family evaluation are, perhaps, even more difficult to conceptualize and administer.

This chapter will examine several issues relevant to expertise in assessing families whose cultural framework differs from the majority of the U.S. population. The topics to be covered include:

1. What is cultural sensitivity?
2. What are the important constructs to assess in families and how might these constructs vary across U.S. minority and recent immigrant groups?
3. How do the most frequently used paper-and-pencil assessment devices appear relative to ethnic diversity concerns?
4. What are some suggestions to promote valid assessment procedures?

Family practitioners rely on valid measurement and interpretations to plan for effective treatments. Families are not diagnosed in the ways in which individuals are (e.g., personality traits or intelligence), but they are frequent consumers of mental health services. Clients from ethnic minority families present interesting assessment concerns for the practitioner.

CULTURAL SENSITIVITY

Culture is an intricate web of meanings through which people, individually and as a group, shape their lives. Culture, however, does not have absolute predictive power concerning the behavior of members of a group. Further, every culture continues to evolve. It is a set of tendencies or possibilities from which to choose.

Cultural paradigms must be recognized and understood. At the same time, these paradigms must be viewed as broadly comprising cultural tendencies that individual families may accept, deny, modify, or exhibit situationally. Forcing a family or an individual to fit within any preconceived cultural model is not cultural sensitivity—it is stereotyping (Anderson & Fenichel, 1989; Steele, 1990).

An acceptance that certain differences and similarities exist in families across cultural groups characterizes culturally sensitive assessments. These differences are neither good nor bad; better or worse; less or more intelligent. The awareness of this possibility and a flexible repertoire of responses are the important components of multicultural assessments of families.

WHAT IS KNOWN ABOUT HEALTHY FAMILIES?

A growing list of competencies or attributes of families that predict or correlate with positive adjustment for the family has appeared. Some of the important constructs include: good communication skills, excellent problem solving, provision of emotional support, authoritative socialization strategies, provision of child supervision, satisfaction with work, positive orientation toward education, good mental health (or at least the absence of serious psychopathology), no substance abuse, physical affection toward children; successful infant attachment, and good marital or relationship quality.

Successful families are good at managing the stresses within their nuclear or extended group and dealing with the press of other environmental demands. Poverty, unemployment, residence in violent neighborhoods, a history of antisocial behavior in the family, and parental failures in school are all risk factors for family and child adjustment.

Some of the family dynamics just mentioned may present fairly straightforward assessment targets (e.g., where do people live; are there two responsible adults or an adaptive network of adults to care for children; are the adults employed). Others, however, may be difficult to measure in any family and hard to interpret across cultural groups (e.g., marital quality, socialization strategies, problem solving) (Beavers & Hampson, 1990; Oster & Caro, 1990).

Other chapters in this volume detail assessment issues with majority culture families. The constructs and methods mentioned in those chapters may also be useful with families from many cultures. The application of identical procedures and interpretative norms may, however, result in unreliable and invalid measurement. Results of analyses of minority members' scores on individual personality measures (e.g., Campos, 1989; Dahlstrom, 1986; Greene, 1987; Padilla & Ruiz, 1975; Velasquez, 1992) point out the dangers of using majority culture expectations to interpret minority performance on tests. Such threats to validity are likely to exist at the family level of assessment as well due to differences among family cultural patterns.

MINORITY GROUPS IN THE UNITED STATES

Brief Descriptions

It is common in both everyday language and in professional literature to describe groups of people using "ethnic glosses" (Trimble, 1990–91). That is, most writers (ourselves included) use the terms Native Americans, African Americans, Hispanic Americans, and Asian Americans as if each of these groups contained very similar people (few within-group differences) and were quite different from each other (many between-group differences). Neither of these assumptions is made safely.

Native Americans

The federal government recognizes 517 separate entities of Native American peoples. The states recognize 36 tribes whose members still speak a total of about 149 different languages with many, many related dialects (LaFromboise, 1988; LaFromboise & Low, 1989; Manson & Trimble, 1982). There are about 2 million Native Americans in the U.S. There are many differences among these peoples whose homes range from the arctic regions of Alaska to the deserts of the Southwest and the shores of New England.

African Americans

African Americans account for about 12% of the U.S. population. African Americans tend to share a group identity based on a common historical experience of racism and oppression. Concepts of cultural orientations and Nigrescence have been used to differentiate individuals within this ethnic group (Cross, 1971, 1978; Thomas, 1971; Parham, 1989; Whatley & Dana, 1989). Four cultural orientations have been described: (a) Afrocentrism; (b) Anglocentrism; (c) bicultural; and (d) marginal. The distinctions refer to an individual's commitment to and pride in traditional African values, or identification with Anglo American priorities, or attempts to be part of both cultures, or finally, to lack a clear commitment to either culture and attempts to survive through cooperation, toughness, suppression of feelings, and a belief in luck and magic (Pinderhughes, 1982).

Nigrescence is a continuum of racial identity that describes an individual's movement from dependence with suppressed rage on white society (i.e., Negromarchy) through steps leading to transcendence that identifies the individual with all of humankind.

Hispanic Americans

By the year 2020 it is estimated that the Hispanic population will grow from 9% of the U.S. total to 15%. There are three major groups of Hispanics (i.e., Mexican Americans, Puerto Ricans, and Cubans). There are, however, another 16 groups of Hispanic Americans that have been identified as ethnic minorities in the U.S. including groups from Central and South American.

The three major groups have different histories of migration to the U.S. and some significant demographic variations among them. Many Mexican Americans came to the U.S. from rural, poverty stricken backgrounds. They arrived with little formal education. In contrast, some groups of Cubans who came were highly educated and relatively affluent. Many of that group thought their stay in the U.S. would be brief. They awaited the overthrow of Fidel Castro in fairly segregated enclaves in southern Florida. (This generalization does not apply to recent waves of poor, mentally ill, and jail inmate Cubans who were probably sent by the Castro government to the U.S.) In contrast, Puerto Ricans (already American citizens) tended to come to New York to find better paying jobs but returned often to their island homes. In fact, the expression Nuyoricans has grown up to describe this group.

Asian Americans

Asian Americans comprise about 32 groups. They represent 4% of the U.S. population and are concentrated in California, New Jersey, Texas, Rhode Island, and Oregon. The primary groups are Chinese, Filipinos, Koreans, Japanese, Asian Indians, and other Southeast Asian groups such as the Vietnamese, Laotians, Cambodians, Hmong, and ethnic Chinese. This Southeast Asian group contains at least an additional 11 cultural groups. Southeast Asians have a birth rate comparable to Hispanic Americans and are, therefore, a fast growing group in comparison to other Asian groups whose birth rate is lower than Anglo-American rates (Leung & Sakata, 1988).

The different groups have distinct immigration and acculturation experiences. Kitano and Daniels (1988) have done a comprehensive review of these processes. Each group has faced violent racism upon entry to the U.S., which continues today for many of the recent immigrants (Starr & Roberts, 1982).

Most of the research on Asian Americans is based on Japanese and Chinese samples (Morishima, Sue, Teng, Zane, & Cram, 1979; Nakanishi, 1988). The more recently immigrated Chinese and other groups have often arrived in the U.S. with major health problems, as victims of terroristic political persecution, or with overwhelming economic deprivation.

Summary

It should be clear from the previous brief paragraphs that generalizations about our usual ethnic glosses are dangerous. In order to provide some guidance, however, to those wishing to improve their cultural competencies with families it is useful to examine cultural patterns associated with each of these groups. It is also useful to comment on how such patterns may change as families interact with the American host culture. These patterns and changes may be described in numerous ways. For the purposes of this chapter, issues related to family interactions and definition and preferred service providers and systems will be highlighted.

WHO IS THE FAMILY?

The definition of family membership may differ across ethnic groups. Individuals from all the groups mentioned above may describe complicated relationships of obedience, cooperation, respect, and obligation to people beyond a nuclear family. This extended family may include individuals who are not blood relatives especially for Native and African Americans. Assumptions, therefore, about roles in family life and the intensity of various relationships beyond the nuclear family require careful attention (McAdoo, 1979; Myers, 1982; Wilson, 1993).

ROLES IN THE FAMILY

Asian and Hispanic Americans may hold very rigid views about appropriate age and gender roles within families. In particular, Asian American families may be strictly organized with male leadership and unquestioning obedience to parents and grandparents. Hispanic American families may exhibit traditional values of *machismo* (role of the father to lead, protect, and provide for the family) and *marianismo* or *hembrismo* (role of the wife and mother to be virtuous, nurture the children, and be submissive to her husband's wishes).

Native American families are more difficult to characterize. Individuals may feel responsibility to many people in their community and a traditional respect for elders. In some tribes, women hold visible and influential roles in both tribal governance and family decision making.

African American families, although overtly headed by males, may be best understood by the mother's and other female relatives' leadership. Female children are socialized to be strong and responsible for family welfare (Boyd-Franklin, 1989; Staples, 1988).

Franklin (1993) presents a case study and analysis of the struggles endured by a middle-class African American family man that illustrates the pervasive effects of racism on families. Hersch (1993) examines the experience of two gifted African American children suggesting the same finding that the experience of unremitting racism affects families and individuals in profound ways—often misunderstood by Anglo American psychologists.

Service Provision

Service providers who are unaware of the cultural expectations of each group are likely to have high drop-out rates from therapy and low utilization from minority groups (LaFromboise, 1988). Some illustrations regarding these expectations may be helpful to the reader.

Asian American families may expect deference and careful courtesy from every person involved in a mental health clinic or office. Providers are often expected to meet and greet the family in the waiting room and direct conversation to the oldest member of the family. These families may evaluate providers upon their obvious expertise in terms of credentials, publications, and other accomplishments. Older male providers will have more immediate credibility than younger females.

Native, Hispanic, and African American families tend to value egalitarianism from the service provider. Families may expect the provider to chat with them and be very friendly and cordial. In fact, they may build rapport more readily if the provider has several connections with them (e.g., friend of a friend, relative, known in another capacity). The usual trappings and distance of professionalism may impede the development of a therapeutic relationship (Bailey, 1987; Farris, 1978; Locust, 1986; Samora, 1979). Native American families expect providers to be respectful, tolerant, accepting of life and other people, family oriented, generous, cooperative, flexible, and to have a sense of humor (Kemnitzer, 1973)! They may respect advisors for the kind of people they are rather than for their specific skills, task orientation, or material possessions (Lewis & Gingerich, 1980).

The Spanish word *simpatia* captures the interactional script expected by some Hispanic Americans and likely useful with Native and African Americans as well. This refers to the providers' tendency to be positive and to avoid negative, competitive, and assertive interactions. Other informative Spanish descriptors of interactional style are *respeto, personalismo, platicando,* and *ambiente.*

> Respeto, or respect, is accorded by younger to older persons, by women to men, and to persons in authority or higher socioeconomic positions. Personalismo refers to a preference for personal, informal, individualized attention in relationships, including those at work and in politics. Platicando, or chatting, is used to create a warm and accepting atmosphere that is called "ambiente" and is characteristic of personalismo. (Dana, 1993, p. 70)

Therapeutic Issues

Members of each minority group may behave in ways that do not match the expectations of Anglo American providers. Further, these clients' basic understandings of health and illness may be unfamiliar to Anglo American providers.

Behavior

African American men and women and Hispanic American men may speak easily on certain topics to service providers from any cultural background, but may be quite reluctant to discuss personal issues at any meaningful depth. Native Americans, Hispanic American women, and most Asian Americans tend to be very quiet. Their silence might be mistaken for resistance. In fact, they have learned that silence in the face of an authority figure is courteous behavior. Among many Native American groups, lots of talking is generally considered impolite behavior. Asian Americans may expect the provider to learn what is wrong in rather indirect ways and provide directives for change. Rehashing family attempts to solve problems may be seen as disrespectful and useless.

Although African American women are likely to speak for the family no matter who is present, women from the other families tend to defer to the adult men. Even if the women disagree with the men or have other therapeutic agendas, it is possible these will not be mentioned unless the women are seen alone.

Service providers might expect very long rapport building periods with African and Native Americans. A relationship called *confianza en confianza* (trusting mutual support) must be established for genuine therapeutic alliances to be forged. African and Native Americans have every reason not to trust Anglo-American providers. The provider may have to prove himself or herself worthy over time. This worthiness will be judged not by the usual trappings of expertise (i.e., how many diplomas on a wall) but by the attitudes, trustworthiness, and availability of the provider (Gibbs, 1988; Gibbs & Huang, 1985).

Even well-intentioned providers can fail this test because they have been taught to interpret certain behaviors in ways that are probably not universally correct. For example, some therapists interpret a client's tardiness or unwillingness to engage in future planning as resistance to therapy. Members from the minority groups, however, may not view appointment times as very important. In fact, they may find the lock step office procedures of many mental health service centers to be offensive or, at least, unhelpful. They may be late for appointments and seem unmoved by the fact they have 50 minutes to discuss their difficulties. Such discussion may take significantly longer or be quite brief. The notion that personal relationships are ordered by time periods may seem very foreign to some clients. They may also not connect to future orientations and long-term planning as being relevant to their current difficulties.

African American families may contain some very angry members. The assertive expression of this anger is frightening to some Anglo American therapists. Its suppression, however, is likely to make genuine communication unlikely (Franklin, 1993). A therapist may have to show the street-smart skill of meeting the unwavering, angry gaze of an African American with calmness, compassion, and perseverance.

Understanding of Difficulties

Most dominant culture members understand physical illness as due to biological difficulties. Their understanding of mental illness is likely to be less clear but often they believe that with personal effort their psychological problems can be alleviated. Whatever their understandings of etiology, majority culture members tend to seek professionally trained, expert help when faced with illnesses.

Hispanic and Native Americans may have a more spiritually based understanding of illness. They may believe illness represents a life that is out of balance because of bad behavior or that evil forces are acting upon the sick or disturbed patient. They may feel more comfortable turning to traditional healers within their own communities to assist them in dealing with illness (Delgado, 1988). Traditional healers often have other jobs (in addition to healing), but still occupy influential positions in many ethnic minority cultures.

Asian American families rarely come to psychologists for emotional or personality problems. Their most frequent use of mental health services concerns vocational and educational counseling (Tracey, Leong, & Glidden, 1986). It is likely they would care for emotionally disturbed family members without professional intervention until such home care became completely impossible (Lin, Inui, Kleinman, & Womack, 1982). Mental illness may still carry a significant stigma in Asian American families representing a failure of the parents to raise children with the appropriate behaviors.

Some Asian Americans may somatize their psychological difficulties. The appearance of physical symptoms due to emotional distress appear commonly in Asian American communities (T.Y. Lin, 1982, 1983, 1990). Neurasthenic reactions may be observed in reaction to a variety of social and personal stresses.

All of the U.S. minorities may have difficulty believing that discussion of difficulties has any value. If their orientations are somewhat external (i.e., the problem is out there and must be fixed by an expert) then Anglo talk therapies appear irrelevant at best. The therapeutic demands for self-disclosure may seem very dangerous given the way most minority groups have been victimized by the dominant culture (Boyd-Franklin, 1993).

Summary and Review

Experts in family assessment may find it useful to pay special attention to a number of issues. A review of existing literature and analysis of our clinical experiences suggest that dominant culture service providers should pay special attention to the following dynamics or constructs. Each of these may vary in ways that make diagnostic impressions based on Anglo-American norms invalid and typical intervention suggestions inappropriate.

Questions about Family Roles

What are the differential expectations toward sons and daughters? Are the son's accomplishments and obedience seen as vitally important to the family's honor and long-term viability? Is the daughter viewed as only a visitor who will someday contribute to her husband's family?

Does the daughter-in-law owe special allegiance and obedience to her mother-in-law?

How influential is the extended family? Is their approval required before decisions can be made?

Are both husband and wife expected to be monogamous? What are the accepted responses toward infidelity?

Are the couple and family comfortable with rigid gender roles? Are the roles complimentary in terms of providing senses of purpose and worth to each member?

How are children to be raised? What are the expectations concerning their behavior in terms of reaching developmental milestones (e.g., toilet training) and in their interaction with adults (e.g., silent, docile, or argumentative and assertive)? What is used to manage their behavior? Considerations of shame and honor may be more powerful than appeals to personal accomplishments or mastery.

How is the family defined? Are there members who are not related by blood or marriage but are nonetheless important sources of support or disturbance?

Personality Factors

Is the family best characterized as optimistic about their abilities to change their situation or pessimistic and fatalistic about their position? Fatalistic world views are common among some minority groups and do not suggest depression or lack of problem-solving skills.

Does the family value independence and individuation or emphasize interdependence? Families may not recognize the value of adult children going off on their own or be impressed by or supportive of individual achievements.

How open is the family? Self-disclosure is valued by mainstream therapists but may be quite offensive to some family members. Because their individual assessments of a situation are considered not important and likely to cause confrontation, talking about personal feelings and opinions may be considered bad manners and irrelevant.

What are the family members' construction of "self?" The Lakota Sioux word *tiospaye* refers to an extended self-concept that includes all family and other relationships necessary for survival. Personal self and needs and rights to become self-actualized may be confusing concepts outside of Anglo American groups.

Belief Systems

How is formal education viewed? Is it seen as equally relevant to men and women? How do family members prefer to learn? Native

American clients report finding informal settings in which they can listen and observe without evaluation or demands for contributions to be the most beneficial.

How powerful is religion or spiritual systems among family members? Sensitivity to religious beliefs is always an important therapeutic issue. This mandate is made more complex by the relative lack of information Anglo American practitioners may have about Native and Hispanic American spirituality and eastern religions.

What is the time orientation of the family? Does a future orientation to problem solving make sense with all families? What are the norms of the family regarding punctuality or scheduling?

How is illness understood? Is there shame? Does a particular symptom represent a punishment? Some Native American groups believed that epilepsy was a punishment for sibling incest. Some Hispanic Americans may believe their difficulties are due to *mal ojo*, that is, an evil curse from another.

Does dominant culture intervention seem relevant to etiological and other cultural beliefs? Should traditional healers from certain groups be involved in treatment programs?

Interpersonal and Interactional Styles

Is rapport and understanding possible if English is used as the second language? Some writers feel that bilingualism is an absolute necessity to really understand what the family is reporting.

What are the parameters associated with personal space? How much touching is considered appropriate? Who can touch whom?

What are nuances of body language? Some Native American groups consider pointing at another to be extremely rude. Some African Americans use what seems to be a signal to move away (i.e., arm and hand waving away from the body) that may actually be an invitation to come closer.

What are the norms of courtesy? Eye contact is sometimes considered to be impolite. In some families only the oldest member should be addressed. How much small talk should be used before (what the service provider considers to be) the session begins? Can first names be used? The safest strategy is to address any older male by a title until given permission to use a first name. How is dress interpreted? Asian Americans may find a casually dressed provider to be unacceptable whereas Native Americans may find those clothed in suits and ties to be too distant to be helpful.

What does yes mean? Among some Southeast Asian immigrant groups a yes means, "I heard you." It does not mean, "I will follow your suggestions."

Does the family value a personal connection to the service provider? In contrast to typical professional norms, some families may want to consult relatives and friends regarding problems. They may come because of knowing the provider in another capacity. The meaning of dual relationships may be difficult to translate to some groups.

Acculturation

All the dynamics suggested in the preceding sections are influenced by the degree to which client families are acculturated to the dominant U.S. culture. Acculturation refers to the learning that occurs among members of minority cultures as a result of their interface with the dominant culture (Padilla, 1980).

Berry (1980) suggested that acculturation occurs in individuals across six dimensions of psychological functioning: language, cognitive styles, personality, identity, attitudes, and acculturative stress. The most obvious measure of acculturation is language. Other signs of increasing acculturation are food preferences, choices of media and entertainment events, knowledge of national history (i.e., which history is known—the new host culture or the original culture), choices of friends for recreational events, and adoption of the norms and values of the host culture.

The level to which minority group members have acculturated to the dominant culture has been shown to have an effect on their mental health status. In general, high levels of acculturation are related to substance abuse, increased risk-taking behaviors, reductions in social support, and general decreases in mental health adjustment ratings (Graves, 1967; Padilla, 1980; Newton, Olmedo, & Padilla, 1982; Szapocznik & Kurtines, 1989).

This finding may appear paradoxical. It seems that current measurement may capture a dimension of acculturation, that is, loss of the culture of origin without ascertaining if another adaptive framework has been developed. Mental health difficulties may arise because individuals have left one system but have little comfort with or acceptance in the other system. African Americans who are described as marginal fit this definition.

Some families may seek professional help because of conflict caused by the discrepancy between the acculturation levels of different generations. Japanese Americans have names for each generation away from birth in Japan (i.e., issei, nisei, sansei, and yousei). A common conflict within this group is the younger generation's rejection of traditional religious, family, and social norms.

Assessment Approaches

There are multiple strategies for evaluating family functioning and multiple targets to consider. Paper-and-pencil normative tests are not as widely used for families as they are for individual assessment. Interviews, observation, and enactments are more frequently utilized.

CRITIQUE OF EXISTING PAPER AND PENCIL FAMILY ASSESSMENTS

Paper-and-pencil measures may not be the most culturally sensitive methodology a practitioner can employ to assess a family from an ethnic minority culture. Bray (Chapter 3 of this volume) notes that most models of family relationships are based on Anglo middle-class families. As a result, most paper-and-pencil measures used to assess family relationships have not been validated with families from diverse ethnic backgrounds.

Family Adaptability and Cohesion Evaluation Scales

Halverson (Chapter 1 in this volume) describes the Family Adaptability and Cohesion Evaluation Scales (FACES; Olson, Portner, & Lavee, 1985) as the benchmark for family assessment. Unfortunately, the norms for the FACES III do not consider cultural and ethnic diversity. The authors of the FACES suggest a practitioner account for cultural ethnic diversity by having family members complete the scale twice—once in reference to how they perceive the family and again for how they ideally would like their family to operate. Olson et al. (1985) also suggest that completion of the Family Satisfaction Scale (Olson & Wilson, 1982) by ethnic minority culture family members will provide helpful information to a practitioner.

If a practitioner wishes to compare a family to the normative group, however, it must be remembered the FACES norm group may not have included members of the particular ethnic culture. Further, a review of certain items that make up the constructs of cohesion and adaptability may give rise to some concern regarding cultural sensitivity.

Family cohesion is defined as emotional bonding that family members have toward one another. It is measured by items such as:

Family members feel very close to each other
Family members feel closer to people outside of the family than to other family members

In our family everyone goes his/her own way
Our family does things together
Family members avoid each other at home
Family members know each other's close friends
Family members consult other family members on their
    decisions
We have difficulty thinking of things to do as a family

Family adaptability is defined as the ability of the marital or family system to change its power structure, role relationships, and relationship rules in response to situation and developmental stress. It is measured by such items as:

Family members say what they want
Each family member has input in major family decisions
Children have a say in their discipline
When problems arise, we compromise
In our family, everyone shares responsibilities
It is difficult to get a rule changed in our family
In our family it is easy for everyone to express his/her
    feelings
Discipline is fair in our family

It seems clear that at least several of these items may mean something in the Anglo American culture and something very different among certain minority families.

Family Environment Scale

Another frequently cited assessment tool, the Family Environment Scale (FES) developed by Moos and Moos (1986), may be used by practitioners to measure the social-environmental characteristics of families from a variety of backgrounds. This scale has been translated into 11 languages including Chinese, French, Korean, and Spanish, which may aid the practitioner who administers it to families with primary languages other than English. In addition, the normative sample includes a small group of Hispanic and African American families. Due to the norming sample not being matched on community size or socioeconomic status, however, the results must be interpreted with caution when used with families from minority cultures.

The FES describes a family's characteristics on the dimension of relationships, personal growth, and system maintenance. The constructs included within these dimensions are cohesion, expressiveness, conflict, independence, achievement orientation, intellectual-cultural orientation, active-recreational orientation, moral-religious emphasis, organization, and control. In name, some of these constructs consider cultural diversity. Because well-constructed norms are not available for minority groups, however, a client's responses may be misinterpreted by a practitioner using the FES for family assessment. Items on the FES that may be problematic include:

> Family members often keep their feelings to themselves
> We fight a lot in our family
> We often talk about political and social problems
> Family members attend church, synagogue, or Sunday School fairly often
> In our family, we are strongly encouraged to be independent
> There is one family member who makes most of the decisions
> Family members strongly encourage each other to stand up for their rights

Like statements on the FACES, the above FES items may have multiple meanings across various minority families.

Other Approaches

Many familiar and innovative methods may be useful with families if a careful analysis is done to insure the methods are congruent with the cultural norms of the family (Patterson, Reid, Jones, & Conger, 1975; Reid, 1978). Parent interview formats have been described by several authors (Aponte, 1976; Fine & Holt, 1983; Friedman, 1969; Golden, 1983).

If family interviewing is impractical, information from the child-administered assessments can also be instructive (Anderson, 1981). For example, the California Test of Personality (Thorpe, Clark, & Tiegs, 1953), Mooney Problem Checklist (Mooney & Gordon, 1950); Offer Self-Image Questionnaire for Adolescents (Offer, 1979); Self-Concept and Motivation Inventory (Farrah, Milehus, & Reitz, 1977) are all general personality tests that have scale scores reflecting family processes.

More specific devices to administer to children include the Behavior Rating Profile (Brown & Hammill, 1983); Child Report of Parent Behavior Inventory (Schaefer, 1965); Child's Attitude toward Mother and Father Scales (Guili & Hudson, 1977); and the Family Relations Test (Bene & Anthony, 1978).

A number of instruments can also be completed by parents to derive information about their child and about their child in the home. Some of these include the Becker Adjective Checklist (Patterson et al., 1975); Revised Behavior Problem Checklist (Quay, 1987); Child

Behavior Profile (Achenbach & Edelbrock, 1991); Eyberg Child Behavior Inventory (Eyberg, Hiers, Cole, Ross, & Eyberg, 1980); and the Parent Daily Report (Patterson et al., 1975).

Another very simple, but useful assessment, goal setting, and monitoring device is an ecomap (Newbrough, Walker, & Abril, 1978). The ecomap graphically represents each system involved with the identified child (e.g., family, church, YWCA, peers, probation) and notes the quality of the relationships among all of the systems. Goals to make the system supportive of change are set and monitored by updates of the ecomap. Essentially, the ecomap turns attention to the qualities of the boundaries surrounding clients as well as to their individual experiences.

Conclusions

Although this brief critique suggests the most frequently cited family assessment tools are not useful for normative comparisons, a therapist may be able to obtain important information under certain conditions. If a measure can be administered in the primary language of the family and the family's priorities match the constructs measured by the instruments, the therapist may use change on the measure following therapy as a means for tracking family members' views on aspects of family life.

INTERVIEWS, OBSERVATIONS, AND ENACTMENTS

Family assessment may be done with the greatest cultural sensitivity and competence using interviews, observations, and enactments. An important axiom to consider is that the solution to any family problem lies within the family's own definition of reality. If practitioners believe this, then a deep understanding of the family ecosystem must be attained before therapists can have confidence in their interpretations and suggestions.

Interviews

An interview format that may be helpful follows. The key ingredients are excellent listening and suspension of personal cultural assumptions. Own up to ignorance when appropriate and ask questions that illustrate an interest in knowing about the family's background.

1. Determine what language should be used. If an interpreter must be used, the person should be one trusted by the family and knowledgeable about nuances in both languages. Even with an interpreter, the validity of the assessment may be compromised.

2. A focus on family strengths will be most respectful. Seeking out family successes and resources is far more useful than trying to determine a psychiatric diagnosis for family members. Many families will not have understandings of difficulties that come close to DSM-IV categories and language difficulties tend to make minority members appear more pathological than they are. In addition, most interventions that will be suggested rely on existing behavioral repertoires. Identification of these is likely to be most critical. For at least these three reasons, an emphasis on strengths is desirable.

3. What are this family's priorities? Service providers make frequent mistakes by assuming what changes are desired by families. Although family therapy may result in clients learning and using strategies modelled or taught by a therapist, therapists should not teach clients to act like Anglo Americans. Therapists aim to make existing systems work within the framework of general understandings of mental health, but must do so with a special sensitivity to cultural variations.

4. What aspects of family life does the family see as important and affecting their priorities? Cause and effect relationships are sensitive to cultural interpretations. It is best to find out what family members believe about how they are involved in problem definition and maintenance before offering an interpretation.

5. What are the family's perceptions of situations and events that affect them? It is common to misconstrue the importance of certain phenomena across cultures. The trust in a therapist will be shattered if a common understanding of what really matters cannot be reached.

6. Check frequently if goals are being met and if services are matching expectations. For example, Sue and Zane (1987) suggest that Asian American clients need some immediate result from therapeutic intervention (e.g., reduction of anxiety, normalization of symptom, relief of depression) for them to continue with services. On the other hand, some Native Americans may take quite a long time before trusting a therapist with important information and may not expect much to change on the basis of their interactions with the therapist.

7. If certain paper-and-pencil instruments must be used, they require scrutiny by culturally aware professionals, community leaders, and family members prior to administration.

8. In contrast to other paper-and-pencil devices (e.g., Moos & Moos, 1986; Olson, Fournier, & Druckman, 1982; Olson, McCubbin, Barnes, Larsen, Muxen, & Wilson, 1982; Olson, Portner, & Lavee, 1989), practitioners might consider careful use of family genograms

(McGoldrick & Gerson, 1985). Genograms focus attention on the complexity of family interrelationships allowing family members to describe the intensity and quality of each of the interactions via graphic representations.

Genograms allow the practitioner and family members to develop hypotheses regarding how a clinical difficulty may be connected to the family system and the evolution of the difficulty over time. McGoldrick and Gerson (1985) provide an interview format that practitioners may find useful. It is a tool for gaining important information from family members about the present living situation, the extended family context, social context, family relationships and roles, and individual issues. Because nuclear and extended family members are included in a genogram, it may be especially suited for use when serving families from minority cultures.

An Illustration

Some of the interpretive pitfalls associated with interviewing minority families may be illustrated by the following. Waterman (1982) suggested a very useful set of questions to use with families who have children with disabilities. Consider each of these from the perspectives of the minority groups described throughout this chapter. (Waterman's questions are paraphrased in italics. Our commentary follows each.)

Do both parents participate with the children? It is a modern Anglo American ideal that both parents have an equitable interaction with their children (especially children with difficulties). Would families from other cultures expect this? Probably not. Who are the caretakers of sick children or children with disabilities in minority families? Can we assume the mother and father of the nuclear family are the most likely ones to shoulder this responsibility?

Are parents overprotective or rejecting or disengaged? What do these terms mean in different cultures? Some Hispanic American girls are never permitted to play out of doors except under the direct supervision of an adult. Is that "overprotective"? Asian Americans may care for their children with disabilities at home and seek help only in the most serious cases. Is that overprotection, rejection, or disengagement? If a child's disability is seen as punishment for family wrongdoings, is that evidence of rejection? Lin et al. (1982) describe a pattern of love, denial, and rejection to characterize Asian American families' reaction to mental illness within the family.

Some Native American families have been seen as rejecting and disengaged toward their children because of the flexible kinship structure in which adults may informally share responsibility for children and the apparently permissive style of parenting that predominates (Attneave, 1982; Locust, 1988; Medicine, 1981).

Do the parents project their anger on each other or on a child? What are cultural expressions of anger? Will it always be recognized by a therapist? How much anger is normative given experiences of racism and oppression? Is anger the most likely emotion to be evoked by a child with a disability? Perhaps guilt, shame, and dishonor are more typical reactions.

Can the children access the parents appropriately? What levels of interaction are normal for different groups? How do children usually get the attention of adults in their culture? Are they supposed to ask for attention?

Is information kept within subsystems? What are the operative subsystems? Some groups may expect women relatives to speak together about family matters or that male elders will be consulted on all decision making. It may be hard to distinguish triangulation in communication when a therapist is not sure who is supposed to know information in certain systems. Anglo American therapists emphasize the husband-wife dyad as appropriately the most intense in a family. This may not be true for many Asian American families (Tamura & Lau, 1992) in which the mother-child dyad (especially between mother and son) is the strongest.

Is nurture and support available within and across subsystems? What are the cultural norms for support? What does nurturing behavior look like? There may be very high expectations for help from extended families that seem unreasonable to an Anglo American therapist, but very normative to certain groups. Expressions of love may be verbal, or physical, or through tangible gifts or goods. Some groups may find expressions of affection to be irrelevant to the quality of their relationships with each other.

Does each system have time alone with its members? To understand alone, a therapist must understand the conception of self. Dominant culture Americans view self in terms of separateness. Many Asians may see self more holistically, feeling identity as belonging to a group of family members, classmates, or company colleagues. In addition, cultural expectations regarding private times may vary as a function of cultural preferences or as a result of economic pressures. There is no word for privacy in Japanese indicating that at least among traditional Japanese the notion of privacy was not valued (Tamura & Lau, 1992). Families who live in one or two rooms, work 16 hours each day, and are responsible to an extended family network are not likely candidates for private times between spouses.

Observations and Enactments

Important family functions can be assessed using behavioral observations. Reliability will vary, of course, depending on the particular techniques and time allotted for the observation. Validity will depend on the practitioner's abilities to choose important observation targets and to interpret the meaning the family members ascribe to the behaviors.

Naturalistic observations are often difficult to arrange. Asking the family to enact various scenarios creates some threats to validity, but does allow the practitioner to see family members in action with each other. Family members can be asked to accomplish a task (e.g., plan an outing or decide on a way to manage a child's school problems) during a therapy session. Choice of the task would be dictated by the presenting priorities and culturally relevant information. Practitioners could gain information about communication patterns, problem solving, family roles, and socialization strategies with just these two tasks.

Another facet of using observational data as the basis for assessment is the possibility of obtaining multirespondent information. In addition to getting individual family members' descriptions of family issues, practitioners can often access teacher descriptions of child behavior. Multimethod and multisource assessments may be very useful as long as family norms for privacy and communication are carefully followed. In some families, individual sessions may be necessary to gather impressions because family members may not confront each other directly.

COMMON MENTAL HEALTH OBJECTIVES

Although mental health probably has many different definitions across U.S. ethnic minority groups (e.g., are you in touch with your feelings or do you successfully repress them for a common good?), there are some goals common to all forms of therapeutic intervention (Madanes, 1990). Each of the goals may be reached in diverse ways depending on cultural expressions and preferences. Whatever the cultural group under consideration, therapists who accept these goals are likely to do less harm than those who do not use them as standards.

Therapists should be seeking information and developing interventions that help them to assist their clients to: (a) control their actions so as to be successful in their chosen tasks; (b) control their thoughts so as to focus their cognitive and emotional energy in productive ways; (c) control violence and anger so that innocent victims are not created and negative cognitive/emotional cycles are avoided; (d) promote empathy so that clients understand the position of others and can choose to use that information if they wish; (e) promote hopefulness in either individual action or collective success—all clients must be able to imagine they will be successful; (f) promote tolerance so that energy can be focused on adjustment and not wasted on hatred of other individuals or groups; (g) encourage forgiveness so that a present or future orientation may be used, thus, allowing for action in the present; and (h) promote harmony and balance that permits a range of human behavior to emerge.

CONCLUSIONS

Careful study of multicultural family measurement issues suggests that culturally sensitive assessment requires broad and deep understandings and a commitment to emic (ideographic/case study knowledge) approaches of assessment. There are many potential sources of confusion when attempting a multicultural practice (Sue, 1991). The most pervasive danger is applying some normative (or etic) constructs to a group without careful validity studies. At this point in time, only emic approaches can be attempted with any safety.

Another problem may be practitioner's beliefs about assimilation versus pluralism (Sue, 1991). Some psychologists may still believe in the melting pot metaphor and expect that ethnic differences will disappear over time. They may assume such homogeneity is preferable to enduring ethnic differences. These practitioners may fear the conflict caused by the clash of cultural norms.

Others believe the differences among the peoples who make up our nation (i.e., a commitment of memory to ethnic group strengths) is what provides the unique and remarkable success of the United States. From this perspective, differences are embraced as complimentary patterns that provide for cultural resilience. Practitioners from this orientation may be interested in acculturation measures as moderators to performance on various psychological tests, but would consider variations among people to be strengths.

Another common cause of confusion, introduced early in this chapter, is a tendency to develop descriptions of group personalities that limit our abilities to recognize individual differences among members of a group. The process of trying to understand minority and recent immigrant groups can inadvertently lead to stereotyping if general statements are confused with personal realities.

Finally, throughout the experience of minority families are the unremitting, humiliating, enraging realities of racism. Those who practice professional psychology must confront racism in their own assumptions and behaviors and learn to identify the effects of racism on their clients. For many of the families who might seek mental health assistance, their everyday life is spent in a toxic environment of hatred, fear, and aggression. We must all be wary of blaming our clients for the environmental stress they endure by using assessment procedures that are insensitive to their contexts.

A challenge of family assessment is to characterize a group of people in meaningful ways. The further challenges of assessing multicultural families are to identify valid targets for measurement and assessment strategies that take into account the costs of being different in the United States of America.

REFERENCES

Achenbach, T.M., & Edelbrock, C. (1991). Revised Child Behavior Profile. Burlington, VT: University Associates in Psychiatry.

Anderson, C. (1981, April). *Family-oriented assessment techniques for school psychologists.* Paper presented at the annual meeting of the National Association of School Psychologists, Detroit, MI.

Anderson, P. P., & Fenichel, E. S. (1989). *Serving culturally diverse families of infants and toddlers with disabilities.* Washington, DC: National Center for Clinical Infant Programs.

Aponte, H. J. (1976). The family-school interview: An eco-structural approach. *Family Process, 15,* 303-311.

Attneave, C. (1982). American Indians and Alaska Native families: Emigrants in their own homeland. In M. McGoldrick, J. K. Pearce, & J. Giordano (Eds.). *Ethnicity and family therapy* (pp. 55-83). New York: Guilford.

Bailey, E. (1987). Sociocultural factors and health care-seeking behavior among Black Americans. *Journal of the National Medical Association, 79,* 389-392

Beavers, W. R., & Hampson, R. B. (1990). *Successful families: Assessment and intervention.* New York: Norton.

Bene, E., & Anthony, J. (1978). Family Relations Test. London, England: NFER Publishing.

Berry, J. (1980). Acculturation as varieties of adaptation. In A. M. Padilla (Ed.), *Acculturation: Theory, models, and some new findings* (pp. 9-25). Boulder, CO: Westview Press.

Boyd-Franklin, N. (1989). *Black families in therapy: A multisystems approach.* New York: Guilford.

Boyd-Franklin, N. (1993). Pulling out the arrows. *Networker*, 17(4), 54-56.

Brown, L. L., & Hammill, D. D. (1983). Behavior Rating Profile. Austin, TX: PRO-ED, Inc.

Campos, L. P. (1989). Adverse impact, unfairness, and bias in the psychological screening of Hispanic peace officers. *Hispanic Journal of Behavioral Sciences, 11,* 127-135.

Cross, W.E., Jr. (1971, July). The Negro-to-black experience. *Black World,* 13-27.

Cross, W. E., Jr. (1978). The Thomas and Cross models of psychological Nigrescence: A review. *Journal of Black Psychology, 5,* 13-31.

Dahlstrom, L. E. (1986). MMPI findings on other American minority groups. In W. G. Dahlstrom, D. Lachar, & L. E. Dahlstrom (Eds.), *MMPI patterns of American minorities* (pp.50-86). Minneapolis: University of Minnesota Press.

Dana, R.H. (1993). *Multicultural assessment perspectives for professional psychology.* Boston: Allyn and Bacon.

Delgado, M. (1988). Group in Puerto Rican spiritism: Implications for clinicians. In C. Jacobs & D. D. Bowles (Eds.), *Ethnicity and race: Critical concepts in social work* (pp. 34-47). Silver Spring, MD: National Association of Social Workers.

Eyberg, S., Hiers, T., Cole, K., Ross, A. W., & Eyberg, S. (1980). *Parent-child interaction training.* Charleston, SC: CAMHC.

Farrah, G. A., Milehus, N. J., & Reitz, W. (1977). *The Self-Concept and Motivation Inventory: What Face Would You Wear?* Dearham Heights, MI: Person-O-Metrics, Inc.

Farris, L. (1978). The American Indian. In A. L. Clark (Ed.), *Culture/childbearing/health professionals* (pp. 20-33). Philadelphia: F.A. Davis Co.

Fine, M. J., & Holt, P. (1983). Intervening with school problems: A family systems perspective. *Psychology in the Schools, 20,* 59-66.

Franklin, A. J. (1993). The invisibility syndrome. *Networker,* 17(4), 32-39.

Friedman, R. (1969). A structured family interview in the assessment of school learning disorders. *Psychology in the Schools, 6,* 162-171.

Gibbs, J. T. (1988). *Young, black, and male in America: An endangered species.* Dover, MA: Auburn House Publishing Co.

Gibbs, J. T., & Huang, L. N. (1989). *Children of color: Psychological interventions with minority youth.* San Francisco: Jossey-Bass Publishers.

Golden, L. (1983). Brief family interventions in a school setting. *Elementary School Guidance & Counseling, 17,* 288-293.

Graves, T. D. (1967). Acculturation, access, and alcohol in a tri-ethnic community. *American Anthropologist, 69*(3-4), 306-321.

Greene, R. L. (1987). Ethnicity and MMPI performance: A review. *Journal of Consulting and Clinical Psychology, 55*, 497-512.

Guili, C. A., & Hudson, W. W. (1977). Child's attitude toward mother and father. *Journal of Social Service Research, 1*, 77-92.

Hersch, P. (1993). Young, gifted and trapped. *Networker, 17*(4), 40-49.

Kemnitzer, L. S. (1973). Adjustment and value conflict in urbanizing Dakota Indians measured by Q-Sort technique. *American Anthropologist, 75*, 687-707.

Kitano, H. H. L., & Daniels, R. (1988). *Asian Americans: Emerging minorities.* Englewood Cliffs, NJ: Prentice-Hall.

LaFromboise, T. D. (1988). American Indian mental health policy. *American Psychologist, 43*, 388-397.

LaFromboise, T. D., & Low, K. G. (1989). American Indian children and adolescents. In J. T. Gibbs & L. N. Huang (Eds.), *Children of color: Psychological interventions with minority youth* (pp. 114-147). San Francisco: Jossey-Bass.

Leung, P., & Sakata, R. (1988). Asian Americans and rehabilitation: Some important variables. *Journal of Applied Rehabilitation Counseling, 9*(4), 16-20.

Lewis, R. G., & Gingerich, W. (1980). Leadership characteristics: Views of Indian and non-Indian students. *Social Casework: The Journal of Contemporary Social Work, 61*(8), 494-497.

Lin, K. M., Inui, T. S., Kleinman, A. M., & Womack, W. M. (1982). Sociocultural determinants of the help-seeking behavior of patients with mental illness. *Journal of Nervous and Mental Disease, 170*, 78-85.

Lin, T. Y. (1982). Culture and psychiatry: A Chinese perspective. *Australian and New Zealand Journal of Psychiatry, 16*, 235-245.

Lin, T. Y. (1983). Psychiatry and Chinese culture. *Western Journal of Medicine, 139*, 862-867.

Lin, T. Y. (1990). Neurasthenia revisited: Its place in modern psychiatry. *Culture, Medicine and Psychiatry, 14*, 105-129.

Locust, C. (1986). *Hopi beliefs about unwellness and handicaps.* Tucson, AZ: University of Arizona

Locust, C. (1988). Wounding the spirit: discrimination and traditional American Indian belief systems. *Harvard Educational Review, 58*, 315-330.

Madanes, C. (1990). *Sex, love, and violence: Strategies for transformation.* New York: Norton.

Manson, S. M., & Trimble, J. E. (1982). American Indian and Alaska Native communities. In L.R. Snowden (Ed.), *Reaching the underserved: Mental health needs of neglected populations* (pp. 143-163). Beverly Hills, CA: Sage.

McAdoo, H. (1979, May). Black kinship. *Psychology Today*, 67-110.

McGoldrick, M., & Gerson, R. (1985). *Genograms in family assessment*. New York: Norton.

Medicine, B. (1981). American Indian family: Cultural change and adaptive strategies. *Journal of Ethnic Studies, 8*(4), 13-23.

Mooney, R. L., & Gordon, L. V. (1950). Mooney Problem Checklist. Cleveland, OH: Psychological Corporation.

Moos, R., & Moos, B. (1986). *Family Environment Scale manual.* Palo Alto, CA: Consulting Psychologists Press.

Morishima, J., Sue, S., Teng, L. N., Zane, N., & Cram, J. (1979). *Handbook of Asian American/Pacific Islander mental health research.* Rockville, MD: National Institute of Mental Health.

Myers, H. F. (1982). Research on the Afro-American family; A critical review. In B. A. Bass, G. E. Wyatt, & G. J. Powell (Eds.), *The Afro-American family: Assessment, treatment, and research issues* (pp. 35-68). New York: Grune & Stratton.

Nakanishi, D.T. (1988). Seeking convergence in race relations research: Japanese-Americans and the resurrection of the internment. In P. A. Katz & D. A. Taylor (Eds.), *Eliminating racism: Profiles in controversy* (pp. 159-180). New York: Plenum.

Newbrough, J. R., Walker, L., & Abril, S. (1978, April). *Workshop on ecological assessment.* National Association of School Psychologists, New York.

Newton, F., Olmedo, E. L., & Padilla, A. M. (1982). *Hispanic mental health research: A reference guide.* Berkeley, CA: University of California Press.

Offer, P. (1979). *The psychological world of the teenager: A study of normal adolescent boys.* New York: Basic Books.

Olson, D. H., Fournier, D. G., & Druckman, J. M. (1982). *ENRICH.* Minneapolis: PREPARE-ENRICH.

Olson, D. H., McCubbin, H. I., Barnes, H., Larsen, A., Muxen, M., & Wilson, M. (1982). *Family inventories.* St. Paul, MN: Social Science, University of Minnesota.

Olson, D. H., Portner, J., & Lavee, Y. (1985). *FACES III.* St. Paul, MN: Family Social Science, University of Minnesota.

Olson, D. H., & Wilson, M. (1982). Family Satisfaction Scale. St. Paul, MN: Family Social Science, University of Minnesota.

Oster, G. D., & Caro, J. E. (1990). *Understanding and treating depressed adolescents and their families*. New York: Wiley.

Padilla, A. M. (1980). *Acculturation, theory, models, and some new findings*. Boulder, CO: Westview Press.

Padilla, A. M., & Ruiz, R. A. (1975). Personality assessment and test interpretation of Mexican American: A critique. *Journal of Personality Assessment, 39,* 103-109.

Parham, T. A. (1989). Nigrescence: The transformation of Black consciousness across the life cycle. In R. L. Jones (Ed.), *Black adult development and aging* (pp. 151-166). Berkeley, CA: Cobb & Henry.

Patterson, G. R., Reid, J. B., Jones, R.R., & Conger, R.E. (1975). *A social learning approach to family intervention, Volume 1: Families with aggressive children*. Eugene, OR: Castalia Publishing Co.

Pinderhughes, E. (1982). Afro-American families and the victim system. In M. McGoldrick, J.K. Pearce, & J. Giordano (Eds.), *Ethnicity and family therapy* (pp. 108-122). New York: Guilford.

Quay, H. C. (1987). Revised Behavior Problem Checklist. Odessa, FL: Psychological Assessment Resources, Inc.

Reid, J. B. (Ed.) (1978). *A social learning approach to family intervention, Volume 2: Observation in home settings*. Eugene, OR: Castalia Publishing Co.

Samora, J. (1979). Conceptions of health and disease among Spanish-Americans. *American Catholic Sociological Review, 22,* 314-323.

Schaefer, E. S. (1965). Child report of parent behavior. *Child Development, 36,* 413-423.

Staples, R. (1988). The Black American family. In C.H. Mindel, R. W. Habenstein, & R. Wright, Jr. (Eds.), *Ethnic families in America: Patterns and variations* (pp. 303-324). New York: Elsevier.

Starr, P. D., & Roberts, A. E. (1982). Attitudes toward new Americans: Perceptions of Indo-Chinese in nine cities. In C. B. Marrett & C. Leggon (Eds.), *Research in race and ethnic relations: A research annual* (Vol.3, Part 2, pp. 165-186). Greenwich, CT: JAI Press.

Steele, S. (1990). *The content of our character: A new vision of race in America*. New York: St. Martin Press.

Sue, S. (1991). Ethnicity and culture in psychological research and practice. In J.D. Goodchilds (Ed.), *Psychological perspectives on human diversity in America* (pp. 51-85). Washington, DC: American Psychological Association

Sue, S., & Zane, N. (1987). The role of culture and cultural techniques in psychotherapy: A critique and reformulation. *American Psychologist, 42,* 37-45.

Szapocnik, J., & Kurtines, W. M. (1989). *Breakthroughs in family therapy in drug abusing and problem youth.* New York: Springer Publishing Co.

Tamura, T., & Lau, A. (1992). Connectedness versus separateness: Applicability of family therapy to Japanese families. *Family Process, 31,* 319-340.

Thomas, C.S. (1971). *Boys no more.* Beverly Hills, CA: Glencoe.

Thorpe, P., Clark, W.W., & Tiegs, E. W. (1953). California Test of Personality. New York: CTB/McGraw-Hill

Tracey, T. J., Leong, F. T. L., & Glidden, C. (1986). Help seeking and problem perception among Asian Americans. *Journal of Counseling Psychology, 33,* 331-336.

Trimble, J. (1990-1991). Ethnic specification, validation prospects, and the future of drug use research. *International Journal of the Addictions, 25*(2A), 149-170.

Velasquez, R. J. (1992). Hispanic American MMPI research (1949-1992): A comprehensive bibliography. *Psychological Reports, 70,* 743-745.

Waterman, J. (1982). Assessment of the family system. In G. Ulrey & S. J. Rogers (Eds.), *Psychological assessment of handicapped infants and young children* (pp. 172-178). New York: Thieme-Stratton.

Whatley, P. R., & Dana, R. H. (1989). *Racial identity and MMPI group differences.* Unpublished paper, Department of Psychology, University of Arkansas, Fayetteville, AR.

Wilson, M. N. (1993). A view of African American family life: Thoughts and implications for social research and intervention. *Focus: Notes from the Society for the Psychological Study of Minority Issues, 7*(2), 14-15.

SIBLING RELATIONSHIPS

Michelle C. Schicke

University of Nebraska-Lincoln

INTRODUCTION

The nature of sibling relationships has been given considerable empirical attention. Research has focused on describing the nature of sibling interaction and roles siblings play in each others' lives, as well as on attempting to support the contention that the sibling relationship can impact children's psychosocial development (Dunn, 1983). The latter purpose has been influenced by two areas: behavior genetics and family systems theory.

Behavior geneticists have proposed that although siblings have roughly half their segregating genes in common, environmental influences operate in a way that makes siblings no more alike than two children chosen at random from the population (Plomin, 1986). Specifically, most environmental influences that affect children appear to be nonshared among family members. Children's psychosocial development, therefore, is influenced mainly by their genetic composition and environmental variables such as peer interactions, sibling treatment of each other, and possibly parental treatment that is those unique to individuals in the same family (Plomin & Daniels, 1987). Rowe and Plomin (1981) stated that interactions between siblings leads to differences between them because they treat each other differently (i.e., due to their natural style of behavior), and because they can play complementary roles that reinforce the differences between them. Therefore, siblings influence the behavior and development of each other by providing different environments for each other.

Systems theory has also impacted sibling research. Carlson in Chapter 2 of this volume discusses the major tenets of systems theory, and they will not be repeated here. According to family systems theory, siblings constitute a major subsystem of the larger family system (Minuchin, 1985), and as such impact the behavior and development of children. The influence of siblings can be direct (e.g., through sibling-sibling interaction) or indirect (e.g., one sibling's presence can affect parental behavior toward another sibling). All members of a family are interrelated and mutually influential parts of the family unit, and therefore no individual (or set of individuals) should be studied in isolation without considering the influence of other parties.

This chapter is premised on the view that sibling relationships are in fact an important part of children's psychosocial development. The first sections of the chapter review research related to sibling relationships. Various aspects and characteristics of such relationships are discussed, and factors related to relationship quality are reviewed. Given that siblings play a prominent role in children's lives, it is proposed that sibling relationships are of significance to both researchers and clinicians working with and studying children and families. The second section of the chapter therefore addresses strategies for assessing sibling interaction and related measurement issues.

CHARACTERISTICS OF SIBLING RELATIONSHIPS

Researchers have devoted a substantial amount of time to studying various dimensions of sibling relationships. The impetus for much of this research is the amount of time siblings spend together and the finding that studying parent-child dyads while disregarding the influence of siblings is misleading. As a result, additional focus has been placed on studying relationships among all family members, including siblings. This section is a review of relevant literature in the area of sibling relationships. The intent is to provide a concise overview of findings related to how siblings behave with one another, and to show that siblings play an important role in children's social and cognitive development. Specifically, reactions of the firstborn to the birth of a new baby, sibling prosocial and aggressive behaviors, attachment, caretaking, teaching, and imitation are   addressed. Although certainly not exhaustive of all aspects of sibling relationships, these characteristics appear to be most often empirically investigated. Because of sibling influence, clinicians and researchers alike should give serious consideration to the impact of the sibling relationship on children's development and psychosocial adjustment.

Reactions to the Birth of a Sibling

From a systems perspective, a new baby represents a dramatic shift in a family's experience of interactional patterns and affective climate (Nadelman & Begun, 1982). Most of the existing research examines the effects of a newborn in two-child families, that is the effects of the newborn on firstborn children. Although marked individual differences have been noted (Dunn & Kendrick, 1982b), many children exhibit behavior change in reaction to the new family member. Furthermore, firstborn children's relationships with parents are altered upon a newborn's birth. These changes have been found to impact the firstborn child's behavior toward the newborn sibling and toward parents.

Firstborns. There is great variation in the way firstborns react to the birth of the second child. Some exhibit problem behaviors, such as increased   crying, clinging, "baby talk," demanding a bottle at night, and problems with toileting (Stewart, Mobley, Van Tuyl, & Salvador, 1987). Some children, however, display no change in behavior or improvements in some   behavior problems after the second child's birth (Nadelman & Begun, 1982). For example, some firstborns show an increase in maturity and independence after the birth of a sibling (Dunn & Kendrick, 1982b). The sex of the firstborn may be a mediator, with boys tending to withdraw and girls showing increased dependence (Nadelman & Begun, 1982; Dunn, Kendrick, & MacNamee, 1981).

Mothers. The birth of a second child also represents dramatic shifts in relationships between firstborn children and other family members. Dunn and Kendrick (1980) reported the time mothers spend interacting with firstborn children declines after the birth of a sibling. Additionally, the frequency of unsolicited positive comments about firstborns' actions decreases, whereas confrontations and comments prohibiting the older child increase. These changes appear to impact firstborns' behavior. Increases in confrontation have been associated with increased negative behavior toward the mother, and increased prohibition by the mother has been found to be related to the frequency with which older children irritate the younger sibling (Dunn et al., 1981). Dunn and Kendrick

(1981a) found that females who played frequently with mothers before the birth of the baby exhibited fewer numbers of prosocial behaviors toward the baby. Fourteen months later these babies were less prosocial toward their older siblings. Less prosocial behavior by females was also associated with playful interaction between the mother and the infant. These effects were not found for males. It was proposed that, for males, decreases in maternal attention may affect other family relationships.

Effects of maternal behavior have been found to affect the behavior of older children toward their siblings several months later as well. Dunn and Kendrick (1982a) reported that when mothers spent a high percentage of time interacting with 8-month-old infants, the firstborn was more likely to make negative approaches toward the baby during the course of a mother-infant interaction 6 months later.

Fathers. Although little attention has been given to fathers' involvement and influence on children's behavior following a sibling's birth, fathers' influence deserves attention. Stewart et al. (1987) observed family interactions prior to and one month after infants' births. They found that firstborn children increased behavior directed toward the father and decreased behavior toward the mother. These researchers suggested that fathers may actually compensate for the decreased attention mothers pay to firstborn children by maintaining their levels of interactions with firstborn children. Dunn and Kendrick (1982b) found that conflicts between mothers and older siblings were fewer when fathers were involved in child care. It appears, therefore, that fathers can play an instrumental role in maintaining some balance within the family system upon the addition of a new child.

Long-Term Effects. It has been suggested that the affective quality of sibling relationships initially established may continue into early childhood (Dunn, 1983). For example, Stillwell and Dunn (1985) found links between the first child's initial interest in the newborn and the affective quality of their relationship 4 years later. In contrast, Abramovitch, Corter, and Pepler (1982) found little stability over an 18-month period in their study of preschool-aged firstborn children and their infant siblings. These differences may be due to variations in observational recording techniques (Dunn, 1983). Nevertheless, the continuity that has been observed may reflect the influence of the first child's personality on the developing sibling relationship, or the stability of parental response to the children and the sibling relationship (Stillwell & Dunn, 1985). That is, continuity may be a function of constant personality characteristics of one of the siblings (e.g., emotional intensity), or interactional patterns learned through consistent parental reinforcement of certain sibling-directed behaviors.

Prosocial/Agonistic Behavior Among Siblings

Probably the most widely studied of sibling relationship characteristics are the occurrence and maintaining factors of siblings' prosocial and agonistic behavior toward each other. Researchers have generally observed sibling interactions and coded interchanges as either positive (prosocial), negative (agonistic, aggressive, etc.), or neutral. Results of many such observations suggest that there is a great deal of interaction between siblings that can be classified as either prosocial or aggressive.

Research concerned with prosocial and agonistic behavior among siblings has often centered around determining characteristics of siblings that lend themselves to the absence or maintenance of such behaviors. Some researchers have concentrated on sibling status variables, such as birth order, sex composition of the sibling pair (i.e., same sex or mixed sex), sex of the children, and age interval between the siblings (Abramovitch, Corter, Pepler, & Stanhope, 1986; Baskett & Johnson, 1982; Corter, Pepler, & Abramovitch, 1982; Dunn & Kendrick, 1981b; Dunn & Munn, 1986; Pelletier-Stiefel et al., 1986). Others have suggested that family constellation variables do not account for much variance in sibling behavior (Brody, Stoneman, & Burke, 1987; Brody, Stoneman, & McKinnon, 1986; Brody, Stoneman, & McCoy, 1992; Bryant, 1982; Corter, Abramovitch, & Pepler, 1983). Instead, these researchers promote studying such variables as temperament of the children involved and parental behavior toward the siblings. Aside from looking at the characteristics that predict certain sibling behavior, some researchers have investigated the stability of prosocial and agonistic behaviors in order to learn how sibling relationship characteristics can affect the behavior of the siblings in the long term.

Family Constellation Variables. The majority of research on sibling aggression and prosocial behavior has focused on differences in the frequency with which such behavior occurs as a function of siblings' position within the family. Specifically, researchers have studied whether agonism and prosocial behavior varies systematically with age spacing between the children, sex of both children, whether the siblings are of the same or different sexes, and sibling birth order.

Regarding age interval between siblings, almost all research points to the lack of a consistent relationship between age spacing of siblings and the amount of conflict or frequency of prosocial behavior between preschool-aged children and their infant siblings (Corter et al., 1982; Dunn & Kendrick, 1981b; Dunn & Munn, 1986; Pelletier-Stiefel et al.,

1986). Nevertheless, Minnett, Vandell, and Santrock (1983) and Stocker, Dunn, and Plomin (1989) found more conflict in wider spaced siblings. Differences in findings could be due to methodology. Minnett and colleagues conducted observations with 7- to 8-year-olds in a school setting (versus home observations), with the subjects unaware of being observed and with mothers absent. Stocker et al. (1989) observed siblings during a marble game. A higher proportion of conflict between wider spaced siblings in this study may have been due to the inability of some of the younger subjects (i.e., second-born children in the large interval group) to understand the game. Some self-report studies with relatively older children have pointed to a trend for greater conflict between siblings closer in age (Burmester & Furman, 1990; Furman & Burmester, 1985). It is possible that older children perceive more conflict with siblings who are more comparable to themselves developmentally, because such children may interact more in general, thus increasing the likelihood of conflict.

Sex of the siblings has also been investigated for its relation to sibling behavior. Some researchers have found that males and females differ in their behavior toward siblings. Among firstborn preschool-aged siblings, girls have been found to be more prosocial and nurturing than boys (Abramovitch, Corter, & Lando, 1979; Corter et al., 1982), although these effects may diminish with age of the siblings (Pepler, Abramovitch, & Corter, 1981). Other researchers have found no sex differences in regards to frequency of conflict or prosocial behavior (Baskett & Johnson, 1982, Dunn & Kendrick, 1981b; Dunn & Munn, 1986; Pelletier-Stiefel et al., 1986).

Brody, Stoneman, MacKinnon, and MacKinnon (1985) suggested that observed sex differences in the amounts of prosocial behavior displayed may be the result of different amounts of interaction by children of different sexes, rather than the effects of gender per se. For example, the finding that older females in same-sex sibling pairs are more prosocial than males in same-sex sibling pairs may be due to the general higher rate of interaction among female siblings than among male siblings. Finally, Abramovitch et al. (1979) suggested that global agonism is not related to sex, but that boys more frequently use physical forms of agonism, whereas girls are more verbal in agonistic encounters.

Unlike interval and sex, consistent evidence exists for the effects of sex composition on rates of prosocial behavior and agonism. Specifically, almost all researchers have concluded that same-sex sibling dyads are typically more prosocial and less aggressive than are mixed-sex dyads (Dunn & Kendrick, 1981b; Pepler et al., 1981). An exception to this is Minnett et al. (1983), who reported that cheating, aggression, and negative behavior were more characteristic of 7- and 8-year-olds in same-sex as opposed to mixed-sex pairs. These differences may be due to the ages of children studied and/or the methodological differences previously discussed.

The effects of birth order on sibling interaction is the family constellation variable most widely studied, and findings in this area are relatively consistent. Older children are typically more prosocial and nurturant than their younger siblings (Abramovitch et al., 1986; Pelletier-Stiefel et al., 1986; Pepler et al., 1981), although between 8 and 14 months of age, younger members increase the amount of prosocial behavior toward their older siblings (Dunn & Kendrick, 1981b). Pelletier-Stiefel et al. (1986) suggested that differences are not due to discrepancies between siblings in cognitive functioning, but rather to relative position in the family. Specifically, these researchers looked at the prosocial behavior and agonism of second-born children when they were the age of the firstborn children at the time of the original study. Firstborns were still higher in their rates of prosocial and agonistic behaviors. Older siblings are also typically more aggressive than their younger counterparts (Abramovitch et al., 1979; Abramovitch et al., 1986).

It appears that, in general, family status variables account for little variability in the affective quality of sibling interaction. The only consistent findings have been that older siblings in the dyad tend to be more prosocial and more aggressive than their younger siblings, and that same-sex dyads are more positive in their encounters. However, these effects may not be due to the status variables per se. Older children may be more prosocial and more agonistic than their younger counterparts simply because their repertoire of social behaviors is larger than that of the younger sibling. The higher frequency of positive behaviors among same-sex siblings may be in part a function of more interaction between these siblings than those of different sexes, which may lend itself to more prosocial behavior. Conversely, it could be that siblings who are more prosocial want to interact more with each other. Many researchers have espoused the view that the key to understanding the marked individual differences in prosocial and aggressive behavior lies not in family status characteristics, but in personality of the individual children and in parent behaviors toward the siblings (Brody & Stoneman, 1987; Dunn, 1988).

Temperament and Family Environment Variables. Because there are such marked individual differences in the behavior of sibling pairs, one possible source of variability is the temperaments of the children involved (Brody & Stoneman, 1987; Dunn, 1988). Brody, Stoneman, and Burke (1987) suggested that sibling dyads including an active, emotionally intense or nonpersistent child are more likely to experience high rates of agonistic behavior. Additionally, these researchers suggested that if both siblings display these temperamental characteristics, an even greater amount of conflict may be evidenced. Conversely, a buffering effect may be noted if only one of the children is active, emotionally intense, or nonpersistent. Although temperament is beginning to receive recognition as a correlate of sibling aggression, research concerned with temperament's relation to the occurrence of prosocial behavior is lacking.

Because sibling interaction occurs in the larger family context, it is important to study parental behavior and influence on the interaction between siblings. Research that has systematically studied parental influence generally has focused on three issues, including the effects of parental presence/absence on quality of sibling interaction, parental response to conflict between siblings, and differential treatment of siblings by parents.

Regarding parental presence, research consistently has shown that siblings get along better when mothers are absent rather than present. Corter et al. (1983) found during home observations that sibling prosocial behavior was lower in the mother's presence, and in a laboratory study young siblings were found to be more aggressive when mothers were present (Corter et al., 1982). Additionally, reports by mothers agree with observations. Corter et al. (1983) found that 72% of mothers reported that their children were more prosocial when they were absent. Corter et al. (1982) suggested that this phenomenon may be due to several factors. First, it is safer for younger children to fight back in the mother's presence. Second, a greater demand for self-control is placed upon children in the absence of adult supervision. Third, negative behavior in the presence of the mother may serve to maintain her attention, thereby reinforcing aggressiveness.

A second parental variable that has been studied is parental response to conflict. The main conclusion reached thus far is that there is a definite link between parental response to conflict and frequency of conflict (Brody & Stoneman, 1987; Brody, Stoneman, & Burke, 1987; Stocker et al., 1989), yet the direction of these effects is not yet clear (Dunn, 1988). For example, Dunn and Munn (1986) suggested that maternal involvement in conflict was associated with an increase in frequency of quarrels, but that children whose parents intervened also showed more mature conflict-resolving strategies (e.g., conciliation, reference to social rules) than did children whose mothers did not intervene. Regarding types of parental involvement, Brody et al. (1986) found that when mothers reportedly used non-punitive child rearing practices, older siblings were less agonistic toward their younger siblings, suggesting that child rearing practices used by parents may affect the development of prosocial orientations in children. Correlations also have been found between maternal discussion of the feelings and needs of one sibling with the other and later friendly behavior by both siblings (Dunn & Kendrick, 1982a).

The most extensively studied area of parental involvement and influence has been differential treatment of siblings. Some research has focused on attempting to determine if parents are discrepant in their treatment of siblings, whereas other research has been concerned with the effects of differential treatment on the quality of sibling relationships.

Many studies have shown that parents are relatively consistent in their treatment of first- and second-born children (Abramovitch et al., 1982). For example, Dunn and Kendrick (1982b) found that mothers who are playful with their oldest child also tend to be playful with the second born. However, some inconsistencies have been found as well. Bryant (1982) found that firstborn siblings in middle childhood receive a fair amount of attention when alone with their mothers, but are relatively neglected when both children are present. Other research has suggested that second-born children receive more attention than older children (Brody, Stoneman, & Burke, 1987; Brody et al., 1992). Dunn and Kendrick (1981b) found that mothers interacted more with their second-born children only if the younger child differed in sex from the firstborn child.

Research that has centered on the effects of differential parental treatment on sibling relationships generally has shown that differential treatment by parents is correlated with frequency of sibling conflict (Dunn, 1988). It has also been suggested that ill will by siblings is evidenced by both children, not only by the child who receives less parental attention (Bryant & Crockenburg, 1980). The effects of differential treatment have far-reaching implications. Stocker et al. (1989) suggested that children's realization that they are treated differently from their siblings and their reactions to this realization may affect a child's well-being and development. It has also been found that perceived differences in parental behavior toward the siblings is associated with emotional adjustment differences among adolescent siblings (Daniels, Dunn, Furstenberg, & Plomin, 1985).

There is evidence for the stability of sibling behavior patterns toward each other, both in terms of prosocial and aggressive behavior. Regarding prosocial behavior, Stillwell and Dunn (1985) found considerable stability over a 3- to 4-year period. Stability is true especially for the older sibling in a dyad (Dunn & McGuire, 1992). Younger siblings have been found to increase amounts of prosocial behavior by age 6 to 8 (Vandell, Minnett, & Santrock, 1987).

Additionally, the reactions of young siblings to the prosocial initiations of older siblings change as later-born siblings grow older, in that such initiations become less welcome. This may be due to the later-born children requiring less nurturance and direction from older siblings as they become more independent and competent (Burmester & Furman, 1990).

More important from a clinical standpoint is the stability and significance of aggressive behavior patterns. Stability in agonistic and conflictual relations has been evidenced over time (Dunn, 1983). Aggressive behavior at home has been associated with aggression among peers in a preschool setting (Berndt & Bulleit, 1985). Furthermore, sibling aggression has been associated with later behavior problems of children (Dunn, 1988; Stillwell & Dunn, 1985). Patterson (1984) reported that coercive behavior by siblings plays a role independent of that of parents in the development of coercive behavior of children. Stillwell and Dunn (1985) concluded that if aggressive behavior does indeed show stability over time, then siblings' influence on aggressive behaviors of children should be seriously considered.

Attachment and Caretaking

Research shows that younger siblings often display the same types of attachment behaviors to their siblings as are typically shown to primary caregivers. Although researchers have not claimed that siblings are the primary attachment figures for infants, related investigations have shown that young children can show attachment behaviors to older siblings as well as to parents. Samuels (1980) claimed that because older siblings, like mothers and fathers, are constant features of infants' social environments, their absence may be disruptive to infants' behavior.

There is a great deal of evidence for attachment characteristics in the sibling relationship. In a laboratory study, Lamb (1978) observed that infants monitored the whereabouts and activities of their preschool-aged older siblings and attempted to maintain proximity to them. Infants have been observed to show signs of distress at the absence of their older siblings (Dunn, 1983; Samuels, 1980), to greet them with pleasure (Dunn, 1983), to use older siblings as a secure base for exploration (Stewart, 1983), and to go to their older siblings when upset (Dunn & Kendrick, 1982a).

One reason attachments may develop is that older children display many of the same caretaking behaviors as parents. Although sibling versions of caretaking behaviors are rudimentary and differ in style from those of parents (Bryant, 1982), older children often assume roles that resemble those of parents, such as providing positive, supportive care and showing physical affection (Pelletier-Stiefel et al., 1986).

Stewart (1983) found in a laboratory study that when parents left the room and infants appeared distressed, many older siblings made attempts to comfort the infant by hugging them or distracting them. This form of supportive caretaking was found to occur more by older sisters than older brothers in mixed-sex sibling dyads. Older brothers did not typically respond with caretaking behaviors toward their younger sisters, but older sisters tended to "smother" their younger brothers. This suggests that, although siblings may make attempts to comfort, they are not as attuned to how to go about it as are parents and other adults.

Teaching

Siblings also can be a source of instruction for children. It has been found that young children learn more effectively if taught by someone close to their own age, and that individuals can learn through the process of teaching someone else (Cicerelli, 1976). Siblings are in a good position to teach and provide modeling and reinforcement for each other, due to a great deal of opportunity to interact.

Research on teaching behavior by siblings has shown, not surprisingly, that older children typically assume the teacher role, whereas younger siblings assume the learner role (Minnett et al., 1983; Stoneman, Brody, & McKinnon, 1984). Because it has been found that people learn from the process of teaching, it is likely that both older and younger siblings in a dyad profit from such instructional interactions.

Regarding sex of the siblings, it appears that older females in a dyad tend to teach more often than do older males (Brody et al., 1985; Cicerelli, 1976). This may be because females are often delegated more caretaking responsibilities than are males, and/or because girls identify more with mothers and female teachers, which influences them to take on roles similar to these prominent adults (Cicerelli,

1976). In addition, younger females in a dyad assume the learner role
more often than do young males. Brody et al. (1985) suggested that
if younger females are more socially engaging and attentive, older
siblings would be more likely to attempt to teach than they would
with boys, whose temperaments often make them difficult to instruct.

Imitation

Aside from direct teaching, siblings can learn from each other
through imitation. For example, Lamb (1978) suggested that one way
infants learn is by repeating a behavior shortly after an older sibling
has done it. Research in this area has focused mainly on how sibling
status variables affect the observance of imitative behaviors in sibling
dyads.

Most research has looked at imitation as a function of birth order,
sex, and sex composition of the sibling dyad. Regarding birth order,
researchers have unanimously agreed that younger siblings imitate
more frequently than older siblings in a dyad (Abramovitch et al.,
1979; Dunn, 1983), although Abramovitch et al. (1979) reported that
20% of imitative behaviors were displayed by firstborn children.
Although older siblings may not be as prone to imitate younger
siblings, these findings suggest that many are interested in the behavior
of their younger siblings.

Investigators have not found sex effects on the frequency of
imitation by younger siblings (Abramovitch et al., 1979; Abramovitch
et al., 1982), but sex composition appears to play a role. Specifically,
imitation is observed to occur more in same-sex than mixed-sex
sibling pairs. Abramovitch et al. (1982) found that imitation decreased
in mixed-sex pairs from the time the younger siblings were 18 months
until they were 36 months old. These researchers suggested that the
younger siblings may have begun to perceive the older sibling as
different, and thus decreased their imitation.

Summary

In conclusion, there is a large body of evidence to suggest that the
sibling relationship in childhood is multifaceted and potentially
important to children's psychosocial development. Siblings' births
may bring about behavior change in firstborn children. Additionally,
the quality of the initial relationship may well be related to the quality
of the relationship years later. Associations have been found between
hostility in the sibling relationship and later adjustment problems of
children. Children can develop attachments to their siblings, and

many display caretaking behavior. Finally, siblings can be a source of teaching and learning for each other, both in terms of direct instruction and imitation.

Although siblings may not be considered the main influence on a child's development, they play an important part in children's lives. Parent-child relationships, although certainly important, do not present the entire picture of a child's family environment. It is also necessary to investigate how sibling relationships mediate parent-child relationships and vice versa. The assessment of sibling relationships is therefore a necessary practice for both researchers and clinicians.

ASSESSING SIBLING RELATIONSHIPS

Researchers have used a variety of methods to collect information about sibling relationships. Parents often serve as a source of information through interviews and various behavior rating scales and checklists. Children themselves, especially those in middle childhood and adolescence, can provide interview and checklist data. Additionally, direct observations of the interactions among various family members can yield a relatively objective perspective on the actual behaviors being displayed by siblings and other family members. The following is an overview of several of the more frequently used methods of measuring sibling relationships. Because each type of measure has unique strengths and weaknesses, it is suggested that the best estimate of the sibling relationship can be gained from multimethod assessment that draws on the perspectives of multiple parties.

Observations

Observations of sibling interaction are the most commonly used method of studying how siblings relate to each other, especially when subjects are young children. Though generally similar in purpose, there is variation among studies in how observations are actually implemented. Points of departure include behaviors or aspects of behavior observed, parties chosen as targets of observation, places at which observations are conducted, types of situation observed, and how collected information is described.

Behaviors to Observe. The selection of behaviors to observe depends in part on the topic of study. For example, many investigators have observed positive and negative behaviors of siblings in order to determine affective quality of the relationship (Abramovitch et al., 1982; Baskett & Johnson, 1982; Dunn & Kendrick, 1981b; Minnett et al., 1983; Stillwell & Dunn, 1985). On the other hand, studies of sibling attachment behaviors focus on behaviors such as the distance an infant is willing to travel from the mother when an older sibling is present (Samuels, 1980), and comforting behaviors emitted by an older sibling when the mother leaves or a stranger enters a situation (Stewart, 1983). Furthermore, there is often some disparity in terms for selected sets of behaviors to be assessed, even among studies purporting to measure similar constructs. For example, positive physical approaches have been termed "physical affection" (Abramovitch et al., 1982), "positive affiliative touch" (Minnett et al., 1983), and "touches affectionately" (Dunn & Kendrick, 1981b). These terms may or may not imply the same behaviors, therefore results of different studies are difficult to compare. Additionally, a construct such as positive or prosocial touch implies at least some degree of inference on the part of the observer, again making cross-study comparisons questionable.

Because most investigators have been interested in interactions between siblings rather than isolated behaviors of children, it has been necessary to employ a system for coding sibling responses to certain child behaviors. Abramovitch et al. (1982), for example, observed child responses to agonistic behavior (e.g., submit, counterattack, no response) and child responses to prosocial behavior (e.g., positive, negative, no response). Depending on how many steps in an interactional sequence the investigator/clinician wants to observe, additional categories of behavior may be necessary (e.g., a child's response to a sibling's counterattack).

Who to Observe. Although it is intuitively appealing simply to observe dyadic interactions between siblings, more information may be gained by including additional family members in the observation. Because interactions between siblings are indirectly impacted by interactions among other family members, it can be helpful to include those such as parents as part of the observation process. For example, Dunn and Kendrick (1980) looked at dyadic interchanges between siblings with mother present and with/without the father present. Such participant variation gives a clearer idea of how sibling interactions are influenced by third parties and family dynamics. This information is essential for researchers, as well as for clinicians attempting to design family-centered interventions.

Where to Conduct Observations. Observations have been conducted in homes (Abramovitch et al., 1982; Brody et al., 1986; Berndt & Bulleit, 1985; Dunn & Kendrick, 1982b; Stillwell & Dunn, 1985), laboratories (Lamb, 1978; Stewart, 1983), and classrooms (Minnett et al., 1983). Discrepant results of sibling relationship studies may well be due to places in which observations were conducted. Lamb (1978) found a much lower rate of interaction between siblings in his laboratory study than have been found in observations conducted in homes. Several factors may contribute to a lowered rate of interaction in a laboratory setting, including the unfamiliarity of the situation, the brevity of observation sessions, and large arrays of novel toys that may distract the siblings from one another (Abramovitch et al., 1982). Despite similarities between laboratory and classroom contexts, Minnett et al. (1983) did not find a lowered rate of interaction in classroom observations. This is possibly because the siblings in the classroom setting were involved in structured tasks.

The most appropriate place in which to conduct observations may partly depend on the types of behaviors to be observed. For example, Dunn and Kendrick (1982a) discussed observations of young children's ability to respond to the feelings of their infant siblings and react appropriately. These authors suggested that in order to see these types of behaviors, children must be studied in situations involving familiar people and familiar situations. Additionally, if the investigator is studying the pattern of family influences on children, it is important to conduct observations in the home (Dunn & Kendrick, 1982a).

Situational Variables. There are several other variables that can be incorporated into an observation of sibling interactions. For example, the researcher/clinician needs to decide whether to conduct unstructured or structured observations, or a combination of both. It may be helpful to vary the situation in order to learn how siblings relate in different situations.

Unstructured or naturalistic observations generally involve instructing the family to ignore the observer and engage in normal activities. Depending on whether triadic interactions involving the mother or father are the focus, observers may instruct parents to refrain from purposely interacting with the children being observed. Additionally, though not completely unstructured, investigators may ask the children to engage in some specific task that is representative of typical shared activities between siblings. Brody et al. (1986) instructed children to watch television, play a board game, and play a construction task. These are activities in which siblings are commonly engaged.

Investigators may want to learn about how siblings relate to one another under certain circumstances. For example, Minnett et al. (1983) observed in unstructured situations, as well as during cooperative and competitive tasks. These researchers asked siblings to wrap a package together (cooperative task), and to play a card tossing game, for which the objective was to toss the most cards into a basket (competitive task). Obviously, there are many other situations that can be manufactured by an observer interested in specific aspects of the sibling relationship (e.g., teaching, conflict resolution).

Somewhat related to level of structure in an observation is whether the observer will provide or restrict access to toys during an observation period. Berndt and Bulleit (1985) brought a toy set to subjects' homes in order to facilitate interaction. As suggested by Abramovitch et al. (1982), however, having novel toys in the situation may distract siblings and decrease interaction. An additional point about toys should be considered. Corter et al. (1982) studied the effects of having one toy versus four toys in an observation session. Although it would seem that four toys would be sufficient to satisfy both children (i.e., they would not be forced to share), these researchers actually found more agonistic behavior in the four-toy condition. They concluded that having four toys increased the opportunity for negative behavior. It is possible that in a situation with many novel toys, an increase in negative interaction that is an artifact of the number of toys, rather than indicative of a general pattern of interaction, may be noted.

The final point about observations to be made here is the use of verbal behavior as data. Although many investigations observed only nonverbal behavior, including verbalizations may give additional information. This may be especially true as talk begins to constitute a larger part of children's total interactions. Some researchers (e.g., Abramovitch et al., 1986) have audiotaped interactions and coded the verbal behavior. Stillwell and Dunn (1985) coded utterances made by children to their mothers about the sibling, and subsequently coded them for their affective tone. As children become older, it may become more important to capture verbal behavior in order to get a more complete picture of the types and quantity of sibling interactions.

Interviews

Another common method of measuring sibling relationships is interviews. The overwhelming majority of these interviews are conducted with mothers, and only occasionally with fathers. Parental interviews can be conducted in person or via telephone. One study (Stillwell & Dunn, 1985) included interviews with children themselves, although this is rare.

Parental interviews. Interviews with parents are valuable for several reasons. First, they provide investigators/clinicians with information concerning sibling interactions in situations other than those in which the observer is present. Second, it is helpful to have information from a variety of sources. Finally, such data provide information about parents' perceptions of their children's relationships. This is often essential information, because parental perceptions themselves may be indirectly related to the quality of sibling relationships.

Interviews with parents generally involve questioning parents about their perceptions regarding certain aspects of their children's behavior toward each other. Stillwell and Dunn (1985) inquired about children's aggression toward their siblings, sharing between siblings, and the quality of the child's relations with his/her sibling. Dunn, Stocker, and Plomin (1990) focused on affection, comforting and concern, helping and teaching, caretaking, aggression, competing, jealousy with mother and with father, time spent together, playing together, pretend play, and quarrels in their maternal interviews.

Another variation of interviewing parents was undertaken by Gottlieb and Mendelson (1990). These researchers studied factors that facilitate the adjustment of a firstborn female child to the birth of a newborn sibling. Among their hypothesized variables was parental support of the firstborn. Parents were contacted by telephone at various times to ask about supportive behaviors directed toward their daughters. Although these investigators did not directly inquire about sibling relationships, this type of data could be a very rich source of information. Specifically, when parents are contacted at several points, the responses given may reflect perceptions of the sibling relationship based on recent occurrences, whereas a single home interview may yield either a parent's global or overall view of the sibling relationship or a view clouded by other factors (e.g., how the parent's day went). If the latter is true, having multiple contacts with parents may lead to an "averaging" out of such extraneous factors. Although this type of information does not have to be gathered by telephone, such a method may be the most economical way to collect the data.

Child interviews. As previously mentioned, the majority of research on sibling relationships has focused on young children. Interviews with children, therefore, have not been commonplace. However, Stillwell and Dunn (1985) did conduct interviews with 6-year-old subjects. In these interviews, children were asked to describe and talk about themselves, their family, and their friends. Among interview items were three that were concerned with siblings (i.e., "Tell me about your brother/sister," "What do you really like about your brother/sister?" and "What is it you don't like about your brother/sister?"). Responses were coded, and numbers of positive and negative utterances were calculated. Child responses quantified in this way significantly correlated with some, but not all, other measures (e.g., child responses correlated with maternal interviews). These results suggest that children of this age and certainly older may add significantly to the total picture of the sibling relationship.

Rating Scales

Some researchers have utilized various types of rating scales in order to measure perceptions of the sibling relationship. Unfortunately, none of these scales is commercially available, which makes them inaccessible to others attempting to measure similar sibling relationship aspects, and makes it difficult to determine the quality of such measures used. Nevertheless, scales for use by parents and children have been developed for use in research projects.

In their study of children's reactions to the birth of a sibling, Nadelman and Begun (1982) used the Child Behavior Questionnaire as a measure of parental perceptions of their children's behavior. This instrument consisted of two parts. The first was a series of eight open-ended questions regarding firstborns' attitudes toward their mothers' pregnancy and postpartum behaviors displayed by the older sibling. These reponses were scored by the investigator using a 5-point behavioral rating scale. The second part required the mother to rank 26 items of her child's behavior using a 5-point Likert scale.

The Sibling Relationship Questionnaire (Furman & Burmester, 1985) is a child report instrument that has been used with children in fifth and sixth grade. The scale is designed to measure children's perceptions of their relationships with siblings in several domains: relative power/status, warmth/closeness, conflict and rivalry. These domains are represented by 15 scales (e.g., nurturance by sibling, companionship, competition, parental partiality for sibling), each consisting of three items. Siblings respond to items using a 5-point Likert-type scale.

Although no commercially prepared measures of sibling relationships exist, there are norm-referenced instruments available for assessing certain aspects of siblings. For example, as many researchers have tried to get away from looking only at the effects of sibling status variables on sibling interaction, many have begun to investigate how child temperament affects the developing sibling relationship. Some investigators have relied upon interview data with mothers for information about children's temperaments (Dunn & Kendrick, 1982b), but it can also be advantageous to use commercially available measures of temperament. For example, Brody, Stoneman, and Burke (1987) used the Activity, Emotional Intensity, and Persistence subscales from Martin's (1988) Temperament Assessment Battery. If the researcher/clinician is interested in normative temperament information, such instruments may be preferred over research-project-developed rating scales and/or interview items.

Comparison of Methods

There are several approaches to measuring sibling relationships, each of which have specific strengths and weaknesses. The following is a comparison of the methods discussed previously, focusing on practical aspects of the methods.

Observations are excellent ways to capture actual observable behaviors that occur, from the perspective of a relatively unbiased observer. However, outside observers are not available during all interactions, hence they will not be privy to all that occurs. Additionally, Dunn et al. (1990) found that negative or agonistic behaviors occurred at such a low frequency that a sufficient sample of such behavior was not collected during an observation period of 30 minutes. These authors therefore suggested that if the focus of the observation is conflict or negative behaviors, observation periods of longer than 30 minutes should be used.

It is also quite possible that subjects' behavior in the presence of an outsider may not be representative of typical behavior. This problem may be mitigated by paying a visit to the family at least once before the observation session, and/or by not recording behaviors of family members until at least 10 minutes after arrival for the observation visit (Dunn & Kendrick, 1980).

Interviews with parents give information that may not be observable or accessible during observation sessions. They do, however, require retrospection on the part of parents, which may result in decreased accuracy. Stewart et al. (1987) resolved this problem in part by having two interviewers question each parental report of a problem to make sure it was a new problem. Despite the bias of parents, Dunn et al. (1990) found that maternal interviews had high test-retest reliabilities. They suggested that this could indicate either that mothers' perceptions of the sibling relationship are relatively stable, although not necessarily related to the children's actual behavior, or that the child behaviors that were the focus of the interview were stable. These authors also found that mothers' reports agreed with brief observations of children's interactions, suggesting that reports given by the mothers were relatively objective.

Child ratings also have their strengths and weaknesses. Such perceptions are strong because they include interactions that occur in a broad variety of social contexts, many of which are not accessible to outside observers. These ratings are not objective, however. Furman and Burmester (1985) suggested that they are "affected by the children's memories, their interpretation of events, and their willingness to report their actual perceptions on a questionnaire" (p. 456).

Which type of data to collect may depend on the focus of the assessment (Dunn et al., 1990). For example, if the researcher/ clinician is interested in considering the global behavior of both older and younger siblings, maternal interviews and unstructured observations may be useful. If interested in a specific aspect of the relationship, however, certain situations may be set up to elicit the types of behaviors that are the focus of study. For example, if interested in assessing directive or controlling behavior, the investigator/clinician may set up a task-like situation, especially one at which the younger sibling is not competent. In general, it appears that the measurement of sibling relationships needs to incorporate data collected from a variety of sources and in a variety of contexts in order to get a broad array of information that can be incorporated into a global picture of the relationship.

Though not comprehensive, this review has examined the most common methods of measuring sibling relationships, focusing on those thought to be most useful for researchers and practitioners. Each of the methods provides its own type of information that varies according to such variables as the perspective taken, the degree of retrospection, and the level of inference required. The best estimate can likely be obtained from a multimethod assessment that focuses on the type of information sought.

CONCLUSION

Whereas it was formerly believed that the influence of families on children's behavior could be investigated by examining parent-child relationships, this is now generally considered insufficient. Siblings are influential in children's lives, and as such should not be ignored when studying children and families. Behavior geneticists have shown that siblings often shape each other's behavior. Family systems theorists posit that because of the reciprocal influence of all family members, families cannot be fully understood without a consideration of the sibling subsystem.

The research reviewed in this chapter suggests that the sibling relationship is a complex one, with siblings playing a variety of roles for each other. The research also supports the view that family status variables play a very limited role in sibling behavior. Therefore, in order to learn about sibling relationships, researchers/clinicians must assess family interactions and dynamics via a multimethod assessment that focuses on the inclusion of all family members.

REFERENCES

Abramovitch, R., Corter, C., & Lando, B. (1979). Sibling interaction in the home. *Child Development, 50,* 997-1033.

Abramovitch, R., Corter, C., & Pepler, D. J. (1982). Patterns sibling interaction among preschool-age children. In M. E. Lamb & B. Sutton-Smith (Eds.), *Sibling relationships: Their nature and significance across the lifespan* (pp. 61-86). Hillsdale, NJ: Lawrence Erlbaum Associates.

Abramovitch, R., Corter, C., Pepler, D. J., & Stanhope, L. (1986). Sibling and peer interaction: A final follow-up and a comparison. *Child Development, 57,* 217-229.

Baskett, L. M., & Johnson, S. M. (1982). The young child's interaction with parents versus siblings: A behavioral analysis. *Child Development, 53,* 643-650.

Berndt, T. J., & Bulleit, T. N. (1985). Effects of sibling relationships on preschoolers' behavior at home and at school. *Developmental Psychology, 21,* 761-767.

Brody, G. H., & Stoneman, Z. (1987). Sibling conflict: Contributions of the siblings themselves, the parent-sibling relationship, and the broader family system. *Journal of Children in Contemporary Society, 19,* 39-53.

Brody, G. H., Stoneman, Z., & Burke, M. (1987). Child temperament, maternal differential behavior, and sibling relationships. *Developmental Psychology, 23,* 354-362.

Brody, G. H., Stoneman, Z., & MacKinnon, C. E. (1986). Contributions of maternal child-rearing practices and play contexts to sibling interactions. *Journal of Applied Developmental Psychology, 7,* 225-236.

Brody, G. H., Stoneman, Z., MacKinnon, C. E., & MacKinnon, R. (1985). Role relationships and behavior among preschool-aged and school-aged sibling pairs. *Developmental Psychology, 21,* 124-129.

Brody, G. H., Stoneman, Z., & McCoy, J. K. (1992). Associations of maternal and paternal direct and differential behavior with sibling relationships: Contemporaneous and longitudinal analyses. *Child Development, 63,* 82-92.

Bryant, B. K. (1982). Sibling relationships in middle childhood. In M. E. Lamb & B. Sutton-Smith (Eds.), *Sibling relationships: Their nature and significance across the lifespan* (pp. 87-121). Hillsdale, NJ: Lawrence Erlbaum Associates.

Bryant, B. K., & Crockenberg, S. (1980). Correlates and dimensions of prosocial behavior: A study of female siblings with their mothers. *Child Development, 51,* 529-544.

Burmester, D. & Furman, W. (1990). Perceptions of sibling relationships during middle childhood and adolescence. *Child Development, 61,* 1387-1398.

Cicerelli, V. G. (1976). Siblings teaching siblings. In V. L. Allen (Ed.) *Children as teachers: Theory and research in tutoring* (pp. 99-111). New York: Academic Press.

Corter, C., Abramovitch, R., & Pepler, D. J. (1983). The role of the mother in sibling interaction. *Child Development, 54,* 1599-1605.

Corter, C., Pepler, D., & Abramovitch, R. (1982). The effects of situation and sibling status on sibling interaction. *Canadian Journal of Behavioral Science, 14,* 380-392.

Daniels, D., Dunn, J., Furstenberg, F. F., & Plomin, R. (1985). Environmental differences within the family and adjustment differences within pairs of adolescent siblings. *Child Development, 56,* 764-774.

Dunn, J. (1983). Sibling relationships in early childhood. *Child Development, 54,* 787-811.

Dunn, J. (1988). Annotation: Sibling influences on childhood development. *Journal of Child Psychology and Psychiatry, 29,* 119-127.

Dunn, J., & Kendrick, C. (1980). The arrival of a sibling: Changes in patterns of interaction between mother and first-born child. *Journal of Child Psychology and Psychiatry, 21,* 119-132.

Dunn, J., & Kendrick, C. (1981a). Interaction between young siblings: Association with the interaction between mother and first-born. *Developmental Psychology, 17,* 336-343.

Dunn, J., & Kendrick, C. (1981b). Social behavior of young siblings in the family context: Differences between same-sex and different-sex dyads. *Child Development, 42,* 1265-1273.

Dunn, J., & Kendrick, C. (1982a). *Siblings: Love, envy, and understanding.* Cambridge, MA: Harvard University Press.

Dunn, J., & Kendrick, C. (1982b). Siblings and their mothers: Developing relationships within the family. In M. E. Lamb & B. Sutton-Smith (Eds.), *Sibling relationships: Their nature and significance across the lifespan* (pp. 39-60). Hillsdale, NJ: Lawrence Erlbaum Associates.

Dunn, J., Kendrick, C., & MacNamee, R. (1981). The reaction of first-born children to the birth of a sibling: Mothers' reports. *Journal of Child Psychology and Psychiatry, 22,* 1-18.

Dunn, J., & McGuire, S. (1992). Sibling and peer relationships in childhood. *Journal of Child Psychology and Psychiatry, 33,* 67-105.

Dunn, J., & Munn, P. (1986). Sibling quarrels and maternal intervention: Individual differences in understanding and aggression. *Journal of Child Psychology and Psychiatry, 27,* 583-595.

Dunn, J., Stocker, C., & Plomin, R. (1990). Assessing the relationship between young siblings: A research note. *Journal of Child Psychology and Psychiatry and Allied Disciplines, 31,* 983-991.

Furman, W., & Burmester, D. (1985). Children's perceptions of the qualities of sibling relationships. *Child Development, 56,* 448-461.

Gottlieb, L. N., & Mendelson, M. J. (1990). Parental support and firstborn girls' adaptation to the birth of a sibling. *Journal of Applied Developmental Psychology, 11,* 29-48.

Lamb, M. E. (1978). Interactions between 18-month-olds and their preschool-aged siblings. *Child Development, 49,* 51-59.

Martin, R. P. (1988). The Temperament Assessment Battery for Children. Brandon, VT: Clinical Psychology.

Minnett, A. M., Vandell, D. L., & Santrock, J. W. (1983). The effects of sibling status on sibling interaction: Influence of birth order, age spacing, sex of child, and sex of sibling. *Child Development, 54,* 1064-1072.

Minuchin, P. (1985). Families and individual development: Provocations from the field of family therapy. *Child Development, 56,* 289-302.

Nadelman, L., & Begun, A. (1982). The effect of the newborn on the older sibling: Mothers' questionnaires. In M. E. Lamb & B. Sutton-Smith (Eds.), *Sibling relationships: Their nature and significance across the lifespan* (pp. 13-37). Hillsdale, NJ: Lawrence Erlbaum Associates.

Patterson, G. R. (1984). Siblings: Fellow travelers in coercive family process. *Advances in the Study of Aggression, 1,* 173-214.

Pelletier-Stiefel, J., Pepler, D., Crozier, K., Stanhope, L., Corter, C., & Abramovitch, R. (1986). Nurturance in the home: A longitudinal study of sibling interaction. In A. F. Fogel & G. Melson (Eds.), *Origins of nurturance* (pp. 3-24). Hillsdale, NJ: Lawrence Erlbaum Associates.

Pepler, D. J., Abramovitch, R., & Corter, C. (1981). Sibling interaction in the home: A longitudinal study. *Child Development, 52,* 1344-1347.

Plomin, R. (1986). *Development, genetics, and psychology.* Hillsdale, NJ: Lawrence Erlbaum Associates.

Plomin, R., & Daniels, D. (1987). Why are children in the same family so different from one another? *Behavioral and Brain Sciences, 10,* 1-60.

Rowe, D. C., & Plomin, R. (1981). The importance of nonshared (E₁) environmental influences in behavioral development. *Developmental Psychology, 17,* 517-531.

Samuels, H. R. (1980). The effect of older sibling on infant locomotor exploration of a new environment. *Child Development, 51,* 607-609.

Stewart, R. B. (1983). Sibling attachment relationships: Child-infant interaction in the Strange Situation. *Developmental Psychology, 19,* 192-199.

Stewart, R. B., Mobley, L. A., Van Tuyl, S. S., & Salvador, M. S. (1987). The firstborn's adjustment to the birth of a sibling: A longitudinal assessment. *Child Development, 58,* 341-355.

Stillwell, R., & Dunn, J. (1985). Continuities in sibling relationships: Patterns of aggression and friendliness. *Journal of Child Psychology and Psychiatry, 26,* 627-637.

Stocker, C., Dunn, J., & Plomin, R. (1989). Sibling relationships: Links with child temperament, maternal behavior, and family structure. *Child Development, 60,* 715-727.

Stoneman, Z., Brody, G. H., & McKinnon, C. (1984). Naturalistic observation of children's activities and roles while playing with their siblings and friends. *Child Development, 55,* 617-627.

Vandell, D. L., Minnett, A. M., & Santrock, J. W. (1987). Age differences in sibling relationships during middle childhood. *Journal of Applied Developmental Psychology, 8,* 247-257.

6

ASSESSING MARITAL QUALITY IN LONGITUDINAL AND LIFE COURSE STUDIES

David R. Johnson

University of Nebraska-Lincoln

INTRODUCTION

Family researchers have been developing measures to assess the quality of the marital relationship for over six decades (e.g., Hamilton, 1929). Indeed, the quality of the husband-wife relationship has been the focus of more research than any other single topic in the field of family study (Spanier & Lewis, 1980). Embedded in these studies are hundreds of varied scales and measures that were designed to assess some aspect of the quality of a marriage (Touliatos, Perlmutter, & Straus, 1990). Lack of consensus on what constitutes marital quality and the absence of any widely accepted and used instruments have contributed to this proliferation of measures. Even scales that enjoy wide use have come under persistent theoretical and methodological criticism (Huston & Robins, 1982; Norton, 1983; Sabatelli, 1988). This state of affairs reflects the different aims of the researchers developing the measures and the evolution over the last several decades of the theoretical and conceptual definitions of the quality of a marriage.

This study was partially supported by grant 5 R01AG04146 from the National Institute on Aging.

The term "marital quality" has only recently been used to refer to concepts and measures that in the past have been called marital adjustment, satisfaction, and happiness (Spanier & Lewis, 1980). Marital satisfaction and happiness both refer to subjective evaluations of positive affect in the marital relationship by one (or both) of the spouses. Marital adjustment signifies both behavioral and evaluative aspects of a marital relationship. These include dyadic cohesion, satisfaction, consensus, interpersonal tensions, and troublesome dyadic differences (Spanier, 1976). A well-adjusted marriage is often characterized by high interaction and cohesion, low levels of disagreement, high levels of commitment to the relationship (i.e., a low likelihood of leaving the relationship), and good communication and problem-solving abilities. Adjustment is clearly seen as multidimensional, composed of several distinct, but closely related concepts (Spanier & Lewis, 1980). The behavioral and evaluative factors that define marital quality are assumed, based on experience in marital counseling and therapy, to be necessary for a harmonious relationship.

Marital quality measures have been created with two quite different aims: the identification of troubled marriages—primarily a clinical aim, and the desire to test theories related to marital functioning and behavior—a basic research aim. There are no necessary theoretical reasons why measures that function well in one capacity cannot also be valid in the other. Practical and methodological matters, however, often play a more important role. For example, it is unlikely that a 250-item marital assessment scale would be used in a national interview survey of married persons in which the quality of the marital relationship is only one focus. This difference in objectives has been a key factor accounting for variation in concepts and methods used to develop the measures and in the criteria applied to evaluate them. This review focuses on issues of marital quality assessment   in nonclinical research settings that use quantitative methods. However, the strong link between family therapy and marital quality research studies—many key researchers are also family therapists—makes it necessary to consider the influence of marital therapy.

Research studies exploring marital quality have, with some notable exceptions, made use of interview or questionnaire data of married respondents collected in one-time (cross-sectional) surveys. This has been the case despite an increasingly awareness that valid answers to some key unsolved issues in the study of marriage over the life course require longitudinal data (Mattessich & Hill, 1987).

It might be expected that reliable and valid measures of marital quality used in cross-sectional studies would be equally applicable to longitudinal samples. Unfortunately, this is not always the case. Many measurement and analysis issues are introduced when inferences are attempted from multiyear samples (Johnson, 1988). Panel analysis raises concerns about the reliability and stability of measures and their ability to reflect changes (Huston & Robins, 1982). The analysis of the dynamics of family development and change requires that the concepts and measures be analytically distinct, particularly when one aspect of the marital relationship is seen as having a causal effect on another (Norton, 1983). A study examining the effect of wife's employment on marital quality could not examine the intervening mechanisms, such as degree of marital interaction or disagreement, which mediate the effect of work on marital happiness or thoughts of divorce (Booth, Johnson, White, & Edwards, 1984) if these are combined in the measure of marital quality.

There have been several reviews of measurement and conceptual issues in assessing the quality of the marital relationship (Sabatelli, 1988; Spanier, 1976; Glenn, 1990; Huston & Robins, 1982; Johnson, White, Edwards, & Booth, 1986; Hicks & Platt, 1970). A recent inventory of marital quality scales is also available (Touliatos, Perlmutter, & Straus, 1990). None have focused on the conceptual and measurement issues raised by the increasing amount of life course research that focuses on the dynamics of the marital relationship. The purpose of this chapter is to critically examine a selected set of conceptual and methodological issues that have relevance to the study of marital quality over the life course.

Life course theory is concerned with explanation of psychological and social changes in individuals as they progress from birth to death within the context of their society (Featherman & Lerner, 1985). Marital life course studies identify factors that account for changes in the husband-wife relationship that reflect the chronological aging of the individuals and the marriage and the changing roles and structures of the family as the individuals move through their marital life cycle (Mattessich & Hill,1987). The effects on the marital relationship of the birth of children, changes in health and well-being caused by aging, children leaving home, retirement, and changes in economic status and assets, are examples of variables that can be examined in a life course perspective. This perspective also focuses on how patterns of behavior and evaluations early in a marriage carry over into later stages of the relationship.

Research on marital quality over the life course has made use of both cross-sectional and longitudinal samples. In cross-sectional studies change can only be inferred by comparing marriages at different life course stages. These findings will be biased to the extent that there are period, cohort, and selection effects (Glenn, 1991). In longitudinal panel and trend studies, such patterns of change can be observed more directly, but additional problems arise while estimating the effects, such as autocorrelated errors and separating reliability from stability.

This chapter begins to approach the issues of marital quality measurement by reviewing issues related to the definition of marital quality that have influenced assessment strategies. This is followed by a selective review of several scales and measures used in studies of the marital life course that exemplify the different conceptual perspectives on marital quality found in the literature. The focus is then turned to a specific examination of conceptual and methodological issues that have emerged as problems in the assessment of marital quality in life course research. Findings from a four-wave panel of marriages studied over a period of 12 years will be used to illustrate and in some cases provide tentative answers to some important methodological and measurement questions. Finally, conclusions are made about the adequacy of current conceptualization and measurement of marital quality for longitudinal studies.

ISSUES IN DEFINING MARITAL QUALITY

Although many different measures have been called marital quality, there has been more convergence at the level of operationalization than at the level of conceptualization. Scale items that are very similar if not identical are often shared by instruments with widely differing labels and conceptual definitions. Most of the measures have employed a self-report questionnaire or survey format responded to by married persons answering as individuals and not as couples. Many have been validated by comparing scale scores of persons in marital therapy with those not in therapy.

Although the available instruments share much in common in terms of the items used, samples studied, and criteria used to assess scale validity, a basic conceptual and theoretical issue repeatedly surfaces in the published reviews of marital quality measures. This issue concerns whether the definition of marital quality and its measurement should include both behavioral and evaluative components and whether single or distinct measures are needed to assess these components (Norton, 1983; Johnson, White et al., 1986). There have been three perspectives on what constitutes marital quality: marital adjustment, global evaluation, and marital quality as a set of variables.

Marital Adjustment Perspective

The concept of marital adjustment has an extensive history in family research and predates the use of the term marital quality (Lively, 1969). Although the concept has received careful theoretical and conceptual clarification (Spanier, 1976; Spanier & Cole, 1976), the general perspective towards assessment has been a pragmatic one. How well does a potential measure differentiate between "well-adjusted" and "poorly-adjusted" marriages? The definition of adjustment, as discussed earlier, includes not only the married person's subjective evaluation of the marriage but also behavioral characteristics that signify adjustment. Married individuals who are satisfied or happy with their marriage are not necessarily in a well-adjusted marriage. The behavior of the couple in terms of their interaction, communication, consensus, agreement, and commitment is all viewed as important for the placement of a married person on an adjustment continuum (Spanier, 1976). An adequate measure must tap domains of individual subjective evaluation as well as dyadic behavior.

Specification of the appropriate domain of content for the universe of items to be included in a marital adjustment scale often begins with qualitative experience gained from working with distressed couples in family and marital therapy. Because the definition of adjustment includes both evaluative and behavioral traits, the universe of items tapping marital adjustment includes both. The ultimate criterion of whether an item is appropriate for inclusion is its ability to distinguish between maladjusted and normal marriages (Locke & Wallace, 1959; Spanier, 1976). There is an explicit recognition that although the concept of adjustment is multidimensional, a single ordering of marriages from high to low adjustment is possible. The two scales most commonly used in family research (as opposed to those whose primary function is to assist in marital therapy with individual marriages) that share this perspective are the Locke-Wallace Marital Adjustment Test (LWMAT; Locke & Wallace, 1959) and Spanier's (1976) Dyadic Adjustment Scale (DAS). Both have been widely used in marital research, including longitudinal and marital life course studies.

A major critique of the adjustment perspective is that by defining the concept to include several behavioral and evaluative properties, its research utility is limited (Norton, 1983; Fincham & Bradbury, 1987), particularly in studies of the interrelationships between characteristics of the marriage. Scales created for prediction purposes can impose less rigorous standards on the content of the domain of items than do those designed to test empirically the interrelationship among a set of theoretically derived and relevant concepts (Nunnally, 1967).

An example of the wide universe of items often allowed for scales focusing primarily on their ability to predict a trait is the Marital Prediction Test developed by Locke and Wallace (1959). The Marital Prediction Test is designed for "forecasting the likelihood of marital adjustment at a future time" (Locke & Wallace, 1959, p. 251). Among the 20 items in the scale are the respondents' educational attainment, age at marriage, church attendance, size of community in which they grew up, parents' approval of their marriage, and general attitudes toward sex. The combination of demographic, background, and evaluative items makes the concept and the measure virtually worthless for research purposes.

Although marital adjustment measures tap a narrower domain of content, choice of items is often guided more by the ability to differentiate among adjusted and maladjusted marriages than by the need to measure a theoretically coherent trait. Because marital adjustment is defined as a multidimensional concept encompassing a wide range of behaviors and attitudes, this conceptualization has limited utility both in the theoretical models of the dynamics of marital relations and in their empirical testing.

Marital Evaluation Perspective

A perspective that restricts the concept of marital quality solely to subjective global evaluations of the satisfaction/happiness of the married partners has gained increasing support in the marital quality literature (Fincham & Bradbury, 1987; Norton, 1983; Sabatelli, 1988). Advocates of the marital evaluation perspective view the concept as a tool for research and theory and not marital therapy. Fincham and Bradbury (1987) argue that combining behavioral and evaluative components in the same concept and scale confounds the description of the marriage with its evaluation. Attempts to explain marital quality with characteristics of the marital relationship are artifacts of the common variance of shared items in the independent and dependent measures. A researcher interested in the extent to which dyadic communication affects marital quality would be making a serious methodological error to use a measure of marital quality based on the adjustment perspective because good communication is in the domain of content of the adjustment concept and is tapped by its measures.

Several recent measures build on this concept of marital quality. Both the Kansas Marital Satisfaction Scale (KMSS; Schumm, Paff-Bergen, Hatch, Obiorah, Copeland, Meens, & Bugaighis, 1986) and the Marital Quality Index (MQI; Norton, 1983) are unidimensional measures of global satisfaction. Single-item measures of marital happiness have been used in many studies and conform to this perspective (Glenn, 1990). Although psychometrically suspect, the single-item measures of marital quality possess the pragmatic advantage of having been included for decades as the only indicator of marital quality on many large national longitudinal surveys (Glenn, 1990; Orden & Bradburn, 1968).

The problem with this perspective is that it takes the term marital quality that has been widely used to refer to a range of both evaluative and behavioral characteristics of the marital relationship and narrows its application to a much smaller set of concepts and measures. Even if there are compelling theoretical and conceptual reasons for restricting the meaning of the term, the practical matter is that the broader meaning of the term marital quality has already been established, a condition that is difficult to reverse in practice. Perhaps another term other than happiness or satisfaction needs to be selected to refer to the global subjective evaluation of the marriage.

Marital Quality as a Set of Traits

Rather than referring to a specific quality of the relationship that can be assessed by a single instrument, this perspective treats marital quality as an umbrella concept encompassing a *set* of marital behaviors and evaluations, each assessed by a separate measure. This is the most widely accepted meaning of the term in the current literature. Recent reviews of research on marital happiness, satisfaction, and adjustment have also adopted this usage (Spanier & Lewis, 1980; Glenn, 1990). The value of defining marital quality in this way can be seen in the conceptual and definitional confusion found in the field before the term was introduced. Hicks and Platt (1970), in a decade review of research on the same set of concepts that are currently called marital quality, reluctantly used the term "marital happiness" to refer to the set of measures because no other term was available.

The use of separate scales to measure the components of marital quality (Johnson, White et al., 1986) and the practice of breaking composite measures such as the Dyadic Adjustment Scale into subscales (Spanier, 1976) both fit this perspective. This allows for a broader definition of marital quality, similar to that used by advocates of the marital adjustment perspective. It also insists on separate definitions and measures of behavioral and evaluative elements of the marital relationship that are needed for research into the dynamics of the marital relationship. It is this use of marital quality that is adopted in this chapter.

SCALES ASSESSING MARITAL QUALITY IN LIFE COURSE STUDIES

Many measures of marital quality have been used to assess change and stability in marriages as they pass through the life course. Cross-sectional studies predominate, but there also have been a few trend studies (separate samples with the same measures surveyed in different years) and panel studies (same sample surveyed two or more times). The measures selected for review were primarily designed for research rather than therapy, represent the range of definitions of marital quality discussed above, and illustrate some major methodological and conceptual issues in the assessment marital quality over the life course.

Orden and Bradburn's Marital Adjustment Balance Scale (MABS)

The Orden and Bradburn Marital Adjustment Balance Scale (MABS) is based on the theoretical model of psychological well-being that assumes that individual subjective happiness is a function of two independent dimensions, one of positive, the other of negative affect (Bradburn, 1969, p. 9). This theoretical model was applied to account for both overall individual and marital well-being.

To develop the MABS, a nine-item scale of marital tensions and a nine-item scale of marital satisfactions were created based on intensive interviews with a small sample of respondents. Other items were included based on their relationship to the general positive and negative affect scales also developed by Bradburn (1969). Respondents were asked to give a yes or no response to a checklist of items. The marital satisfactions measure included items measuring companionship and sociability, which were also treated as separate subscales (Orden & Bradburn, 1968). These included items tapped affection, sharing a good laugh, spending an evening chatting with one another, doing things together with friends, eating out together, and going out together for entertainment. The marital tensions subscale included a set of situations that caused disagreements or problems in the marriage in the last few weeks, such as being tired, irritating personal habits, household expenses, being away from home, and not showing love.

The subscales, which were a simple summation of the number of yes responses, were found to be correlated with a single-item measure of marital happiness (Taking all things together, how would you describe your marriage? Would you say your marriage was very happy, pretty happy or not too happy?) but were not significantly correlated with one another (Orden & Bradburn, 1968). The marital satisfactions and tensions subscales were combined into a single composite 11-point scale to create the Marital Adjustment Balance Scale.

Orden and Bradburn validated the scale primarily based on its strong relationship to the marital happiness item and the similar correlations of MABS and happiness with variables such as socioeconomic status and gender. Although the word adjustment is used in the title, it was not constructed or validated by score comparisons of well and poorly adjusted couples as determined by therapists. They do not report any indices of internal consistency of test-retest reliability for the scale.

The study in which the scale was first used involved two to four waves of panel data over a period of one year. Because all items were included only on a later wave, patterns of change for the entire scale were only available for samples interviewed in Waves II and III. Test-retest correlations (computed from cell frequencies presented in tables [Bradburn, 1969]) for marital tensions (collapsed into three ordinal categories) were .4 for both men and women. It was not possible with the data presented to compute the correlations for the satisfactions subscale or the total MABS.

This scale is important because it was used in one of the first attempts to evaluate quantitatively in a panel study the relationship between change in different components of the marital relationship. Based on an analysis of cross-classifications, Bradburn (1969) concluded that change in marital tensions was associated with change in marital happiness but change in marital satisfactions was not. For this analysis, the scale was disaggregated into its components and was not treated as the single balance measure. This practice was also noted in other studies making use of the scales (e.g., Burke, Weir, & DuWors, 1979).

The MABS was developed from a specific theoretical model of well-being applied to marriages in which the ultimate dependent variable is a subjective global evaluation of the marriage (happiness). Thus, it appears to fit the conceptualization of marital quality as a global subjective evaluation of the marriage. Orden and Bradburn (1968) even discuss whether the researcher should use their scale or the single-item measure of marital happiness. They conclude that the MABS would be preferred primarily because of its greater precision (more categories). Yet the scale itself does not include evaluative measures and might be seen primarily as assessing marital behavior. The measure of tensions comes closer to a marital problems scale (Johnson, White et al., 1986) and the positive affect measure primarily taps spousal interaction and, to some extent, intimacy.

The relatively low test-retest correlations of the tensions subscale in the MABS and the acknowledgement by Bradburn (1969) that the positive affect items performed poorly in accounting for change in marital happiness suggest that this scale and its components may not be useful for longitudinal studies. The observed independence of the tensions from marital sociability and companionship subscales is not necessarily consistent with findings from other studies using similar measures. Johnson, White et al. (1986) found strong correlations between a marital problems index (similar to the MABS tension subscales) and marital interaction. It is possible that application of the psychometric scaling techniques available to researchers today to data collected using these scales would help clarify some of the issues related to their reliability and stability. The MABS itself taps several marital behaviors and is multidimensional. This scale has the conceptual advantages of not combining behavioral and evaluative components and being derived from a theoretical model of psychological well-being. However, its problems and uncertainties outweigh these advantages.

The Locke-Wallace Marital Adjustment Test

This widely used scale was created to provide a short 15-item test of marital adjustment at a time when most of the available scales averaged around 150 items (Locke & Wallace, 1959). It was created to provide a short, easily administered scale for use in research settings. Items were selected from previous scales that best discriminated high and low adjustment in the original studies and covered the important domains of content as evaluated by the authors. Reliability was judged as high (.90 using the Spearman-Brown formula) and the scale discriminated well between respondents in mal- and well-adjusted marriages judged by clinical criteria.

The Locke-Wallace Marital Adjustment Test (MAT) has an important place in family research because it represents the first short instrument geared to researchers from the marital adjustment and marital therapy perspective. As a measure of marital quality it clearly fits the conceptual definition marital adjustment, because the domain of item content includes both behavioral and evaluative components.

It has often been used as a criterion to evaluate the validity of other marital quality scales (Spanier, 1976).

Included in the scale are a marital happiness item, a set of items about disagreements, marital interaction, and questions about whether the respondents would have ever married or would marry the same person again. A scaling system is present for weighting items, although there is little explanation of how these were derived. For example, the single item of marital happiness has a weight three to seven times greater than other items.

Use of the scale in other samples has confirmed its reliability (Margolin, 1978) and several reported studies have examined the factorial structure of the items in the scale (Kimmel & Van Der Veen, 1974; Locke & Williamson, 1958) and its overall reliability and validity (Cross & Sharpley, 1981). Several factor analyses all support the scale as multidimensional, although there has been little agreement on the number of dimensions (from one to eight). Kimmel and Van Der Veen (1974) found only one factor when men and women were combined in the same analysis, but found two distinct factors for husbands and wives when analyzed separately. They also reported that these factors have high test-retest stability. In a small sample of 44 couples tested a little over 2 years apart, the test-retest correlations were between .69 and .78 for the separate factors for husbands and wives. They concluded that both factors appear to tap stable and enduring characteristics of the marital relationship.

Because Locke has published several versions of the marital adjustment scale with varying sets of items, few of these validity and factorial structure studies report on the same scale. This has made it difficult to judge the dimensionality of the scale or provide information on how best to form subscales to separate out substantively important behavioral and evaluative components. The small number of items in the scale contributed to the wide use of the measure but made its potential disaggregation into useful subscales more difficult. As a result, the scale would not be very useful for life course studies examining the dynamics of the components of the marital relationship.

Spanier's Dyadic Adjustment Scale

The Dyadic Adjustment Scale (DAS) is the most widely used indicator of marital quality in the literature, with over 1,000 studies making use of the scale (Touliatos, Perlmutter, & Straus, 1990). It was also conceived in the marital adjustment tradition where the primary criterion for the scale was its ability to distinguish between well-adjusted and failing marriages (Spanier, 1976). A unique feature of the scale was that items were worded in a way that made the scale appropriate for nonmarital dyads (e.g., a cohabiting couple).

The pool of items considered for the scale was selected from among all previously published adjustment instruments. Additional items were added to fill gaps in domains the author believed were not well represented in the pool. The final composite scale consists of 32 items and taps both behavioral and evaluative components of the relationship. The DAS includes a global happiness item and 15 items tapping agreement in different areas of the relationship, thoughts of divorce, temporary separations, quarreling, marital interaction, and displays of affection. Twelve of the 15 items in the Locke-Wallace MAT are included in the DAS. This results in a close correspondence between these two scales; Spanier (1976) reported a correlation of .86 between the DAS and the MAT.

Selection of items from the pool for inclusion in the DAS involved several criteria. A critical factor was the ability of the item to discriminate between a sample of divorced persons who answered the scale based on recollection of the last months of their failed marriage and a sample of currently married persons. Highly skewed items were also excluded. A final step excluded items with low factor loadings. A coefficient alpha reliability of .96 was reported for the total scale.

Subscales of the DAS were created to reflect the multidimensional nature of marital adjustment. These were developed by factor analysis and consist of four subscales: Dyadic Consensus (13 items), Dyadic Satisfaction (10 items), Dyadic Cohesion (5 items), and Affectional Expression (4 items). All the subscales except Affectional Expression had coefficient alpha reliabilities exceeding .85. Confirmatory factor analysis in a second sample of divorced and separated persons generally confirmed the four factors (Spanier & Thompson, 1982), but another factor analysis of married respondents did not (Sharpley & Cross, 1982).

Because of its widespread use, the DAS has often been the focus in critical reviews of the measurement of marital quality. Several problems with the scale have received the most emphasis. Because the DAS includes behavioral and evaluative items, the concern has been raised that this confounds and limits analysis of marital processes (Norton, 1983; Fincham & Bradbury, 1987). The practice observed in many studies of using the subscales rather than the composite measure partially alleviates this concern (e.g., Belsky, Spanier, & Rovine, 1983). However, the subscales do not separate behavioral and evaluative dimensions that need to be measured separately in causal and longitudinal models of marital processes (Johnson, White et al., 1986). For example, the Dyadic Satisfaction subscale included behavioral reports (e.g., frequency of quarrels, discussion of divorce or separation, frequency of marital interaction) as well as evaluative items (marital happiness, feelings about the future of the relationship)

Norton (1983) raises concerns about the arbitrary weighting of items in the DAS. Although most of the items can contribute up to 5 points each to the scale, two can only contribute 1 point, two 4 points, and one 6 points. Their relative contribution reflects only the number of response categories and not the discriminating power of the item. Coupled with the variable number of items in each subscale, these lead to disproportionate contribution of certain domains of content to the total scales score that are unrelated to their conceptual importance or discriminating power. This is not a serious problem for the researcher who is willing to discard the recommended scoring of the DAS in favor of weighting to equalize the contributions of items and subscales to the total scale score (Norton, 1983).

Several methodological concerns have been directed to the definition and structure of the subscales. Because they were defined by factor analysis they can be questioned when factor analyses in other samples do not reproduce the same structure. Although a close fit to the four-factor structure was confirmed by Spanier and Thompson (1982), Sharpley and Cross (1982) found a very different factor structure. Crane, Busby, and Larson (1991) also failed to reproduce the four factor structure among both distressed and nondistressed couples. Unfortunately, none of these studies used large or representative samples. Spanier and Thompson's (1982) sample was of divorced persons responding about their failed marriages, Sharpley and Cross did not say where they got their 95 married respondents, and Crane, Busby, and Larson used a sample of 253, containing both couples in therapy and nondistressed couples. Because the subscales were defined by factor analysis, Sabatelli (1988) raises the concern that they are not true scales because no attempt was made to define a universe of content for the dimensions from which to select the items.

Methodological and conceptual concerns about the DAS raise questions about its utility in studies examining the dynamics of the marital relationship over the course of the marriage. However, many studies examining family life cycle issues have used the DAS. The DAS and its subscales were used in a longitudinal panel study of the effects of the birth of a child on the marital relationship (Belsky, Spanier, &Rovine, 1983). Couples were interviewed before the birth of a child, and 3 and 9 months after the birth, for three waves of data.

The study examined the changes in mean scores for wives and husbands over the three waves of the subscales and composite DAS. Stability of the subscale and total scores was also reported. Additional measures of marital functioning and marital interaction were also included in the study. Significant mean declines were found over the three waves for the total scale, cohesion, and affectional expression. The total scale score was found to be highly stable, particularly for wives. Correlations between the first and third waves were .82 for wives and .69 for husbands. The subscales were less stable, with Satisfaction the most stable for both genders (r = .81 for wives and .60 for husbands) and Affectional Expression and Gender Cohesion the least stable (rs from .69 for wives to .43 for husbands). They conclude that the study observed real and reliable mean declines in components of marital adjustment over the period of the birth of a child, but that the relative rank order of the married persons on marital adjustment changed little over this marital life cycle transition.

Because of criticism directed toward the DAS and its subscales, Belsky, Lang, and Rovine (1985) replicated the study, substituting another set of scales that separately measured different aspects of the marital relationship. No attempt was made in either study to examine the causal process through which the addition of a child influenced the dynamics of the relationship between the spouses. The findings of the two studies were remarkably similar, suggesting that some conceptual and methodological criticism of the DAS in longitudinal studies may be unjustified.

The Kansas Marital Satisfaction Scale

The Kansas Marital Satisfaction Scale (KMSS) is the shortest scale in the marital quality literature, being composed of only three items. Yet its validity and reliability have been very carefully and completely evaluated in published studies (Schumm, et al., 1986) and it has been used in family life cycle studies (Anderson, Russell, & Schumm, 1983). It strictly fits the conceptualization of marital quality as global evaluation of the marriage. The three items measure satisfaction with spouse, the marriage, and the marital relationship. The scale has the advantage of being short, and concurrent validity studies found it to be correlated highly with the Dyadic Adjustment Scale. It has also been shown to be stable over a 10-week period (r = .71) (Mitchell, Newell, & Schumm, 1983).

Anderson, Russell, and Schumm (1983) used the KMSS in a cross-sectional study to test research questions about the relationship between marital quality and stage in the family life cycle. The KMSS was used to measure the global assessment of marital satisfaction and several other scales were included to measure other aspects of the marital relationship (regard, empathy, discussion, and self-disclosure) that were viewed as causes of marital satisfaction. They found that marital quality (using the five scales, including KMSS, as a set in a MANOVA) showed a curvilinear relationship with family life cycle (lowest levels when the oldest children were from 5 to 12 years of age), which replicated findings from previous studies with other scales.

Although no panel studies have been reported that include this scale, the availability of three items gives it several advantages over the single-item measure of marital happiness to be reviewed below. How well the three items would serve as multiple indicators of a latent variable of marital satisfaction in structural equation path models is not known but deserves further exploration.

The Nebraska Marital Quality Scales

As part of a panel study of a national sample of married persons designed to assess factors predicting marital instability over the life course, Johnson, White et al. (1986) devised a set of five scales to measure five theoretically important dimensions of marital quality. Combinations of these scales have been used in many research studies based on a four-wave panel of married persons followed over 12 years. The marriage characteristics assessed were selected because of their theoretical importance in a model of the marital process and were proposed to account for the effects of wife's paid employment in the labor force on the likelihood that the marriage would end in divorce or permanent separation (Booth, Johnson, White, & Edwards, 1984). Scale items were selected based on a review of the literature, seeking items that fell within the theoretical domain of content for the concepts. Pretest of a national sample of 300 married persons was used to evaluate and modify some scales. The final versions of the scales were developed from the larger study of over 2,000 married respondents through item analysis. The five measures are Marital Happiness, Marital Interaction, Marital Disagreement, Marital Problems and Marital Instability (or Divorce Proneness).

Marital Happiness was defined as an individual level property reflecting positive and negative feelings about the marriage, and is conceptually equivalent to the Kansas Marital Satisfaction Scale and other global evaluative measures. Eleven items were included in the scale. Seven measured happiness with aspects of the relationship and four were global assessments of the relationship. The scale had a coefficient alpha reliability of .86.

Marital Interaction was defined as the amount of interaction of the couple in day-to-day activities. It consists of five items tapping eating main meals together, shopping, visiting friends, working on projects around the house together, and going out. The alpha reliability of the scale was .63 and yields one factor in factor analysis.

Marital Disagreements was designed to test for the presence and severity of disagreements between the spouses. Four items tap disagreements, frequencies of quarrels, and physical abuse. Because of different numbers of response categories in the items, each item was z-scored before the items were summed. The reliability was relatively low (alpha = .54).

Marital Problems assesses the extent to which personal traits and behaviors of the spouses contribute to problems in the marriage. It measures a collective property of the relationship reflecting a dyadic condition. Respondents were asked to indicate if 13 potential trouble spots in the marriage caused problems in their marriage due to either their behavior or the behavior of their spouse. Included where such things as getting angry easily, won't talk to each other, has irritating habits, drinks, or uses drugs. The alpha reliability was .76.

Marital Instability (also called Divorce Proneness) is defined as the propensity to divorce and included both cognitive and behavioral components. This includes thoughts about divorce and specific actions such as talking to a friend or spouse, seeing an attorney, separating, etc. There are 13 items in the scale and its alpha reliability is .91 (Booth, Johnson, & Edwards, 1983). This scale was validated primarily by its ability to predict divorce or permanent separation. Those who scored high on the scale were nine times more likely to divorce within 3 years than those exhibiting no instability on the scale. The five subscales are substantially intercorrelated. A confirmatory factor analysis of the scales found two correlated factors, one included marital happiness and marital interaction, the other marital instability, marital problems, and marital disagreements. Because of the need to retain separate scales for the conceptually distinct aspects of the marital relationship, no attempt was made to combine them into two composite measures.

Several research studies have made use of these scales included on a national longitudinal telephone survey of a sample of married persons. Many have examined one or more aspects of marital quality over the marital life course with either cross-sectional data from one of the earlier panels or two and three wave panel data (Booth & Edwards, 1989; Booth, Johnson, White, & Edwards, 1986; Johnson, Amoloza, & Booth, 1992; White, 1983; White & Booth, 1985; White &

Booth, 1991; White & Edwards, 1990; Zuo, 1992). Three of these studies exemplify how these measures can be used to improve our knowledge about the dynamics of marital processes.

White (1983) examined the reciprocal relationship between marital happiness and marital interaction with cross-sectional data from the 1980 wave of the national study. Making use of two-stage least squares, she tested the reciprocal relationship between marital happiness and marital interaction. Because she was using cross-sectional data, certain untestable assumptions were required to identify mathematically the set of equations needed to test the reciprocal relationship. Her results suggested that marital happiness was more likely to influence marital interaction than viced versa.

Zuo (1992) replicated White's findings using the same sample but included the information gained in three waves of interviews conducted in 1980, 1983, and 1988 with the same respondents. Panel data allowed a different set of assumptions to identify the equations. Zuo also treated happiness and interaction as latent variables and used the scale items as multiple indicators. This adjusted for the biasing effect of measurement errors in panel models. A reciprocal effect was found in the second wave that confirmed White's (1983) findings. In the third wave, however, the findings suggested approximately equal effects of happiness on interaction and interaction on happiness.

Johnson, Amoloza, and Booth (1992) examined the degree of stability and developmental change in the five measures over the first three waves (8 years) of the panel study for 1,043 respondents continuously married over the period. Developmental change was measured by the mean changes in marital quality scores that were due to the passage of time. Marital Happiness and Interaction were found to undergo significant declines over the 8-year period. No significant changes were found for the other measures. This pattern of change was the same for both married men and women and for respondents at different marital durations, although short-term marriages (under 5 years of marriage in the first wave) showed significantly greater declines than other groups in happiness and interaction.

Johnson, Amoloza, and Booth (1992) also examined the stability of the marriages. A procedure that separates reliability from stability in panel studies with three or more waves was used (Wiley & Wiley, 1970). This assured that the differences in the reliability of the scales did not bias a comparison of their stabilities. Structural equation models were used to estimate the relative stability of gender and marital duration groups. All the measures were found highly stable over the 8 years of the panel study. Correlations between waves over approximately 3 years when adjusted for attenuation due to reliability were found to be in the .8 to .9 range. Overall, no component of marital quality was more stable than the other. The only difference found for any of the five subscales was significantly less stability in marital problems among respondents' marriages of less than 5 years.

It is possible that the highly stable nature of the marital quality items may reflect stable characteristics of the individuals or the tendency of persons to consistently report similar evaluations regardless of their actual relationship. Johnson, Amoloza, and Booth (1992) examined the 37 persons in the panel study who had divorced and remarried by the third wave. The correlations of marital quality they reported while still in their first marriage were compared to the reports they provided for their second marriage. These correlations were very low, mostly negative, and nonsignificant, suggesting that persons appear to take the conditions of the dyad into account in their ratings.

Research studies making use of the Nebraska Marital Quality Scales in multiwave panel models would not have been possible, or would have been more limited, if the marital quality measures had not been separated into separate scales. A problem with the measures is that some scales do not meet normal criteria for satisfactory reliability ($r_{xx} > .8$). Use of large samples and models that incorporate assumptions about measurement error can go a long way to eliminate this as a serious concern. The five scales do not encompass all the characteristics of the marital relationship that are normally viewed as important. Measures of intimacy, communication, and cohesion are omitted and would need to be added for some models of the marital process.

Single-Item Measurement of Marital Happiness

Generally, reviews of assessment instruments discount or ignore single-item measures (e.g., Norton, 1983; Sabatelli, 1988). The difficulties in estimating reliability and obtaining sufficiently high levels of it, the lack of precision afforded by restricted response categories, and the limited domain of content that can be covered by single-item measures often leave little to recommend. In the field of marital quality, measurement of marital happiness by a single item not only has a long history but also a large and significant body of current use, particularly in issues related to cohort, period, and selection effects in marital quality over the life course (Glenn, 1991). This reflects the availability of only one item indicating marital happiness/satisfaction on many large national surveys.

The General Social Survey, an annual interview survey of a national sample of respondents, has included a one-item measure of marital happiness since 1973. This represents a unique and valuable source of trend data that can help separate cohort and period effects from changes in individuals as they traverse the marital life course (Glenn, 1990). The recent and widely available National Survey of Families and Households (NSFH; Sweet, Bumpass, & Call, 1988), which contains over 7,000 items on a national probability sample of over 13,000 persons, includes only one item tapping marital happiness/satisfaction and one item tapping divorce proneness. These data will be available soon in panel form because the second wave of a 5-year panel has recently been completed. Several other large national surveys contain only single indicators of important marital quality concepts (Kolb & Straus, 1974).

The single-item measure of happiness takes several forms and varies primarily in the number of response categories. The most common form asks the respondents to evaluate how happy they are with their marriages. Three response categories are most common (very happy, pretty happy, not too happy), although the NSFH data make use of a 7-point scale (from very happy to very unhappy). Although there has been no explicit attempt to estimate the reliability and validity of this item, evidence from several sources can be used for this purpose. A similar happiness item is found in most marital quality measures, including the Locke-Wallace MAT, Spanier's DAS, the Nebraska Marital Happiness Scale, and several other scales not reviewed here. Orden and Bradburn (1968) used the single-item report of marital happiness to validate their balance scale.

Factor analyses of these scales often show that the single global item of marital happiness generally has the highest communality of any item (Sharpley & Cross, 1982), suggesting it is the best single item indicator of the scales. Responses to the item appear stable. Orden and Bradburn (1968) found high test-retest correlations for the item in a short-term panel study (correlations using gamma between .82 and .94).

A major criticism of the single-item measure of marital happiness is that it is highly skewed. In most samples 60% to 80% of the respondents select the most happy category; a very small proportion, normally less than 3%, select the not too happy response in the most common three-category version of the item. Studies using this item over the last five decades generally find similar patterns (Orden & Bradburn, 1968; Glenn, 1991). The item normally remains skewed even when more categories are available. The NSFH contains seven response categories, but the modal response is still in the highest happiness category.

The marital happiness item has been most extensively analyzed by Glenn and his associates, primarily using data collected in large national data sets (Glenn & Weaver, 1978a; Glenn & Weaver, 1978b; Glenn & McLanahan, 1982; Glenn, 1989; Glenn, 1991). Glenn (1991) concludes that the item is unlikely to be biased in assessing change in trend studies, although he acknowledges that it may be biased by social desirability. He compared annual trends in the percent responding very happy from 1973 through 1988 and found a significant decline in this percent over the period. This was the first study to find a trend in the United States in the last two decades toward lower reported levels of marital happiness.

Reliance on single-item measures of marital quality is not recommended. When the use of such measures is the only way to make inferences about trends or to access large, nationally representative, longitudinal samples, then more effort needs to be devoted toward assessing the psychometric properties of these indicators so they can be used in the most valid manner.

METHODOLOGICAL ISSUES IN ASSESSING MARITAL QUALITY IN LIFE COURSE RESEARCH

In this section four methodological issues in the assessment of marital quality are examined. These issues have been selected because of their relevance to the study of the marital relationship over the course of the marriage. The first issue examined is social desirability response tendency in marital quality scales. Some scholars have discounted any attempt to measure married persons' evaluation of their marriage because of the strong tendency to want to report the marriage in a positive light. The evidence for this is examined and the consequences for life course studies is explored. The second issue is the influence of selection effects on inferences made from research findings on married persons. Selection of persons out of the pool of married persons through divorce is an increasing problem that affects both cross-sectional and longitudinal studies. A third issue returns to the problem of single-item indicators of marital quality. Focusing on the marital happiness item, estimates of reliability and stability in panel studies are developed. The final issue examines problems in estimating the reliability and stability of marital quality in panel studies. For several of these issues, data from the four waves of a national sample of married persons were used to illustrate problems and suggest solutions.

Marital Conventionalization and Marital Quality

A study by Edmonds (1967) introduced the concept and measurement of marital conventionalization to the marital quality literature. Marital conventionalization is the tendency for married persons to rate their marriage in more positive terms than is actually true of the relationship. The method of assessing conventionalization was modeled after the techniques used to measure social desirability. Both include several statements that are unlikely to actually occur to which the respondent is asked to give a true or false response. Methodological concerns have been raised by the high correlations (r = .3 to .7) that have been observed between marital conventionalization and a variety of evaluative measures of marital quality (Fowers & Pomerantz, 1992). This has led some family scholars to question the value of subjective assessment of marital quality (Hicks & Platt, 1970; Edmonds, 1967). For example, some researchers have found that when marital conventionalization is controlled, the effect of other variables on marital satisfaction/adjustment is substantially reduced (Edmonds, Withers, & Dibatista, 1972).

The important question for the assessment of marital quality is whether this tendency to give improbably high ratings to marriages is itself an indicator of marital quality or is a contaminant that biases most marital quality measures. Recent research provides a strong indication that conventionalization is more a measure of marital quality than it is a measure of a marital social desirability response tendency. In an extensive review of the research on marital conventionalization, Fowers and Pomerantz (1992) conclude that it behaves more as another indicator of marital satisfaction than a social desirability response set. This argument is supported by factor analyses that find that the items load on the same factor as marital satisfaction items (Hansen, 1981), and by the low relationship of conventionalization to other social desirability measures.

There is some empirical evidence of a substantial relationship between religiosity and marital conventionalization (Edmonds, Withers, & Dibatista, 1972). Some researchers in marital happiness have discounted the relatively strong effects of the importance of religion in the respondent's life (Glenn & Weaver, 1978a) as reflecting merely a response bias. Concern that marital quality measures are highly biased by marital social desirability led Glenn (1991) to examine whether the decline in marital happiness observed over the last two decades reflects only increases in openness about intimate relationships and the subsequent lesser need to exaggerate. Although there have not been trend studies of changes in marital conventionalization over time, indirect evidence suggests that declines in marital happiness are not the products of response biases. Glenn (1991) argued that if marital happiness is being more accurately measured in recent years, this should also increase the relationship between marital happiness and other variables such as general happiness. The virtually unchanged relationship between these two types of happiness over a 14-year period makes it unlikely that more honest reporting accounts for the observed decline in marital happiness.

Similar logic can be applied to the strong relationship between the perceived importance of religion in life and marital happiness. If the higher marital quality of more religious persons is primarily a reporting bias, one would expect that the relationship between evaluative marital quality variables and behavioral ones would be weaker among highly religious than among less religious married persons. Booth and Johnson (1992) examined the relationship between marital happiness in 1980 and the occurrence of a divorce or separation within the next 8 years. Marital happiness and importance of religion were both found to be significant and strong predictors of subsequent divorce. Much, but not all, of the effect of religious importance on divorce was through marital happiness. The effect of marital happiness on divorce, however, did not vary by level of religious importance as would be the case if marital happiness had a different meaning for religious and non-religious people. Therefore, it is unlikely that the high marital happiness levels of more religious persons can be discounted as a response bias.

One additional piece of evidence from life course research casts doubt on the likelihood that measures of marital quality are heavily biased by personal response tendencies unrelated to the nature of the marital relationship. If variance in marital quality was primarily a trait unrelated to the marital relationship, it would be expected that as a person moves from one marital relationship to another, there should be a consistency in their tendency to evaluate any marriage. The low, mostly negative and nonsignificant correlations over time between marital quality scale scores in 1980 when respondents were married to one spouse and in 1988 when they were married to another spouse make it unlikely that factors not related to the marriage are responsible for the responses (Johnson, Amoloza, & Booth, 1992).

Although much more research needs to done on the intriguing tendency for people to view their marriages in very positive and exaggerated ways, particularly in longitudinal and trend studies, the body of evidence points to marital conventionalization as another measure of marital quality and not a source of potential bias in drawing conclusions about patterns of change in marriages over the life course.

Selection Effects

There has been much research on marital quality over the family life cycle that makes use of cross-sectional samples to reach conclusions about how marital quality varies as a marriage moves through the stages of the family life course (Burr, 1970; Rollins & Cannon, 1974; Anderson, Russell, & Schumm, 1983; Spanier, Sauer, & Larzelere, 1979). It is undoubtedly clear to these researchers that the results could be seriously biased by selection and cohort effects. For example, differences in marital happiness between marriages of 5 and 25 years duration may not reflect the effect of duration on happiness. Not only is the group of couples who have been married for 25 years likely to be in a select group of surviving marriages, they also are likely to have gotten married in a period with different cultural, social, and economic climates than those married 5 years ago. Differences in marital happiness may not reflect a change at all, but represent a difference in marriage cohorts and the different social and marital characteristics of marriages that survive 25 years in a society with high divorce rates.

Most studies of the effects of socioeconomic, background, and structural variables on marital quality only study currently married persons. It is possible, however, that variables strongly related to marital quality may show no effects in such an analysis (Glenn & Weaver, 1978a). For example, if the presence of a premarital birth is strongly related to low marital quality in a subgroup of respondents, it is likely that this group would be selected out due to divorce. A study of the relationship between marital happiness and the presence of premarital birth using a sample of current married respondents may find no effect because the group with the largest effects has been selected out.

Glenn and Weaver (1978a) used a similar argument to account for the small or nonexistent effects of several social, economic, and demographic variables on marital happiness in several national surveys. For example, early age at marriage, which has been found to be a strong predictor of divorce (Bumpass & Sweet, 1972), was not significantly related to marital happiness. They argue that the surveys they examined were conducted (1973-1975) when divorce rates were increasing rapidly and selection of unhappy marriages out of the pool of currently married persons was high. This would attenuate the effect of such variables in the cross-sectional analysis.

The selection argument has also been used to explain the highly skewed distribution of many marital happiness and satisfaction variables (Glenn & Weaver, 1978a; Orden & Bradburn, 1968). The very small proportion reporting their marriages as not too happy may reflect that such persons move quickly out of marriage.

Because marital happiness is a strong predictor of divorce, selection should affect both the distribution of marital happiness scores and the relationship of happiness to social variables. However, other evidence raises serious doubts that selection alone is the basis for negative findings and the small proportion reporting low happiness. Donohue and Ryder (1982) examine both issues. Studies since 1938, when divorce rates were much lower, find nearly identical distributions on the responses to a global marital happiness item to those found in recent decades where disruption due to divorce is more common. If the selection argument were valid, earlier studies should find a larger proportion of unhappy persons, which they do not. They also replicate Glenn and Weaver's (1978a) regression analysis that used data from the 1970s with similar national survey data from the 1960s. Because divorce rates were lower in the 1960s, they argued that the selection effect should be smaller. The effects of social and demographic variables on marital happiness were very similar in both decades. This finding makes it unlikely that the higher selection into divorce in the 1970s was attenuating the findings.

One solution to the selection problem in making inferences from cross-sectional data is to study a closed population, one in which few people enter or leave. This is difficult in marital quality research because it makes no sense to assess the marital quality of persons who have not yet married or are no longer married. One possible solution is the concept of marital success (Glenn, 1990; Glenn, 1991). Marital success distinguishes marriages that are still intact with both partners viewing it as satisfactory from failed marriages or marriages in which at least one partner views it as unsatisfactory. Glenn (1991) combines information on divorce and separation with marital happiness rating to classify marriages as successful or not. He then empirically examines trends in marital success by years since first marriage and by period. Although the measure is relatively crude, some of his findings present a sobering view of the chances for marital success in the 1980s. For persons in the 1980s who were first married 20 to 24 years ago, only 32.5% are classified as successful in their marriage. Even lower rates are found for selected demographic groups (Glenn, 1989).

One of the most widely accepted findings in change in marital quality over the life course is that the likelihood of divorce declines with marital duration (Bumpass & Sweet, 1972). However, there is evidence that this effect, with the possible exception of declines in the first 2 or 3 years, is primarily the result of selection. High-risk marriages are selected out early, leaving only those with relatively low risks in the pool of married persons. Johnson, Amoloza, and Booth (1992) found in a sample of married persons followed over 8 years that mean scores on the Nebraska Divorce Proneness Scale did not decline and that the scale was very stable. Use of panel data allows some control for the problem of selection, but even here care must be taken. Panel studies are susceptible to high attrition rates, particularly panels followed over many years. The marriages that remain may be selective in many ways that can bias the findings. For example, although there was no evidence that persons leaving the three-wave panel of marriages had higher scores on Divorce Proneness or any of the other marital quality scales, it is possible that unspecified factors select out persons more subject to change. If so, this would reduce the external validity of the findings.

Single-item Measures of Marital Quality

A significant portion of the research on marital quality relies upon single-item measures of marital happiness. Almost all of the research making use of large, nationally representative samples relies on single-item measures (Glenn, 1990). These items are frequently highly skewed in the positive direction, have only three to seven response categories, and have unknown reliability and stability.

Low reliability and limited response categories are not serious problems when the item is used as a dependent variable in regression-based models in large samples (Johnson & Creech, 1984). Both tend to introduce random errors that attenuate statistical power rather than bias the estimates of effects. Concerns continue to persist, however, that the low reliability and precision of single-item measures may contribute to the inability of studies using the single-item indicator to replicate findings from smaller samples that make use of multiple-item scales (Donohue & Ryder, 1982). The more serious problems occur in panel studies. Difficulties in estimating the reliability affect the ability to accurately estimate stability. Estimation of change is hampered by ceiling and floor effects introduced by skewed distributions and few response categories.

Methods for estimating the reliability of single-item measures in panel models have been developed, but have not been applied to the basic marital happiness item. Panel models designed to explore the causal linkages between marital quality and other aspects of the marital relationship (e.g., Zuo, 1992) need to include information on the measurement error in the indicators used to avoid biasing the results. This section makes a contribution to these unsolved problems by comparing regression results from the single-item happiness measure with those from a more psychometrically sound scale and by exploring the reliability and stability of the item in a four-wave panel model.

When Donohue and Ryder (1982) ruled out selection as an explanation for the small and generally nonsignificant effects of socioeconomic and demographic variables on marital happiness found by Glenn and Weaver (1978a), another explanation for the generally negative findings from large national surveys regarding these variables was needed. One suggestion was that perhaps the single-item happiness measure was so flawed that it produced meaningless results. If this were the case, then regression models making use of the single item should yield weaker results than models that measure marital happiness with a reliable multi-item scale. A test of this is found in Table 1. Two regression models are computed for the 1980 wave of the four-wave panel study discussed elsewhere in this chapter. Most of the demographic and social variables used as predictors by Glenn and Weaver (1978a) and Donohue and Ryder (1982) are included. One model uses the Nebraska Marital Happiness Scale (Johnson, White et al., 1986) as the dependent variable. The other uses the standard global happiness item with three response categories (very happy, coded 3; pretty happy, 2; and not too happy, 1). Standardized regression coefficients (betas) are reported so the relative effects can be compared.

The analyses provide some evidence that the poorer measurement properties of the single-item measure attenuate the effects, but other findings cannot be so clearly interpreted. More variance is explained in the scale than in the item (5.6% to 4.9% but the difference is not substantial. Five of the independent variables were statistically significant related to the scale whereas only four reached significance when the item was the dependent variable. However, only two variables were significant in both models: respondent is nonwhite and religion is important in life. Gender, age, and total family income were only significant in the scale regression, whereas education and husband's occupational status were only significant for the item regression. The direction of all the effects (whether significant or not) was the same in both models. Generally, the results conclude that the single-item measure of marital happiness is quite robust. Differences found may be more substantive than methodological. There is little

Table 1. Comparison of regression models in which marital Happiness is measured by the single item global Happiness and measured by the Marital Happiness Scale. (N = 1,888)

Independent Variables	Global Happiness Item Beta	Marital Happiness Scale Beta
Age of Respondent in Years	-.045	-.109*
Total Annual Family Income	.033	.075*
Years of Schooling Competed	-.087*	-.046
Husband's Occupational Status	.071**	.033
Wife Work Full Time	-.015	-.037
Wife Work Part Time	.007	.002
Respondent's Gender (M=1)(F=2)	-.050	-.128*
Respondent is Non-White	-.116*	-.085*
Religion importance in life	-.164*	-.165*
Children under age 5 in HHold	.004	.001
Children under age 12 in HHold	-.040	-.053
Number of Children under 18	-.053	-.065
R-Squared	.049	.056

* Statistically significant at the .01 level.

indication in this analysis that findings from studies making use of the single-item measure of marital happiness are suspect.

Application of single-item measures in panel data may be more problematic. To date, the only panel analyses employing the single item were by Bradburn (1969) and Orden and Bradburn (1968). They report results of the test-retest stability of the global happiness item with three-response categories and make some inferences about change in marital happiness relative to change in positive and negative affect (Bradburn, 1969). Making use of cross-classification techniques, Bradburn (1969) concluded that changes in marital happiness over the short period of their panel were more likely to reflect changes in negative than in positive affect in the marriage. A nonconventional analysis method used in the study limits further exploration of these results for biases and methodological problems.

As was clearly shown by Duncan (1969), causal panel analyses that do not consider measurement error can produce results that are seriously biased. Therefore, estimates of the reliability and stability of single-item measures are needed. Heise (1969) presented a method for estimating the reliability and stability of indicators in panel studies with three or more waves. This technique has been applied to estimate the reliability of single items on public opinion surveys (Alwin & Krosnick, 1991; Jagodzinski & Kühnel, 1987). Data from the national four-wave panel are used to provide reliability and stability estimates for the single-item happiness indicator.

Test-retest correlations have generally been the only method available for estimating the reliability of single-item measures. Such correlations, however, are likely to be affected by both the reliability and true score change in the measure. The method, originally proposed by Heise (1969) and modified by Wiley and Wiley (1970), separately estimates reliability and stability if three or more waves of panel data are available and if certain assumptions are made. Figure 1 presents a basic model for such an analysis. The variables in circles are unmeasured variables representing the true score component of marital happiness (MH) in each of the panel years. The indicators in the rectangles are the measures of marital happiness, in this case the global happiness item (GH). The λ coefficients are estimates of the relationship between the true score and the measure, and the λ coefficients are the measurement errors in the indicators. The MH variables are assumed to be related to one another in a simplex or lag-1 manner. This means that MH at time t is only directly related to marital happiness at time t+1. Any relationship between MH_1 and MH_3 is through MH_2.

Further restrictions are required to identify mathematically the equations. Two alternative sets have been proposed. The first assumes that the reliability is the same in each wave (Heise, 1969). In Figure 1, all the ε coefficients (in their standardized form) would be assumed to be equal. This reduces the number of unknowns sufficiently to just identify a three-wave and to overidentify a four-wave model by 2 degrees of freedom. The second choice is to assume that the measurement error variances of the indicators are the same for each wave (Wiley & Wiley, 1970). The degrees of freedom are the same in both models. Both can be estimated with three or more waves of data available with LISREL VII (Jöreskog & Sörbom, 1988).

The correlations among the four waves of data for the global happiness item are presented in Table 2. Given that each wave is 3 to 4 years apart, the test-retest correlations are quite high, averaging around .5 for adjacent waves. The mean score declines steadily over the 12 years, which is a pattern also found for the Marital Happiness Scale.

Estimates of the reliability and stability for the two alternative models are presented in Table 3. The equal reliability model yielded a reliability score (calculated as the square of the standardized lambda

Figure 1. Four-wave path model for Global Happiness as single indicator of Marital Happiness.

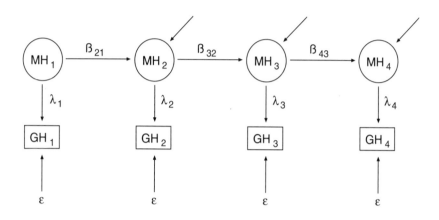

Table 2. Correlations, means and standard deviations among the for the global happiness item in the four waves. $(N = 945)$

	Wave 1	Wave 2	Wave 3	Wave 4
Wave 1	1.0000			
Wave 2	.5298	1.0000		
Wave 3	.4494	.4849	1.0000	
Wave 4	.4150	.4276	.5076	1.0000
Means	2.7027	2.6227	2.6081	2.5572
S. D.	.4817	.5141	.5332	.5692

coefficient in the model) of .563. The equal error variance model found the lowest reliability in Wave 1 and the highest in Wave 4. Stabilities were high in both models. The stability was highest from the first to the second wave. The standardized stability between these waves for the equal error variance model exceeded 1, an illogical value that suggests specification errors in the model. Other stability estimates were in the .85 to .95 range, which are still extraordinarily

Table 3. Reliability and stability coefficients for the single global happiness
item using the equal reliability and the equal error variance models.

	Equal Reliability model	Equal Error variance model
Reliability		
Wave 1	.563	.484
Wave 2	.563	.549
Wave 3	.563	.578
Wave 4	.563	.630
Stability		
Waves 1 - 2	.942	1.019
Waves 2 - 3	.855	.854
Waves 3 - 4	.901	.848

high. Either MH is an extremely stable trait over a 12-year period, or
the model is misspecified in some way and yields invalid results.

There is a good basis for questioning the equal error variance
model. Because the marital happiness item is so highly skewed, the
mean score is closely related to the standard deviation. The proportion
of persons saying they are not too happy is so small that the item
effectively behaves like a dichotomy. For dichotomous items the
standard deviation is a perfect, but nonlinear, function of the mean
score ($sd = \sqrt{pq}$). Because the standard deviations vary with the means
scores it makes more sense to assume that reliabilities are equal and
differences in variances are a function of error and not the latent trait.
The more mathematically meaningful estimates from the equal
reliability model support this view.

Because the global happiness item is part of the Nebraska Marital
Happiness Scale (Johnson, White et al., 1986), an estimate of reliability
can be computed from an item analysis of the scale. For the 1980
wave, the corrected item-total score correlation of the global item with
the scale was .692. Correcting for the higher reliability of the multiple-
item scale (r_{xx} = .851), this would yield an estimated reliability for the
global item of .563. This is identical to that obtained in the four-wave
model assuming equal reliabilities.

Although the convergence of estimates from internal consistency
and test-retest methods should increase confidence in the accuracy of
this estimate of the reliability, the very high stability over 3 or more
years implied by such a reliability estimate questions this confidence.
One resolution is to consider the latent variable implied by the marital

happiness item. The measurement model implies that MH is tapping global happiness, free of measurement error. However, the lag-1 model specifies that MH has a direct causal effect on MH in the next wave. It may be reasonable to assume that this is an incorrect model. Marital happiness, even free of measurement errors, may not be causally related to happiness in subsequent years. Instead, MH may be an outcome of other unmeasured characteristics of the marital environment that are quite stable and autocorrelated to a lag-1 process. If this were the case, the reliability of the global happiness indicator would be underestimated and the high stability coefficients would reflect that latent trait and not marital happiness net of measurement error.

Hargens, Reskin, and Allisson (1976) were confronted with a similar problem while trying to estimate measurement error in indicators of scientific productivity. They conclude that when only a single indicator is available, it is not possible to infer the nature of the unmeasured variable estimated by the model. Attempts by Jagodzinski and Kühnel (1987) to solve this problem making use of polychoric correlations suggests a possible solution. The solution proposed here builds on their work, but has not been presented in this form in literature.

A model assuming two latent traits is shown in Figure 2. Marital Happiness free of error (MH) is not assumed to directly affect itself in subsequent waves. Another latent variable, labelled Marital Environment (ME), has effects on MH and is causally related to itself in a lag-1 pattern. The problem with the model is developing a method of estimating both the measurement errors in the global happiness indicator and the effects of Marital Environment. The model is underidentified and no solution in the single variable case has been found in the literature. Combining a polychoric model with a four-wave path model is a key to estimating this model (Jöreskog & Sörbom, 1988; Jagodzinski & Kühnel, 1987).

A polychoric correlation provides an estimate of the relationship between two unmeasured continuous and normally distributed variables implied by crudely categorized indicators with a small number of ordered response categories (Jöreskog & Sörbom, 1988). The tetrachoric correlation is the version of this coefficient used for dichotomous variables. The cross-classification of the categories of the two indicators is fit to a model which assumes that this pattern was generated by two normally distributed, continuous variables. Polychoric correlations are correlations between the indicators after removing the effects of categorization errors.

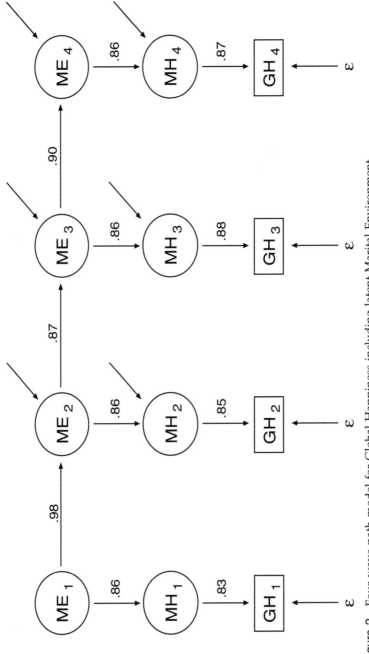

Figure 2. Four-wave path model for Global Happiness including latent Marital Environment.

In the four-wave panel model, polychoric correlations are used to estimate the relationship among the unmeasured MH variables. Fitting the Hiese model extended to four waves to these correlations yield estimates of the paths among the unmeasured variables. The parameters linking MH and the global happiness indicators were estimated in a second stage by a LISREL model for the correlations among the indicators. The estimates from the first stage were set as fixed values and the paths between MH and GH were estimated.

Standardized path coefficients estimated in this model are presented in Figure 2. Marital Environment was very stable between waves and strongly affected Marital Happiness (.86). The paths from MH to GH range from .825 to .875, which imply reliabilities from .68 to .76. These are higher than the previously estimated reliability of the marital happiness item. The model is also consistent with the theoretical expectation that happiness would be expected to show reasonable instability over time (Campbell, Converse, & Rodgers, 1976). Test-retest correlations for MH implied by the model are approximately .7 between adjacent waves. These are more reasonable than the correlations in the .8 to .9 range found in the first model.

It is clear from this analysis that establishing the reliability and stability of single-item marital quality indicators is not a simple task. Multiple indicators of marital happiness would have simplified the task and reduced the need for as many untestable assumptions. Other possible sources of error in these models, such as serially correlated measurement errors, which could not be addressed here, might also have been evaluated (Johnson & Amoloza, 1989). Although these qualifications suggest that single-item measures should be avoided whenever possible, the overall conclusion reached about this single-item measure of global marital happiness is that it is a reliable and robust indicator of happiness. Confidence can be placed in previous findings making use of the item and future use of this and similar items in life course studies appears warranted.

Marital Quality Scales Used in Panel Studies: Reliability and Stability Issues

Most marital quality measures are multiple-item scales that have been psychometrically evaluated to one degree or another (Sabatelli, 1988). Internal consistency reliability is normally (but not always) computed, the factor structure is examined, and occasionally test-retest reliability results are reported. None of these steps guarantee that the scale will behave acceptably when used in panel models designed to assess the causal structure and process of marital change over the life course. In estimating such models it is normally necessary to incorporate estimates of measurement error to avoid biased estimates. Although internal consistency is generally adequate as an estimate of reliability in cross-sectional studies, reliability based on over-time correlations becomes very important in panel designs. Problems arise when internal consistency and test-retest reliability estimates do not coincide.

Johnson and Amoloza (1989) examined three marital quality scales (Marital Happiness, Marital Interaction, and Marital Disagreements) in a three-wave panel. The test-retest was higher than internal consistency reliability for one scale, the two estimates where approximately the same for another, and internal consistency was highest in a third. Serially correlated measurement errors were generally found responsible for the difference when test-retest exceeds internal consistency reliability. When internal consistency was highest, the misspecification of the causal lag among the unmeasured variables appears responsible. As shown in the analysis of the global happiness item, estimates of reliability can greatly affect those of stability.

Large differences between test-retest and internal consistency reliability estimates pose problems for the researcher. The normal solution to these problems is to have multiple indicators for all important variables. Although two or more scales may be used as indicators for each variable (Johnson, White et al., 1986), scales are often disaggregated into subscales or separate items (e.g., Zuo, 1992; Johnson & Amoloza, 1989). Disaggregation of scales that are multidimensional presents a problem because each dimension must be represented by a separate latent variable in the model analyzed. Because each latent variable should have at least two indicators, models can quickly become unmanageable. For example, assume a researcher is exploring the relationship between the quality of the marital relationship and psychological depression in a three-wave panel study. Measures of marital happiness, disagreements, and interaction would be needed to explore the reciprocal relationship to depression. Additionally, five or six control and background variables (marital duration, gender, socioeconomic factor, children, etc.) would be needed. If each of the marital quality and depression variables were measured by disaggregating them into the separate items, and the Nebraska Marital Quality Scales were used, then these three scales would require 18 indicators per wave, depression may take 7 more, and the controls at least 6 (assuming no multiple indicators for these). Over the three waves, this model would have 93 indicators.

The model could be simplified using only one indicator for each variable and correcting them for attenuation due to unreliability by estimating the error variances from internal consistency reliability estimates (a procedure often proposed—e.g., Hayduk, 1989). Alternatively, the error variances with single indicators could be estimated by imposing restrictions on the lagged process using models similar to those used to evaluate marital happiness indicators discussed above (Werts, Jöreskog, & Linn, 1971). Both approaches carry the risk of seriously misspecifying the model and producing biased results.

This problem is illustrated with an analysis of the reliability and stability of the Nebraska Marital Happiness Scale making use of the same four-wave dataset discussed above. Table 4 presents the correlations, means, and standard deviations for the scale in each of the four waves for all respondents with complete data and married to the same person over the 12 years of the study. Over this period, mean scale scores declined and the standard deviations increased.

Three separate estimates of reliability and stability were computed. The Heise model assumes equal reliabilities, the Wiley and Wiley model assumes equal error variances, and the third model corrects the covariance matrix for attenuation with coefficient alpha as the reliability estimate. A comparison of the alternative models is presented in Table 5. The most conspicuous difference is the large discrepancy in reliability, and subsequent stability, between the panel and the correction for attenuation models. The scale is much less reliable and far more stable when panel methods are used.

Table 4. Correlations, means, and standard deviations among the Marital Happiness Scale across the four waves. ($N = 900$)

	Wave 1	Wave 2	Wave 3	Wave 4
Wave 1	1.0000			
Wave 2	.6199**	1.0000		
Wave 3	.5546**	.6123**	1.0000	
Wave 4	.5183**	.5225**	.6334**	1.0000
Mean	29.17	28.50	28.22	27.97
S. D.	3.406	3.657	3.826	4.150

** Statistically significant at .01 level.

Table 5. Reliability and Stability of the Marital Happiness Scale across four waves for three alternative models.

	Model		
	Equal Reliability (Heise)	Equal Error Variance (Wiley & Wiley)	Correction For Attenuation (Alpha)
Reliability			
1980	.689	.621	.831
1983	.689	.671	.850
1988	.689	.706	.865
1992	.689	.745	.882
Stability			
Wave 1–2	.913	.964	.738
Wave 2–3	.878	.878	.714
Wave 3–4	.907	.870	.725

It is likely that the same problem noted for the analysis of the global happiness item may be occurring here (Figure 1). An unmeasured variable, labelled Marital Environment, may be driving the stability of Marital Happiness. With only one indicator of Marital Happiness, there are not enough degrees of freedom in the model to estimate the effects. The required multiple indicators can be obtained by disaggregating the scale into separate items. However, with 11 items in this scale, this would produce an unwieldy model. A compromise is to create subscales from among the items to yield at least two indicators.

The Marital Happiness Scale items were factor analyzed to aid in identifying two or three meaningful subscales. Although all items had their highest loadings on the first unrotated factor, a good indicator the scale is unidimensional, two- and three-factor rotated solutions were explored. A three-subscale solution was the most satisfactory. The items in each scale are shown in Table 6. Scales created were (A) intimacy, (B) companionship, and (C) relationship satisfaction. Correlations, means, and standard deviations among the subscales in all waves are given in Table 7. Figure 3 presents the path model fit to the data. The model was fit to both the observed covariance and correlation matrices. Models based on covariance allow the retention of the metric of the indicators. This insures that the unmeasured variables of the same concept are equivalent across waves, and is generally preferred (Alwin & Jackson, 1980). In this case, however, the highly skewed subscales create a mathematical dependence between the group means and standard deviations. These artifactual fluctuations across the waves in the standard deviations affect the covariances, not the correlations. Here, the analysis of the

Table 6. Marital Happiness Scale items and subscales.

Subscale A

1. How happy are you with the amount of understanding you received from you (husband/wife)? Would you say you are very happy, pretty happy, or not too happy with this aspect of your marriage? (response categories the same for items 1 thru 7)
2. With the amount of love and affection you receive?
3. The extent to which you and your spouse agree about things?
4. With your sexual relationship?

Subscale B

5. With your spouse as someone to take care of things around the house?
6. With your spouse as someone to do things with?
7. With your spouse's faithfulness to you?

Subscale C

8. Taking all things together, how would you describe your marriage? Would you say that your marriage is very happy, pretty happy or not too happy?
9. Compared to other marriages you know about, do you think your marriage is better than most, about the same as most, or not as good as most?
10. Compared to your marriage three years ago, is your marriage getting better, staying the same, or getting worse?
11. Would you say the feeling of love you have for your (husband/wife) are extremely strong, very strong, pretty strong, not too strong, or not strong at all?

Table 7. Correlations, means and standard deviations among the three marital happiness subscales in the four panel waves. ($N = 943$)

	HA1	HB1	HC1	HA2	HB2	HC2	HA3	HB3	HC3	HA4	HB4	HC4
Correlations												
HA1	1.000											
HB1	.584	1.000										
HC1	.543	.432	1.000									
HA2	.537	.365	.421	1.000								
HB2	.421	.513	.396	.564	1.000							
HC2	.368	.297	.563	.597	.471	1.000						
HA3	.481	.347	.335	.537	.430	.411	1.000					
HB3	.378	.455	.296	.371	.517	.314	.619	1.000				
HC3	.384	.279	.437	.402	.348	.492	.638	.522	1.000			
HA4	.459	.324	.352	.481	.374	.358	.561	.413	.464	1.000		
HB4	.342	.387	.274	.302	.452	.273	.427	.507	.389	.635	1.000	
HC4	.365	.297	.417	.369	.301	.434	.460	.386	.552	.679	.566	1.000
Means	10.064	8.090	10.979	9.807	7.928	10.710	9.731	7.830	10.630	9.636	7.80	10.476
Standard Deviations	1.789	1.125	1.194	1.864	1.199	1.345	1.909	1.251	1.419	1.996	1.272	1.590

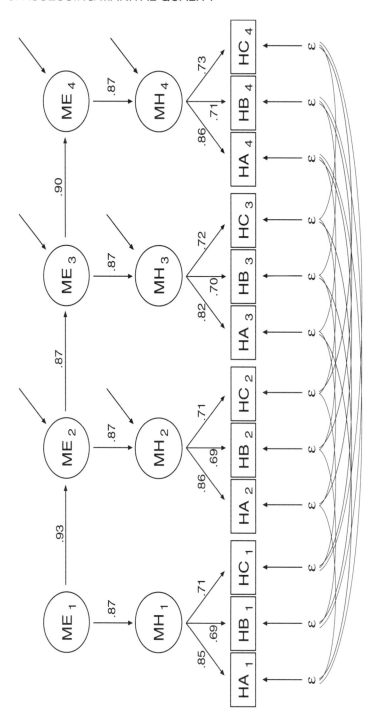

Figure 3.   Four-wave path model for three-indicator Marital Happiness with latent Marital Environment variable.

correlation matrix is more reasonable. To ensure comparability across waves in the unmeasured variables, the paths from the MH to the indicators and their error terms are allowed to vary by indicator but are constrained to be the same for each wave.

The model in Figure 3 also assumes that measurement errors of the same scale are correlated across waves. This is the usual assumption in multiple indicator panel models (Jöreskog & Sörbom, 1988). It accounts for the part of the variance that indicators do not share in common that may be correlated across time. The estimates appearing on the model are from the analysis of the correlation matrix. Estimates for the error terms and their intercorrelations are omitted from the diagram to simplify the figure.

Comparisons of the estimates in Figure 3 with those from the model fit to the single happiness item in Figure 2 show remarkable similarities. The pattern of effects among Marital Environment (ME) and Marital Happiness (MH) are almost identical. Perhaps more surprising is the estimate of the relationship between the indicators and MH. The square of this estimate is the measure of reliability. The single-item global happiness scale is found to be about as reliable as the most reliable of the subscales (A: Intimacy). It is considerably more reliable than the four-item scale in which it is included.

This anomaly may reflect two things. Subscale C includes two items (9 and 10) with the lowest item-total score correlations in the Marital Happiness Scale that may be suppressing the subscale's reliability. The model in Figure 3 also includes autocorrelated measurement errors not found in the global happiness model. These errors can include part of the reliability variance in the scale that is not included in the effect from MH to the indicator (Alwin & Jackson, 1980).

An important outcome of this exercise is the stability estimates of marital happiness free of measurement error. The stability estimates are not present as parameters in the model, but can be calculated from the coefficients. The correlations of MH among adjacent waves are r_{12} = .695; r_{23} = .670; and r_{34} = .693. These moderately high estimates of stability raise doubts about the high levels of stability reported for the single indicator panel models in Table 5.

This analysis was designed to illustrate some issues and problems that arise in panel models that require attention in panel studies of marital quality over the life course. The influence of the latent Marital Environment variable is intriguing and is substantively as well as methodologically important. The findings suggest that there are very stable traits in marriages that are strongly linked to marital happiness.

Panel models that include other indicators of marital quality and other more direct measures of the marital environment are needed. Such models will need to demonstrate close attention to the reliability and measurement issues discussed throughout this chapter.

SUMMARY AND CONCLUSIONS

This chapter has examined in a selective way the assessment of marital quality. Although many ways of assessing the quality of marriage have been proposed, it is clear that the variety of measures reflects basic conceptual issues about the meaning of the term. Three perspectives were identified: the marital adjustment perspective with its roots in marital therapy and identification of troubled and well-adjusted marriages, the global satisfaction view that seeks to restrict the definition of marital quality to subjective evaluation of the whole marriage, and a more eclectic approach that groups a series of separate concepts under the umbrella term of marital quality but seeks separate measures for each. The third perspective has the widest acceptance and use in the literature and is consistent with researchers seeking to assess aspects of marital quality in causal life course models.

The next objective was to more closely examine specific measures of marital quality that might have utility in life course studies. The review was restricted to scales and measures with relatively small numbers of items that were designed primarily for research and not clinical purposes. Basic criticisms and concerns raised about the measures and examples of their use in life course research were discussed. More attention was given to an evaluation of the single-item measure of marital happiness than in previous reviews of marital quality measures because most studies making use of large and nationally representative samples employ crude, often highly skewed, single-item measures. Scales found most appropriate for life course work were those that measured only one trait of the marital relationship well.

Four methodological issues in the assessment of marital quality were reviewed. The conclusion that could be drawn from the discussion of methodological issues in the assessment of marital quality is that, with some care in selection of scales, analysis method, and the interpretation of the results, these problems do not seriously impair the ability of the researcher from making valid statements about the quality of marriages. Marital conventionalization, or the tendency of persons to report their marriage in a more positive light than it actually was, has cast doubt on the validity of evaluative measures of marital quality. More recent research suggests that this tendency is not a typical survey response bias like social desirability, but may be a valid component of how people see these marriages. The fact that marital happiness scales, often viewed as highly contaminated by marital social desirability, are strong predictors of behavior such as divorce, even among groups susceptible to reporting high marital satisfaction, suggests that marital quality measures may not be biased enough to reduce their utility as research tools.

Selection effects from failed marriages are a special problem for researchers making use of cross-sectional data to make inferences about life course changes, but also present problems when longitudinal data are available. In some cases, especially with panel data, it is possible to estimate the effects of selection and take them into consideration in the analysis models.

The problems of single-item measures, quite prevalent in the analysis of marital quality, are examined in detail by concentrating on the global marital happiness item with three response categories. The review of previous work and an empirical analysis of the behavior of the item in four-wave panel suggests that the measure is quite robust and reliable. This reduces concerns that findings from studies using the single-item indicator should be discounted as not sufficiently valid.

The final issue examined concerned problems in estimating the reliability and stability of marital quality measures in panel studies. A panel model for multiple indicators of marital quality was proposed and partially applied to four-wave panel data. This analysis suggested that splitting scales into two or more indicators may be necessary to estimate stability in a valid manner.

Some conclusions can be drawn from this exploration of the measurement of marital quality. First, the debate over what should be called marital quality should be ended. Most researchers now recognize the need to assess the various components of marital quality in separate scales. Use of marital quality to refer only to global assessment of the marital relationship appears too limited and removes a term that has been useful in characterizing research on the marital relationship.

Second, because of resource constraints, work should concentrate on creating short, unidimensional scales for the components of marital quality. Family researchers should work to add these to some of the regular national surveys that are the only real source of large and nationally representative samples. Third, although scales should be short, the researcher should be able to subdivide the scales when two or more indicators of each construct are needed to estimate panel models of marital quality. Fourth, there is evidence that a single-item scale of marital happiness may be more robust and less biased than expected and appears to be a valid replacement of complete scales of marital happiness. Research making use of single-item marital evaluation measures, particularly when large representative samples are available, has been found to be clearly worth pursuing when more complete scales are not available. Finally, multiwave, multivariate models of the causal relationships between marital quality and other marital variables require multiple indicators of constructs and careful specification of the models to avoid serious bias introduced by the reliability of the measures.

REFERENCES

Alwin, D. F., & Jackson, D. J. (1980). Measurement models for response errors in surveys: Issues and applications. In K. F. Schuessler (Ed.), *Sociological methodology: 1980* (pp. 69-119). San Francisco: Jossey-Bass.

Alwin, D. F., & Krosnick, J. A. (1991). Aging, cohorts and the stability of sociopolitical orientations over the life span. *American Journal of Sociology, 97*, 169-195.

Anderson, S. A., Russell, C. S., & Schumm, W. R. (1983). Perceived marital quality and family life-cycle categories: A further analysis. *Journal of Marriage and the Family, 45*, 126-139.

Belsky, J., Lang, M. E., & Rovine, M. (1985). Stability and change in marriage across the transition to parenthood: A second study. *Journal of Marriage and the Family, 47*, 855-865.

Belsky, J., Spanier, G. B., & Rovine, M. (1983). Stability and change in marriage across the transition to parenthood. *Journal of Marriage and the Family, 45,*567-577.

Booth, A., & Edwards, J. N. (1989). Transmission of marital and family quality over the generations: The effect of parental divorce and unhappiness. *Journal of Divorce, 13,* 41-58.

Booth, A., & Johnson, D. R. (1992). *Religious change and change in marital quality.* Unpublished manuscript.

Booth, A., Johnson, D. R., & Edwards, J. N. (1983). Measuring marital instability. *Journal of Marriage and the Family, 45,* 387-394.

Booth, A., Johnson, D. R., White, L. K., & Edwards, J. N. (1984). Women, outside employment and marital instability. *American Journal of Sociology, 90,* 567-583.

Booth, A., Johnson, D. R., White, L. K., & Edwards, J. N. (1986). Divorce and marital instability over the life course. *Journal of Family Issues, 6,* 421-442.

Bradburn, N. M. (1969) *The structure of psychological well-being.* Chicago: Aldine.

Bumpass, L. L., & Sweet, J. L. (1972). Differentials in marital instability: 1970. *American Sociological Review, 37,* 754-766.

Burke, R. J., Weir, T., & DuWors, R. E. (1979). Type A behavior of administrators and wives' reports of marital satisfaction and well being. *Journal of Applied Psychology, 64,* 57-65.

Burr, W. R. (1970). Satisfaction with various aspects of marriage over the life cycle: A random middle class sample. *Journal of Marriage and the Family, 32,* 29-37.

Campbell, A., Converse, P. E., & Rodgers, W. L. (1976) *The quality of American life: Perceptions, evaluations, and satisfactions.* New York: Russell Sage Foundation.

Crane, D. R., Busby, D. M., & Larson, J. H. (1991). A factor analysis of the Dyadic Adjustment Scale with distressed and nondistressed couples. *American Journal of Family Therapy, 19,* 60-66.

Cross, D. G., & Sharpley, C. F. (1981). The Locke-Wallace marital adjustment test reconsidered: Some psychometric findings as regards its reliability and factoral validity. *Educational Psychology Measurement, 41,* 1303-1306.

Donohue, K. C., & Ryder, R. G. (1982). A methodological note on marital satisfaction and social variables. *Journal of Marriage and the Family, 44,* 743-747.

Duncan, O. D. (1969). Some linear models for two-variable panel analysis. *Psychological Bulletin, 72,* 177-182.

Edmonds, V. H. (1967). Marital conventionalization: Definition and measurement. *Journal of Marriage and the Family, 29,* 681-688.

Edmonds, V. H., Withers, G., & Dibatista, B. (1972). Adjustment, conservatism and marital conventionalization. *Journal of Marriage and the Family, 34,* 96-103.

Featherman, D. L., & Lerner, R. M. (1985). Ontogenesis and sociogenesis. *American Sociological Review, 50,* 659-690.

Fincham, F. D., & Bradbury, T. N. (1987). The assessment of marital quality: A reevaluation. *Journal of Marriage and the Family, 49,* 797-809.

Fowers, B. J., & Pomerantz, B. L. (1992, November). *Reconceptualizing marital conventionalization: Examining psychological, relational and cultural explanations.* Paper presented at the 22nd annual Theory Construction and Research Methodology Workshop, Orlando, FL.

Glenn, N. D. (1989). Duration of marriage, family composition, and marital happiness. *National Journal of Sociology, 3,* 3-24.

Glenn, N. D. (1990). Quantitative research on marital quality in the 1980s: A critical review. *Journal of Marriage and the Family, 52*, 818-831.

Glenn, N. D. (1991). The recent trend in marital success in the United States. *Journal of Marriage and the Family, 53*, 261-270.

Glenn, N. D., & McLanahan, S. (1982). Children and marital happiness: A further specification of the relationship. *Journal of Marriage and the Family, 44*, 63-72.

Glenn, N. D., & Weaver, C. N. (1978a). A multivariate, multisurvey study of marital happiness. *Journal of Marriage and the Family, 39*, 269-282.

Glenn, N. D., & Weaver, C. N. (1978b). The contribution of marital happiness to global happiness. *Journal of Marriage and the Family, 43*, 161-168.

Hamilton, G. V. (1929). *A research in marriage.* New York: Albert and Charles Boni.

Hansen, G. L. (1981). Marital adjustment and conventionalization: A reexamination. *Journal of Marriage and the Family, 43*, 855-863.

Hargens, L. L., Reskin, B. F., & Allisson, P. D. (1976). Problems in estimating measurement error from panel data: An example involving the measurement of scientific productivity. *Sociological Methods and Research, 4*, 439-458.

Hayduk, L. A. (1987). *Structural equation modelling with LISREL: Essentials and advances.* Baltimore: Johns Hopkins University Press.

Heise, D. R. (1969). Separating reliability and stability in test-retest correlations. *American Sociological Review, 34*, 93-101.

Hicks, M. W., & Platt, M. (1970). Marital happiness and stability: A review of the research in the sixties. *Journal of Marriage and the Family, 32*, 553-574.

Huston, T. L., & Robins, E. (1982). Conceptual and methodological issues in studying close relationships. *Journal of Marriage and the Family, 44*, 901-925.

Jagodzinski, W., & Kühnel, S. M. (1987). Estimation of reliability and stability in single-indicator multiple-wave models. *Sociological Methods and Research, 15*, 219-258.

Johnson, D. R. (1988). Panel analysis is family studies. *Journal of Marriage and the Family, 50*, 949-955.

Johnson, D. R., & Amoloza, T. O. (1989, April). *Assessing reliability using internal consistency and three-wave panel methods: A synthesis and empirical exploration.* Paper presented at the Midwest Sociological Society Annual Meeting, St. Louis, MO.

Johnson, D. R., Amoloza, T. O., & Booth, A. (1992). Stability and developmental change in marital quality: A three-wave panel analysis. *Journal of Marriage and the Family, 54*, 582-594.

Johnson, D. R., & Creech, J. C. (1984). Ordinal measures in multiple indicator models: A simulation study of categorization errors. *American Sociological Review, 48,* 398-407.

Johnson, D. R., White, L. K., Edwards, J. N., & Booth, A. (1986). Dimensions of marital quality: Towards methodological and conceptual refinement. *Journal of Family Issues, 7,* 31-49.

Jöreskog, K. I. G., & Sörbom, D. (1988). *LISREL 7: A guide to the program and applications.* Chicago: SPSS.

Kimmel, D., & Van Der Veen, F. (1974). Factors of marital adjustment in Locke's marital adjustment test. *Journal of Marriage and the Family, 36,* 57-63.

Kolb, T. M., & Straus, M. A. (1974). Marital power and marital happiness in relation to problem-solving ability. *Journal of Marriage and the Family, 36 ,* 756-766.

Lively, E. L. (1969). Towards a conceptual clarification: The case of marital interaction. *Journal of Marriage and the Family, 31,* 108-114.

Locke, H. J., & Wallace, K. M. (1959). Short marital adjustment and prediction tests: Their reliability and validity. *Marriage and Family Living, 21,* 251-255.

Locke, H. J., & Williamson, R. C. (1958). Marital adjustment: A factor analysis study. *American Sociological Review. 23,* 562-569.

Margolin, G. (1978). Relationships among marital assessment procedures: A correlational study. *Journal of Consulting and Clinical Psychology, 46,* 1556-1558.

Mattessich, P., & Hill, R. (1987). Life cycle and family development. In M. B. Sussman & S. K. Steinmetz (Eds.), *Handbook of marriage and the family* (pp. 437-469). New York: Plenum Press.

Mitchell, S. E., Newell, G. K., & Schumm, W. R. (1983). Test-retest reliability of the Kansas Marital Satisfaction Scale. *Psychological Reports, 53,* 545-546.

Norton, R. (1983). Measuring marital quality: A critical look at the dependent variable. *Journal of Marriage and the Family, 45,* 141-151.

Nunnally, J. C. (1967). *Psychometric theory.* New York: McGraw-Hill.

Orden, S. R., & Bradburn, N. M. (1968). Dimensions of marriage happiness. *American Journal of Sociology, 73,* 715-731.

Rollins, B. C., & Cannon, K. L. (1974). Marital satisfaction over the family life cycle: A reevaluation. *Journal of Marriage and the Family, 36,* 271-282.

Sabatelli, R. M. (1988). Measurement issues in marital research: A review and critique of contemporary survey instruments. *Journal of Marriage and the Family, 50,* 891-917.

Schumm, W. R., Paff-Bergen, L. A., Hatch, R. C., Obiorah, F. C., Copeland, J. M., Meens, L. D., & Bugaighis, M. A. (1986). Concurrent and discriminant validity of the Kansas Marital Satisfaction Scale. *Journal of Marriage and the Family*, *48*, 381-387.

Sharpley, C. F., & Cross, D. G. (1982). A psychometric evaluation of the Spanier dyadic adjustment scale. *Journal of Marriage and the Family*, *44*, 739-741.

Spanier, G. B. (1976). Measuring dyadic adjustment: New scales for assessing the quality of marriage and similar dyads. *Journal of Marriage and the Family*, *38*, 15-28.

Spanier, G. B., & Cole, C. L. (1976). Towards clarification and investigation of marital adjustment. *International Journal of Sociology of the Family*, *6*, 121-146.

Spanier, G. B., & Lewis, R. A. (1980). Marital quality: A review of the seventies. *Journal of Marriage and the Family*, *42*, 825-839.

Spanier, G. B., Sauer, W., & Larzelere, R. (1979). An empirical evaluation of the family life cycle. *Journal of Marriage and the Family*, *41*, 27-38.

Spanier, G. B., & Thompson, L. (1982). A confirmatory analysis of the dyadic adjustment scale. *Journal of Marriage and the Family*, *44*, 731-738.

Sweet, J. A., Bumpass, L. L., & Call, V. R. A. (1988). Design and content of the National Survey of Families and Households (Working Paper NSFH-1). Madison, WI: Center for Demography and Ecology, University of Wisconsin.

Touliatos, J., Perlmutter, B. F., & Straus, M. A. (1990). *Handbook of family measurement techniques.* Newbury Park, CA: Sage.

Werts, C. E., Jöreskog, K. G., & Linn, R. L. (1971). Comment on "Estimation of measurement error in panel data." *American Sociological Review*, *36*, 110-113.

White, L. K. (1983). Determinants of spacial interaction: Marital structure or marital happiness. *Journal of Marriage and the Family*, *45*, 511-519.

White, L. K., & Booth A. (1985). Transition to parenthood and marital quality. *Journal of Family Issues*, *6*, 435-449.

White, L. K., & Booth A. (1991). Divorce over the life course: The role of marital happiness. *Journal of Family Issues*, *12*, 5-21.

White, L. K., & Edwards, J. N. (1990). Emptying the nest and parental well-being: An analysis of national panel data. *American Sociological Review*, *55*, 235-242.

Wiley, D. E., & Wiley, J. A. (1970). The estimation of measurement error in panel data. *American Sociological Review*, *35*, 112-117.

Zuo, J. (1992). The reciprocal relationship between marital inter-action and marital happiness: A three-wave study. *Journal of Marriage and the Family, 54,* 870-878.

Section Three

Assessment of Special Challenges
Faced by Families

The previous two sections of the volume described family assessment related to the usual issues faced by families. In this final section, the papers are concerned with assessment approaches with families facing particular challenges. Chapters concerning divorce, aggressive children, and the effects of a child with a disability on family and child functioning comprise the third section.

Dr. Paul Amato notes that empirical investigation into the impact of divorce on children lacks the theoretical base that would provide a solid foundation for future research. Amato suggest that current research includes too many dependent variables which results in weak outcomes. Studies also fall short when global constructs are assessed with lack of attention to the specific indicators that form those constructs. Many of the instruments currently in place for assessing outcomes have questionable reliability and validity. This results from small, nonrandom samples being used with multiple item measures. Amato offers a review of causal models of the effects of divorce and provides a thorough critique of each with its associated measurement approaches.

Elaine B. Werth tackles the difficult assessment challenge of measuring the effects of family/parent training for families who have aggressive children. With youth violence a national priority for reduction, the need to develop and validate approaches to help families cope with and change the behavior of aggressive children is critically important.

Dr. Marjorie Padulla considers families who have had to organize around a member's disability. The assessment challenges include finding measures that: (a) emphasize strengths, not just pathological elements of the family's experience; (b) can gather information from all family members including the person with the disabilities; (c) allow for a broad focus on family dynamics not just on the relationship of family members to the person with the disability; and (d) have psychometric qualities that allow for confident use with the special families.

ISSUES IN MEASURING THE EFFECTS OF DIVORCE ON CHILDREN

Paul R. Amato

University of Nebraska-Lincoln

The divorce rate in the United States has been increasing steadily for the last century, from 7% of first marriages in 1880 to over 50% in recent decades (Weed, 1980). Even though the divorce rate leveled off in the 1980s, current estimates indicate that nearly two-thirds (64%) of all first marriages will end in divorce or permanent separation (Martin & Bumpass, 1989). Currently, more than one million children experience parental divorce every year in this country (U.S. Bureau of the Census, 1989, p. 92). This increase in the likelihood of marital disruption, and the large number of children involved, has generated public concern about the consequences of divorce for children's well-being.

People who hold traditional attitudes believe that a two-parent family is necessary to ensure children's successful socialization and development. Consequently, traditionalists see any departure from the two-parent family as necessarily being problematic. Several observers have criticized this perspective, referred to as a "family deficit model," as being simplistic (Demo, 1992; Marotz-Baden, Adams, Buech, Munro, & Munro, 1979). They point out that alternative family forms, such as single-parent families, can serve as successful environments for children's development. In recent years, ideological debates over divorce and single-parent families have appeared in both the popular press and academic journals (see Etzioni, 1992, for a discussion).

Nevertheless, in spite of the debate at the ideological level, good reasons exist for assuming that parental divorce has the potential to create problems for many children.

First, both mothers and fathers are important resources for children. Research has consistently shown that a high level of parental support and a moderate level of parental control and supervision promote children's development and well-being (Maccoby & Martin, 1983; Rollins & Thomas, 1979). As such, the departure of one parent—usually the father—from the household following marital dissolution represents the loss of a potentially important resource for children. Furthermore, for a period of time following divorce, custodial mothers tend to be less affectionate toward their children and punish them more severely and less consistently than do married mothers (Hetherington, Cox, & Cox, 1982). Divorce also exposes children to high levels of interparental conflict—both prior to and following marital disruption. Not surprisingly, research shows that interparental conflict is associated with deficits in children's well-being, regardless of family type (Emery, 1982). In addition, children living with custodial mothers are likely to experience economic hardship (Weitzman, 1985). Finally, divorce initiates a series of life changes (such as moving and changing schools) that may be stressful to children. Any of these factors—parental loss, poor quality parenting, interparental conflict, economic hardship, and stressful life changes—might place children of divorce at increased risk for a variety of problems.

During the last three decades, psychologists, sociologists, and other social scientists have carried out a large number of studies dealing with the impact of divorce on children. Several scholars have reviewed this literature in a qualitative fashion (e.g., Emery, 1988; Demo & Acock, 1988). More recently, Bruce Keith and I carried out a meta-analysis of 92 of these studies (Amato & Keith, 1991a). Our meta-analysis showed that children of divorce, compared with children in continuously intact two-parent families, score slightly but significantly lower on measures of academic ability, conduct, psychological adjustment, self-esteem, and social competence. Divorce is also associated with poorer quality mother-child and father-child relationships.

These results would appear to indicate that divorce has broad negative implications for children's functioning and well-being.

However, as we noted in the meta-analysis, many of these studies contain serious methodological limitations. To assess how methodological factors might affect study results, we created a simple index of study quality based on the following criteria: (a) a random selection of children, (b) a large sample size (defined as being greater than the median), (c) the use of appropriate control variables in analyses (or the matching of subjects on relevant variables), and (d) the use of multiple- rather than single-item measures of outcomes. Curiously, we found a tendency for methodologically weak studies to show stronger effect sizes than methodologically strong studies—at least in relation to measures of academic achievement and conduct (Amato & Keith, 1991a).

I attribute this finding to the "publish if significant" effect. Assume that journal editors accept manuscripts for publication if they are methodologically strong *or* if they show significant effects, all things being equal. If this is the case, then methodologically strong manuscripts may be published even if they show small or nonsignificant differences between groups. On the other hand, methodologically weak manuscripts get accepted for publication only if they show a relatively large and significant difference between groups. As a result of this process, across a large number of studies, poorer quality studies will show more deleterious effects of divorce, on average, than better quality studies.

Unfortunately, most studies of divorce cluster near the lower end of our study quality index. To illustrate this point, I used the 92 studies from the meta-analysis and added another 37 studies based on samples of divorced children only (studies not included in the meta-analysis). Of these studies, 92 (71%) have scores of 0, 1, or 2. Correspondingly, 26 studies (20%) have a score of 3 and only 11 studies (9%) have a perfect score of 4. This suggests that there is room for additional work on this topic—work that improves methodologically on studies conducted thus far.

In this chapter, I discuss issues in measuring the impact of divorce on children. Some of my comments deal with traditional measurement problems, such as reliability and validity. However, it is not realistic to separate measurement issues from other general problems that arise in study design and data analysis, so my discussion touches on a variety of topics. My intention in discussing measurement and other methodological issues is to increase researchers' awareness of some common problems in this area and to provide suggestions for improving our ability to estimate more accurately the effects of divorce on children.

I begin by considering problems associated with the selection of dependent variables and how researchers go about measuring these. In particular, I argue that (a) the selection of dependent variables is rarely guided by theory, (b) few researchers have attempted to measure beneficial outcomes of divorce, and (c) we know little about *adjustment to divorce*, as opposed to other kinds of child outcomes. After this I discuss the merits of various sources of data on children: children's self-reports, parents' reports, teachers' reports, and direct observation. Finally, I discuss the importance of using causal models to guide data analysis. As I argue, the failure to use adequately specified causal models leads to a considerable degree of confusion among researchers in estimating the effects of divorce on children.

TWO RESEARCH APPROACHES: EFFECTS OF DIVORCE VERSUS ADJUSTMENT TO DIVORCE

Researchers often refer to the "effects of divorce on children" or to "children's adjustment to divorce" as if the two phrases mean the same thing. But this practice reflects a certain conceptual carelessness. The first conceptualization refers broadly to any consequences that parental divorce might have for children's functioning and quality of life, whereas the second refers specifically to how children have coped with divorce-related stress.

These two conceptualizations reflect different research strategies. To study the effects of divorce, researchers compare a sample of children in divorced families with a sample of children living in continuously intact two-parent families. Through matching or the use of covariates, the two samples are "equated" on variables that are likely to be related to both parental divorce and children's outcomes (such as parents' education and race). Children in both samples are then measured on some outcome, and it is assumed that observed differences between the samples are due to divorce. In other words, to estimate the extent to which divorce brings about certain effects, it is necessary to adopt a quasi-experimental design with a "control" group of children from nondivorced families.

On the other hand, to assess children's adjustment to divorce, it is necessary to examine a sample of children who have *all* experienced parental marital dissolution. Researchers administer some instrument that measures how well children have coped with divorce-related stress. Researchers then correlate scores on this measure with other variables (such as time since divorce or parental income) to see what factors promote children's adjustment. In other words, studying children's adjustment to divorce does not require a comparison group of children from intact families; indeed, calculating "divorce adjustment" scores for such a group makes no sense.

Researchers, however, often confuse these two strategies. For example, imagine a researcher who selects a sample of children in divorced and intact families and administers measures of teacher-rated school grades and popularity with classmates. Suppose that the researcher finds no significant difference between the two groups of children on either measure. Would the researcher be justified in concluding that the children in this sample have adjusted to divorce satisfactorily? This would not be correct, for the children may be within the normal range in terms of school grades and popularity but poorly adjusted to specific aspects of the divorce itself (for example, feeling resentment toward one or both parents or longing for a parental reconciliation). Similarly, suppose that the researcher finds that children of divorce score significantly lower on these outcomes. Could the researcher conclude that these children are poorly adjusted to the divorce? Not necessarily, for the children might be well-adjusted to the divorce itself (for example, holding positive feelings toward parents and accepting the permanence of the separation), and the differences could be due to other factors brought about by divorce, such as a decrease in household income or a change of schools.

A corresponding error is made by many researchers who carry out within-group analyses of children of divorce. Researchers often correlate measures of children's functioning, such as school grades and popularity, with variables such as family income or the quality of parent-child relationships. If the correlations are positive and significant, the researcher may conclude that high family income and good parent-child relationships promote children's adjustment to divorce. But this conclusion is misleading. Income and the quality of parent-child relationships may be similarly associated with children's functioning in intact families; as such, these correlations tell us little about how children adjust to the particular difficulties surrounding parental divorce. To understand what factors promote children's adjustment to divorce, it is necessary to measure divorce adjustment directly.

In short, I argue that studies of children's *adjustment to divorce* are different in nature from those that address the *effects of divorce* on children. Adjustment to divorce cannot be studied with a between-group design; this makes no more sense than comparing single and married individuals on a measure of marital adjustment. Furthermore, adjustment must be measured directly; measures of academic achievement, psychological well-being, and social relations are not the same as adjustment to divorce. Measures of these more general constructs may be related to adjustment to divorce, but this is an empirical question. Both kinds of studies are useful, but they provide us with different types of information.

In the discussion below, I consider the two types of studies separately. I begin by addressing some issues in measuring the effects of divorce on children. After this, I discuss issues relating to adjustment to divorce.

MEASURING THE EFFECTS OF DIVORCE ON CHILDREN

Previous studies have used a variety of outcomes to assess the effects of divorce on children. In our meta-analysis (Amato & Keith, 1991a), we collapsed these outcomes into eight categories. *Academic achievement* included scores on standardized achievement tests, school grades, teachers' ratings of children's achievement, and parents' reports of school success. *Conduct* was based on measures of aggression, behavior problems, and delinquency. *Psychological adjustment* involved measures of depression, anxiety, and happiness/satisfaction. *Self-concept* included self-esteem, perceived competence, and internal locus of control. *Social adjustment* was based on measures of popularity, loneliness, or cooperativeness. *Mother-child relations* and *Father-child relations* included any references to the quality of the parent-child relationship. We also used a residual *Other* category.

The extent to which these categories are represented in the literature can be seen in Table 1. Columns 1 and 2 contain the number and percent of studies that utilized a particular outcome. In other words, 33 studies reported group comparisons of academic achievement, and this represented 35.8% of all published studies. (These percentages add to more than 100 because many studies used multiple outcomes.) The third column shows the number of independent samples relevant to a particular outcome. A single study reported data on more than one independent sample, if, for example, analyses were conducted separately for boys and girls or for blacks and whites. For example, the 33 studies included a total of 39 separate tests of the hypothesis that children in divorced and intact samples differ in academic achievement. The fourth column shows percentages based on the total number of comparisons. In other words, out of all comparisons made between children in divorced and intact samples, academic achievement was the outcome 13.7% of the time.

Table 1. Frequency of Outcomes Appearing in Studies of Children
of Divorce and Mean Effect Size for Each

	Studies		Comparisons		$\overline{X}$ Effect
Type of Outcome	N	%	N	%	Size
Academic achievement	33	35.8	39	13.7	-.16*
Conduct/behavior	42	45.7	56	19.7	-.23*
Psych adjust	37	40.2	50	17.6	-.08*
Self-concept	28	30.4	34	12.0	-.09*
Social adjustment	30	32.6	39	13.7	-.12*
Mother/child relations	20	21.7	22	7.7	-.19*
Father/child relations	17	18.5	18	6.3	-.26*
Other	18	19.6	26	9.2	.06
Total studies	92	244.5			
Total comparisons			284	99.9	

* $p < .001$.

For interested readers, I also present the mean effect size for each
category of outcome. The effect sizes are calculated as the difference
in means between children in divorced and intact families on the
dependent variable, divided by the within-group standard deviation.
Negative signs indicate that children in the divorced group exhibited
a lower level of functioning or well-being than did those in the intact
group.

Table 1 tells us that the 92 studies included data on a total of 225
child outcomes, or between two and three per study. The most
common outcome was conduct, which appeared in nearly one-half of
all studies (45.7%). Similarly, of all comparisons, measures of conduct
represented about one-fifth (19.7%) of all dependent variables.
Psychological adjustment was the second most common outcome; it
was included in 40% of all studies and represented 18% of all dependent
variables. Compared with the more individualistic outcomes
represented in the first five categories, measures of mother-child and
father-child relationships are less common and appear in only 22%
and 18.5% of all studies, respectively.

These results indicate that available studies cover a range of child
outcomes. Furthermore, the data in column 2 reveal that it is common
for studies to mix outcomes from more than one domain of child
functioning. Overall, these results suggest that social scientists have
cast a broad net in attempting to document the effects of divorce on
children. Readers will also note that the effect sizes are uniformly

negative and significant, with the exception of the Other category. This suggests that the consequences of divorce for children are consistent across a variety of domains of functioning. However, the effect sizes are also generally weak. Across all outcomes, the median effect size represented .14 of a standard deviation difference between groups.

Should we conclude then, that the effects of divorce on children are broadly negative but weak? Unfortunately, the data in Table 1 must be interpreted in the light of three common problems in the selection of outcomes. These problems involve (a) the theoretical relevance of outcomes, (b) the reliability and validity of measures, and (c) the absence of outcomes that might reflect strengths acquired through divorce.

Theoretical Relevance Of Outcomes

In relation to the first point, studies often include measures of dependent variables that have only a tenuous theoretical link to divorce. A perusal of this literature reveals that authors rarely provide a theoretical rationale for the selection of outcomes. Although cynical, it seems likely that some researchers include multiple outcomes in the hope that at least a few will show statistical significance. When all of these measures are lumped together across studies, the average effect size is weak. If researchers were to include dependent variables with closer theoretical connections to divorce, the average effect sizes might be larger than those in Table 1.

Furthermore, researchers often fail to define constructs (either nominally or operationally) with enough specificity to capture the probable effects of divorce. For example, research suggests that divorce may have some undesirable consequences for aspects of children's self-concept. According to Wallerstein and Kelly (1980), young children, because they are egocentric, sometimes blame themselves for their parents' divorce. This tendency is exacerbated by the fact that many parents do not discuss the reasons for divorce with their children, especially when children are young. Also, interparental conflict tends to interfere with the closeness of the parent-child relationship, both prior to and following divorce (Grych & Fincham, 1990; Hetherington, Cox, & Cox, 1982). Because children may shoulder some of the responsibility for interparental conflict, and because they receive less positive feedback from parents around the time of parental separation, they may come to see themselves as troublemakers in the family who are undeserving of parental love.

Many studies use self-concept as a dependent variable, which is an appropriate starting point. But rather than delineate those aspects of the self-concept most relevant to children's divorce experiences, most researchers simply rely on a measure of global self-esteem, such as the Piers-Harris Children's Self-Concept Scale. (For examples, see Berg & Kelly, 1979; Cooper, Holman, & Braithwaite, 1983; and Stephens & Day, 1979.) Consider the item content of this scale. The Piers-Harris contains 80 statements that yield a total self-esteem score. (It is also possible to calculate subscale scores, but researchers have rarely reported data on these.) Examples of items include "I am smart," "I am strong," "I am good at making things with my hands," "I have nice hair," and "I have lots of pep" (Piers & Harris, 1969). It is not clear why children of divorce should differ from other children in their self-ratings for these items. Not surprisingly, studies that employ self-esteem as a dependent variable tend to yield weak effect sizes (see Table 1).

In contrast, other items on the Piers-Harris scale seem especially relevant to children of divorce, such as "I cause trouble to my family," "I am an important member of my family," and "My family is disappointed in me." A scale based on items similar in content to these might yield larger differences between children in disrupted and intact families than scales that measure broader constructs. In other words, the specific effects of divorce are likely to "wash out" when researchers employ global measures as dependent variables. Consequently, researchers should utilize or develop measures of constructs that are more closely related to children's divorce experiences. Until researchers develop more explicit links between parental divorce and measures of dependent variables, most studies will probably continue to find small differences between groups.

Reliability and Validity of Measures

Another problem in the literature on children of divorce has to do with the reliability and validity of instruments used to measure child outcomes. A large number of studies use measures that have unknown reliability and validity. Across the 92 studies of children of divorce that we examined for our meta-analysis (Amato & Keith, 1991a), authors provided information on reliability only 36% of the time. Even fewer authors presented information on validity.

Of those studies that reported reliability coefficients for measures of dependent variables, the mean was .79, the standard deviation was .10, and the median was .81. This indicates that the average reported reliability was at an acceptable level. However, one-half of all coefficients were .80 or less, and 43 percent were .75 or less. This indicates some room for improvement. Furthermore, it is reasonable to assume that scale reliability was lower in studies that did not report this information than in studies that did.

Because the assessment of dependent variables in this area of research is often crude, a good deal of random measurement error is present. This means that the effect sizes reported in Table 1 are likely to be underestimates of the true effect size. Better estimates of effect sizes will emerge when researchers use more reliable indicators of child outcomes. Before carrying out a study, researchers should be more vigilant in searching for theoretically relevant instruments with established reliability and validity. As a general rule, researchers should create their own instruments only when they are reasonably certain that an appropriate one does not exist for their purpose.

Problems with measurement error are bound up with two styles of research represented in the literature on children of divorce. Some studies are based on small convenience samples of children but employ multiple-item measures with good reliability and validity. But although strong on measurement, the small and nonrandom nature of the samples means that the results cannot be generalized beyond the study itself. On the other hand, survey researchers generally work with large and randomly selected, representative samples. But because of the great expense of carrying out large-scale surveys, researchers usually attempt to include as many variables as possible so that the data set can be used for a variety of purposes. Consequently, surveys frequently employ short scales or single-item indicators of constructs. Because scale reliability increases with the number of items, all things being equal, short scales tend to have low reliability. And unless information on test-retest reliability is available (which is usually not the case), single-item indicators have unknown reliability. For these reasons, studies based on survey data, compared with other studies, tend to report lower reliability coefficients and are more likely to report no information at all. In other words, studies with the best generalizability tend to have the poorest quality measurement— a frustrating situation.

The obvious solution to this problem is to combine the best of the two research strategies within a single study. One can envision a study based on a large and representative sample of children that includes relevant measures of child outcomes with a sufficient number of items to attain high reliability. (Instruments, of course, should be valid as well as reliable.) However, decreasing measurement error requires cutting down on the total number of variables in the study.

This means that the survey could not be multi purpose; it would have to be designed with the specific purpose of measuring the consequence of divorce for children. Such a study would represent a distinct advance on previous survey research on this topic, because virtually all analyses have been carried out using data sets constructed for other purposes. Of course, it would be costly to carry out a large scale survey concentrating on only a single topic. Nevertheless, social concern about this issue would appear to be a sufficient justification for funding.

Problem-Oriented View of Divorce

Another measurement issue in assessing the effects of divorce on children has to do with the fact that researchers have tended to adopt an exclusively problem-oriented view of divorce. Underlying most of this research is the assumption that divorce is a major stressor for children, and as such, is likely to lead to behavioral, psychological, or academic problems. This is a reasonable assumption. However, researchers have rarely considered the other side of the coin, that is, the possibility that experiencing divorce may provide children with certain benefits.

Based on qualitative data, Weiss (1979) argued that children in single-parent families "grow up a little faster." Many single parents have full-time jobs as well as the major responsibility for household management and child care. Not surprisingly, these single parents often experience role overload. Consequently, children in these households must learn to do many things for themselves, such as cooking, cleaning, or washing clothes. Older children often assume a major share of household responsibility, and in a sense, become co-managers of the household. Although these responsibilities may represent a burden if they are excessive or if children are too young, other children may experience enhanced maturity, autonomy, and self-confidence.

Two other qualitative studies support Weiss's (1979) thesis. Reinhard (1977) found that adolescents from divorced families were especially likely to describe themselves as self-reliant. Similarly, Dunlop and Burns (1988) found that adolescents believed that they had acquired strengths and a sense of responsibility from living in a single-parent family. Overall, these studies suggest that the effects of divorce on children are not entirely negative, and that positive outcomes are also common.

In an attempt to test Weiss's (1979) thesis, Gay Ochiltree and I used a measure of everyday life skills (Amato & Ochiltree, 1986; 1987a). Because this is one of the few quantitative studies that searched for positive outcomes of divorce, I will discuss it in some detail. To develop this measure, we presented a sample of Australian children between the ages of 8 and 16 with a list of 40 everyday activities. We first asked if children knew how to perform the task; if they responded positively, we then asked how often they performed each. The purpose of the pretest was to identify items relevant to children in these age groups and to omit items with little variance. For example, "cleaning shoes" appeared to be out-of-date, because few children reported ever cleaning their shoes. We also retained items that reflected an equal number of traditionally male and female activities. The final instrument was based on 20 items including: make a bed, wash the dishes, sweep or vacuum, use a washing machine, iron clothes, make a simple meal, hammer a nail, mow a lawn, wash a car, and replace a light globe.

We included the instrument in a survey of 402 children, selected randomly from schools in the state of Victoria in Australia. The sample was constructed so that half of the children lived in single-parent families (most of these formed through divorce) and half lived in continuously intact two-parent families. Both the child and one of his or her parents responded (separately) to the 20 questions about life skills. The alpha reliability coefficient for this instrument was .83 for children and .87 for parents. The correlations between parents' and children's reports were .38 for younger children and .48 for adolescents (both $p < .001$). We were able to confirm that children of divorce benefit in at least one important way: They have a greater knowledge and performance of everyday skills than do children raised in traditional two-parent families. This difference was only slightly smaller among older adolescents than among younger children, suggesting that children do not lose the advantage as they grow older (Amato & Ochiltree, 1987a).

Other research has suggested additional advantages that may accrue to children of divorce. Single mothers usually increase their participation in the paid labor force, either following or in anticipation of marital dissolution. Numerous studies have shown that children of employed mothers have less stereotyped views about the roles of men and women than do other children (Spitze, 1988). In addition, daughters of employed mothers have higher occupational expectations than do daughters of nonemployed mothers (Spitze, 1988). These effects may be reinforced by seeing mothers in the role of chief decision maker in the family. In a society that is becoming more egalitarian, and in which most women are employed, one can argue that these outcomes are beneficial. To the extent that divorce moves mothers into the paid labor force and places them in a position of power in the household, divorce may have a positive effect on children—especially daughters. However, relatively little research has examined these notions, and the available studies yield contradictory results (Barber & Eccles, 1992).

Overall, few researchers have searched for possible strengths that children might acquire as a result of parental divorce. To gain a more balanced view, future studies should attempt to conceptualize and measure characteristics of children that might be enhanced through experiencing parental divorce and life in a single-parent family. Qualitative studies of children and divorce may be useful for gaining insights into what these beneficial outcomes might be.

MEASURING ADJUSTMENT TO DIVORCE

In contrast to the large number of studies that have searched for broad effects of divorce on children, relatively few have concerned themselves specifically with how children adjust to divorce itself. In an early piece of research that followed this approach, Kelly and Berg (1978) used a projective Family Story Test to generate children's emotional and attitudinal reactions to parental separation and divorce.

One of the most thorough research efforts along these lines was carried out by Kurdek and his colleagues (Kurdek & Berg, 1983; Kurdek, Blisk, & Siesky, 1981; Kurdek & Siesky, 1980). Because this is one of the few comprehensive efforts to measure adjustment to divorce, I will describe their efforts in some detail. The authors give slightly different accounts of the instruments in different publications, so the descriptions below are based on Kurdek and Berg (1983).

One of the scales that emerged from this program of research was entitled, Children's Attitudes Toward Parental Separation Inventory (CAPSI). The CAPSI contains 60 items with a "yes" and "no" (or agree/disagree) response format. The scale contains six subscales with 10 items each: peer ridicule and avoidance, fear of abandonment, hope of reunification, paternal blame, maternal blame, and self-blame. Kurdek and Berg (1983) do not provide reliability coefficients for the subscales, but Cronbach's alpha for the entire scale is .78. A parallel version of this instrument is also completed by parents, and this yields a reliability coefficient of .79. The parent and child forms correlate at .41.

Understanding the Divorce is a nine-item questionnaire. The items refer to children's understanding of the meaning of divorce, acceptance of the parents' divorce, hopes of parental reconciliation, attributions of blame for the divorce, parent personalities, and friends' reactions to the divorce. The questions are open-ended and the interviewer records children's responses verbatim. Questions include "What does it mean when two people get divorced?" and "Why don't your Mom and Dad live together anymore?" The researcher then assigns a point for each answer that represents "adjustment." For example, this would include responses indicating (a) that parents don't live together because they are incompatible, (b) that the parents will not live together again, (c) that the child does not blame him/ herself for the separation, and (d) that the child has told friends about the divorce. The sum of points across all items forms a total score. Independent coders agree at 96% on whether a point should be allocated for a particular answer; however, Cronbach's alpha for the scale is only .50.

Children's Emotional Reactions to the Divorce is a measure of parents' perceptions of the extent to which children display a variety of positive and negative feelings *following the separation*. Items include personal growth and self-knowledge, increased happiness, independence and responsibility, relief from conflict, loneliness, sadness, helplessness, confusion, guilt or self-blame, and nervousness. After negatively-worded items are reverse coded, items are summed to provide a total score reflecting positive adjustment; Cronbach's alpha for this scale is .81.

Research conducted by Kurdek and Berg (1983) with these measures revealed a number of significant associations. Age was positively correlated with children's CAPSI scores and with parent-rated children's emotional reactions. Girls scored higher than boys on both the Children's CAPSI and on parent-rated children's emotional reactions. In addition, both measures were positively associated with mother's divorce adjustment and negatively associated with the degree of interparental conflict.

In general, children's specific divorce adjustment was positively related to more global measures of behavioral adjustment. Overall, the pattern of correlations provides evidence for the construct validity of the CAPSI and the emotional reactions measure. The Understanding the Divorce scale, however, yielded few significant correlations with other variables, possibly because of problems with internal consistency.

The work of Kurdek and his colleagues is noteworthy because it represents a serious effort to measure children's *adjustment to divorce* as opposed to adjustment in general. Nevertheless, several limitations of this work are evident. First, the internal consistency reliability of the Understanding Divorce scale is low, suggesting either that the number of items is too small to form a reliable estimate, or that the scale is not unidimensional.

Second, and more importantly, it is not clear whether these three scales tap the full meaning of the "adjustment to divorce" construct. In other words, the content validity of these measures is not well established. To establish content validity, it is necessary to enumerate the various dimensions implicit in the construct of adjustment to divorce. Perhaps the best sources for this purpose are in-depth, qualitative studies of children of divorce. Researchers have carried out relatively few such studies; yet, these studies yield a number of insights into the particular problems that divorce generates for children and how children deal with these (Amato, 1987; Kurdek & Siesky, 1979; Mitchell, 1983; Wallerstein & Kelly, 1980; Wallerstein & Blakeslee, 1989; Weiss, 1979).

Based on these studies, a list of the main challenges that divorce poses for children would include the following:

1. *Understanding the reason for the parents' decision to divorce.* Many parents do not tell their children the reasons for separation; this results in a considerable degree of confusion—especially for younger children.

2. *Dealing with anger toward parents.* Children often blame one or both parents for the divorce. "Forgiving" parents for the divorce is necessary for maintaining positive parent-child relationships.

3. *Feelings of being abandoned by the noncustodial parent.* Because the noncustodial parent has left, children may feel rejected. Children need to accept that the departure of the noncustodial parent is not a reflection of the parent's feelings for the child. Children must also come to grips with situations in which the noncustodial parent visits infrequently or not at all.

4. *Fearing abandonment by the custodial parent.* Young children may fear that their custodial parent will leave one day, just as the noncustodial parent did. They may also worry about who will take care of them if their custodial parent dies.

5. *Dealing with feelings of self-blame and guilt.* Because young children are egocentric, they may believe that they are somehow responsible for the divorce. For example, they might think that if they had behaved better, the divorce could have been avoided.

6. *Feelings of embarrassment or shame.* Children may fear ridicule, especially from other children. For this reason, they may lie about their parents' status to other children.

7. *Hopes of parental reconciliation.* Accepting the permanence of divorce if often difficult but necessary if children are to adapt

to a new life in a single-parent family. False hopes can also interfere with the acceptance of stepparents.

8. *Feelings of guilt for choosing to live with one parent rather than the other.* Children may express a wish to live with one parent, either before or after the separation. They may feel remorse for having "rejected" the other parent, particularly if both parents want custody.

9. *Dealing with feelings of sadness and loss of parental attention.* For children who understand that parental reconciliation is unlikely, a period of mourning for the intact family may occur.

10. *Preoccupation with the divorce.* Some children may ruminate on the divorce to the extent that it interferes with school and peer activities. Children need to concentrate on their own lives.

11. *Feelings of powerlessness and fatalism.* Divorce and the life changes that follow are generally beyond the control of children. Consequently, children may feel that nothing they do makes a difference.

12. *Feeling anxious about future intimate relationships.* Adolescents, in particular, may worry that they, like their parents, will be unable to have a successful long-term intimate relationship.

13. *Accepting parental dating.* Children may find it difficult to see their parents dating. This may also involve acknowledging that parents are sexual beings.

Children must deal with most of these challenges following divorce. Presumably, a well-adjusted child is one who has mastered each. Of course, some children may successfully cope with some of these tasks but not with others.

From reviewing this list, it is clear that some of these challenges are covered in the measures developed by Kurdek and his colleagues, such as dealing with anger toward parents, self-blame, hopes of reconciliation, feelings of abandonment, and embarrassment around other children. However, other dimensions of divorce adjustment are not represented in Kurdek's measures, such as guilt over custody arrangements, accepting parental dating, and anxiety about intimate relationships.

In principle, it should be possible to construct an instrument that measures each of these dimensions of adjustment. Multiple items could be written for each dimension, and a factor analysis could confirm the underlying dimensionality. A researcher could administer such an instrument in an interview format for younger children, whereas a self-administered questionnaire might be appropriate for adolescents. Given that children may be more successful at meeting some challenges than others, subscale scores as well as a total adjustment score are necessary. Needless to say, such an instrument would have clinical as well as research applications. Given the potential usefulness of such an instrument, it is curious that so little work has been done in this direction.

SOURCES OF DATA

A central issue in attempting to determine the effects of divorce on children, or children's adjustment to divorce, is the appropriate source of data. Previous studies have relied primarily on four sources: children's self-reports (or scores on standardized tests), parents' reports, teachers' reports, and direct observation by researchers.

Frequency of Use of Various Sources

All four sources of data are popular among researchers studying children of divorce. Table 2 provides data on how often researchers have used each, depending on the type of outcome in question. These data are taken from our meta-analysis of 92 studies described above (Amato & Keith, 1991a). The last row in Table 2 indicates that across all outcomes, the child was the most common source (54%), followed by parents (18%), researchers (17%), and teachers (12%). However, the frequency of sources varies with the choice of dependent variable.

For studies of academic achievement, the child is the most common source. Not surprisingly, given the domain of interest, teacher's views are also frequently sought out. Researchers may tend to avoid parent's reports because they assume that parents are biased favorably toward their children (i.e., parents may be reluctant to report that their children are doing poorly at school). Studies of children's conduct, in contrast, are most likely to rely on parents' reports or the direct observation of behavior by researchers. Actually, for this outcome, all four sources appear regularly in the literature. Psychological adjustment is based most often on questioning of children, although parents' reports, teachers' reports, and direct observation are also commonly used. Studies of self-concept usually rely on self-reports; given the nature of the domain, this seems inevitable. Social adjustment is most often measured by questioning children themselves, although all sources are represented in the literature with some frequency.

Children's reports clearly dominate studies of mother- and father-child relations. Presumably, researchers tend to avoid parental ratings

Table 2. Frequency and Percentage of Comparisons Based on Data
From Four Sources

		Child	Parent	Teacher	Researcher	Total
Academic achievement	n	21	4	8	6	39
	%	(54)	(10)	(21)	(15)	(100)
Conduct	n	13	16	11	15	55
	%	(24)	(29)	(20)	(27)	(100)
Psych adjustment	n	22	13	5	10	50
	%	(44)	(26)	(10)	(20)	(100)
Self-concept	n	30	2	0	2	34
	%	(88)	(6)	(0)	(6)	(100)
Social adjustment	n	17	8	5	8	38
	%	(45)	(21)	(13)	(21)	(100)
Mother-child relations	n	17	2	1	2	22
	%	(77)	(9)	(5)	(9)	(100)
Father-child relations	n	17	0	0	1	18
	%	(94)	(0)	(0)	(6)	(100)
Total	n	137	45	30	44	256
	%	(54)	(18)	(12)	(17)	(101)

because they are likely to be contaminated by social desirability. (How many parents will admit that they have a poor relationship with their children?) And although teachers may be good judges of what goes on in the classroom, they probably do not have enough information to be good judges of parent-child relationships. However, it is surprising that so few studies of parent-child relationships are based on direct observation by researchers.

Advantages and Disadvantages of Various Sources

Each source has certain advantages and disadvantages. Children may be the best source to report on their own feelings. On the other hand, young children may have a difficult time understanding questions or responding articulately. Furthermore, their limited reading ability constrains the use of self-report questionnaires. Amato and Ochiltree (1987b) found that children as young as 8 years of age could respond lucidly to interview questions dealing with divorce and that the resulting data quality was reasonably high; however, traditional interview methods did not work well for children younger than this.

Parents know their own children better than anyone else does. As such, they can report on children's behavior over a long time span and across a variety of situations. Furthermore, they can report on the behavior of very young children for whom self-report data are not possible. However, social desirability is a problem: As suggested above, many parents are probably reluctant to say negative things about their children—especially parents who may be feeling guilty for having obtained a divorce. In addition, parents may not be aware of many of their children's behaviors—especially those that occur outside the home.

Teachers have the advantage of being relatively "objective" outsiders. Furthermore, they know children in a different context from that of parents: school as opposed to home. On the other hand, some researchers have suggested that teachers are biased against children of divorce. In a study by Santrock and Tracy (1978), student teachers viewed a videotape of a boy at home and in peer interaction. Those who believed that the child was from a divorced family rated him lower in happiness, emotional adjustment, and ability to cope with stress than did other teachers. In a similar study conducted by Ball, Newman, and Williams (1984), teachers read about a child identified as living in either an intact or a divorced family. Compared with the child from an intact family, teachers expected the child from a divorced family to have more problems at school and not to perform as well in the classroom. These studies suggest that if teachers know the family background of their students, their ratings may reflect expectations as much as reality.

Behavioral ratings based on direct observation can attain a relatively high level of objectivity, especially if the raters are blind to the family type of the child. Furthermore, researchers using this method observe actual behavior, rather than reports of behavior. However, it is possible to observe behavior for only a short time period in a specific situation. Behaviors with low base rates, as well as covert behaviors, are difficult to observe. Furthermore, children may know that they are being observed, thus generating problems of reactivity. Observational studies are also relatively expensive, which makes them impractical for many researchers.

Studies that use multiple sources to measure dependent variables are preferable to those that use a single source, all things being equal. Correlations between children's, parents', teachers', and observers' ratings of children's behavior tend to be low (Achenbach, McConaughy, & Howell, 1987). For this reason, using two or more sources can compensate for the disadvantages of each and provide a more rounded assessment of divorce effects. If two sources lead to the same conclusion (say, that children of divorce exhibit more behavior problems than other children), researchers will have more confidence in their findings than if only a single source were used. Similarly, if all sources generate consistently null findings, then researchers can be reasonably confident about the findings.

Although multiple sources are desirable in studies that examine the effects of divorce on children, problems arise when the two sources yield discrepant results. What if data based on teachers' reports yield significant differences but data based on parents' reports do not? Should the researcher conclude that the parents' data are biased and that the teacher data are more objective? Or should the researcher conclude the reverse? Similar dilemmas emerge for any pair of methods. Within any particular study, therefore, it is difficult to reconcile diverging results based on different sources. Meta-analytic methods of accumulating results across a large number of studies may provide clearer information on this issue.

Source and Mean Effect Size

These considerations raise the question of whether the choice of source affects the results of the study. Do some sources reveal stronger effects of divorce, on average, than others? Table 3 provides data relevant to this question. This table presents the mean effect sizes from our meta-analysis (Amato & Keith, 1991a), based on whether data came from children, parents, teachers, or direct observation. I omitted data for self-concept, mother-child relations, and father-child relations because almost all of these studies are based on children's reports.

Table 3 reveals a certain degree of consistency. For all outcomes, regardless of source, the effect sizes are negative; this indicates that

Table 3. Mean Effect Size By Source of Data

	Child	Parent	Teacher	Observation
Academic Achievement	-.17***	-.06	-.04	-.24***
Conduct	-.24***	-.18***	-.17***	-.32***
Psychological Adjustment	-.18***	-.06*	-.08	-.03
Social Adjustment	-.19***	-.04	-.14**	-.14**

* $p < .05$.   ** $p < .01$.   *** $p < .001$.

children in divorced families scored more poorly on these measures than did children in continuously intact two-parent families. Nevertheless, variations in the magnitude of mean effect sizes are apparent, and some attain significance whereas others fail to attain significance. To explore this issue further, I carried out significance tests for each outcome to see if mean effect sizes differed across sources at higher than chance levels. These tests involved the Hedges and Olkin (1985) H statistic for effect sizes. All four tests were significant ($p < .05$ for academic achievement, and $p < .001$ for conduct, psychological adjustment, and social adjustment).

Studies based on parents' reports generally found small differences between children from divorced and intact families, and in two out of four cases, as Table 3 indicates, the mean effect size was not significant. This is consistent with the notion, noted above, that parents are reluctant to admit that their children are doing poorly. Such a tendency on the part of parents would lower the variance of the dependent variable and obscure differences between groups. This suggests that researchers should probably avoid using parents as the sole source of data on children's outcomes, with the possible exception of studies that focus on conduct.

It is also interesting to note that in two out of four cases, mean effect sizes based on data provided by teachers are low and nonsignificant. As noted above, studies by Santrock and Tracy (1978) and Ball, Newman, and Williams (1984) found evidence that teachers are biased in their evaluation of children from divorced families. However, the results from Table 3 indicate that effect sizes based on teachers' ratings tend to be weaker than those based on data obtained from children themselves—especially for measures of academic achievement and psychological adjustment. This result provides little support for the notion that teachers stereotype children of divorce and exaggerate the differences between them and children from intact families. It is possible that teachers hold relatively low expectations for children of divorce but assess them in ways that minimize the differences between them and other children. This would occur if, in an attempt to be fair, teachers use different assessment criteria for children from divorced families. Teachers may rate a given level of performance for a child in a single-parent family higher than the same level of performance for a child in an intact two-parent family; they may allocate grades on the same basis. To the extent that teachers are aware of children's family types, this would blur the distinctions between them, resulting in low effect sizes. Although this notion is intriguing, it has never been tested empirically.

Table 3 also shows that questioning children themselves and directly observing children's behavior are the approaches that yield the largest and most consistent differences between groups. The one exception is that observational studies of children's psychological adjustment do not produce significant differences between groups. Given that the dependent variable is intrapsychic, this is not surprising. Overall, these results suggest that researchers working in this area should avoid using parents or teachers as their only sources of data on children's outcomes.

Multiple Sources and Studies of Children's Divorce Adjustment

Multiple sources of information are also useful in studies dealing with factors that influence children's divorce adjustment. Unfortunately, these studies often rely on the same source for information on both the independent and dependent variables. For example, some studies have tested the hypothesis that the custodial mother's psychological adjustment facilitates children's divorce adjustment. However, if data on both the mother's and the child's adjustment come from the mother (the most common situation), then a significant association may reflect either a causal association between variables or *same-source bias*.

Not surprisingly, studies that measure mothers' and children's well-being independently tend to find weaker associations between variables (and hence weaker support for the hypothesis) than do studies that use the same source (Huntley, Phelps, & Rehm, 1987; Kalter, Kloner, Schreier, & Okla, 1989). Nevertheless, same-source bias cannot account for the entire pattern of findings, because a few studies that used independent sources also supported this hypothesis (e.g., Kanoy, Cunningham, White, & Adams, 1984). Clearly, studies of divorce adjustment that use different sources for independent and dependent variables provide more certainty in conclusions than do studies based on a single source.

CAUSAL MODELS OF THE EFFECTS OF DIVORCE ON CHILDREN

As noted above, researchers who study the effects of divorce on children adopt a quasi-experimental design involving a comparison group of children from intact two-parent families. But because researchers cannot randomly assign children to divorced and nondivorced groups, it is difficult to know whether observed differences between groups are due to divorce or some factor associated with divorce. For example, couples who divorce tend to be of lower social class, on average, than couples who do not divorce (White, 1990). Parental social class is also known to be inversely associated with a number of academic and behavioral problems in children (White, 1982). Consequently, some or all of the differences between children in divorced and intact families may be due to social class rather than divorce.

Studies that fail to use appropriate control variables to statistically "equate" groups generally overestimate the effects of divorce on children. In our meta-analysis (Amato & Keith, 1991a), we calculated mean effect size separately for studies that did and did not use control variables. (We considered the matching of children to be equivalent to using control variables.) In relation to measures of academic achievement, the mean difference between children in divorced and intact families was -.25 of a standard deviation (p <.001) for studies that did not use control variables (that is, only reported zero-order differences between groups), and -.10 (p <.01) for studies that used control variables. The difference between coefficients was significant (p <.001), indicating that studies that do not use control variables tend to show bigger "effects" of divorce on children's academic achievement than do other studies. A similar pattern was apparent for two other dependent variables: self-concept and mother-child relations.

The use of control variables is not as common in this body of studies as one might hope. In our sample of studies, out of 284 comparisons, only 78 (27%) involved statistical controls or the matching of children. More recent studies were more likely to use control variables than were earlier studies, but the general failure to address this problem is disheartening.

Unfortunately, even researchers who employ control variables often use them incorrectly, resulting in a great deal of conceptual confusion. In particular, there is little attempt to separate control variables that precede and follow divorce in time; often researchers lump them together and add them to the regression equation in a single step. (Alternatively, in analysis of covariance designs, researchers treat them all simultaneously as covariates.) This practice makes it impossible to interpret the resulting statistics.

It is useful to think about this issue in traditional path analytic terms. The zero-order difference between children in divorced and intact families on some outcome (that is, the simple difference in means between groups) is represented by the unstandardized regression coefficient with no control variables in the model. Let us say that the standard deviation for some dependent variable is 20 and the unstandardized regression coefficient is 10; this means that the effect size is .5. The regression coefficient (or the effect size) reflects the *total association* between parental divorce and the dependent variable.

To estimate the causal impact of divorce, it is necessary to control for variables that precede both parental divorce and the measurement of children's outcomes, because they could be a cause of both. For example, as noted above, parental social class precedes both parental divorce and children's well-being. As such, some or all of the association between parental divorce and children's well-being is likely to be spurious. Other variables that precede divorce and children's outcomes and may affect both include parental age (or year of birth), parental race, parental employment status prior to divorce, child age (or year of birth), and child sex. When we add these variables to the regression equation, the resulting partial unstandardized regression coefficient for divorce can be thought of as an estimate of the *total effect* of parental divorce on children. Let us say that the partial unstandardized coefficient is 5, which is equivalent to the adjusted mean difference between groups. The effect size, based on the original standard deviation, is now .25. This means that half of the original association between divorce and the dependent variable was spurious. Note that the accuracy of this estimate depends on having all of the necessary control variables in the model.

At this point another question arises: Is the effect of divorce on children direct, or is some of its effect mediated by other variables? For example, divorce often results in a number of life changes that may be stressful for children, such as moving and changing schools (Hodges, Buchsbaum, & Tierney, 1984). To determine the extent to which stressful life changes mediate the impact of divorce on children, a measure of this variable (such as a total score from a stressful life events schedule) could be added to the regression equation with all predivorce control variables in the model. Imagine that the partial unstandardized regression coefficient (or the adjusted mean difference) drops to 3, and the corresponding effect size is .15. These statistics now reflect the estimated *direct effect* of divorce on children. This also tells us that 40% of the total effect of parental divorce is indirect, that is, mediated by stressful life events (i.e., ((5-3)/5) X 100).

Path analytic procedures allow us to decompose the original association between parental divorce into total, direct, and indirect estimated effects. To do this, however, requires that one have a theory that allows variables to be ordered in some manner. Unfortunately, researchers often violate this logic. For example, many studies employ household income as a control variable (see Guidubaldi, Cleminshaw, Perry, & McLoughlin, 1983). This is based on the knowledge that divorce often results in a dramatic decline in standard of living for custodial mothers and their children (Weitzman, 1985). However, this procedure is confusing because, to a large extent, current income reflects earlier (predivorce) income. Therefore, when we control for current income, it is not clear whether we are testing for spuriousness or whether we are assessing the extent to which income mediates the impact of divorce on children. Suppose we find that a significant zero-order association between divorce and a dependent variable no longer is significant with current income in the equation. Does this mean that divorce has no effect on children because low income both causes divorce and lowers children's well-being? Or does it mean that low income explains why divorce lowers children's well-being, that is, that income *mediates* the impact of divorce on children? Theoretically, these are entirely different interpretations, but we cannot tell which is correct from the analysis. (Incidentally, matching children on income results in the same confusion.)

This problem could be solved by including a measure of earlier (predivorce) household income in the regression model. Variables could be added in the following steps: (a) control variables and Time 1 (predivorce) household income, (b) parental divorce, and (c) Time 2 (postdivorce) income. Because Time 1 income is in the model, the regression coefficient for Time 2 income would reflect the *change* in income over the time period of the study. Such a model would allow one to estimate the extent to which income at Time 1 causes both divorce and child outcomes, and the extent to which a decline in income at Time 2 mediates the impact of divorce on children. Although this example is couched in terms of multiple regression, more advanced techniques, such as LISREL modelling, follow the same logic.

An analysis like the one described above might involve longitudinal data. Alternatively, it could rely on retrospective data on household income. Presumably, both divorced and nondivorced parents could be asked about household income in a specific reference year, provided that the reference year preceded all cases of marital dissolution for the divorced group. Unfortunately, no study has carried out such an analysis, to my knowledge.

The main point here is many researchers fail to employ control variables in a theoretically meaningful way. As a result, their assessments of the effects of divorce on children are often uninterpretable.

SUMMARY AND CONCLUSION

At this time, we know a great deal about the effects of divorce on children. We know, for example, that children in divorced families, compared with children in continuously intact families, score slightly but significantly lower across a range of measures of general functioning and well-being. We also know something about the factors that are associated with better or poorer outcomes among children of divorce. For example, children appear to do better when they have close relationships with both parents, when mothers and fathers are psychologically well adjusted and provide competent parenting to children, when post-divorce conflict between parents is minimal, when levels of household income are adequate, and when post-divorce life changes are few (see Amato, in press, and Emery, 1988 for reviews). Interestingly, we also know that adults who experienced parental divorce as children score lower than other adults, on average, on a variety of measures of well-being, including socioeconomic attainment, psychological adjustment, and marital quality (Amato & Keith, 1991b). This indicates that the gap between children from divorced and continuously intact families persists well into adulthood.

However, measurement and other methodological problems are common in this area of research. Firmer knowledge about the consequences of parental divorce for children's lives will become available when researchers address some of these limitations. In summary, I provide a list of common problems and suggestions for dealing with these below.

1. Researchers often include dependent variables with little theoretical relevance to the topic of divorce. Researchers should develop and use measures of child outcomes based on what we know about the ways in which divorce affects children's lives.

2. Researchers often employ measures with modest or unknown reliability and validity. Researchers should use established measures with proven reliability and validity whenever possible. Survey researchers should increase scale length to improve reliability, even though this decreases the number of variables included in survey questionnaires.

3. Few studies have searched for positive outcomes of divorce. Researchers should use or construct measures of dependent variables that provide a more balanced view of the consequences of divorce for children.

4. Few studies have specifically addressed children's adjustment to divorce itself. Additional work is required to produce multidimensional measures of divorce adjustment that have good content validity and a sufficient number of items to attain an adequate level of reliability.

5. Most studies are based on a single source of data. Studies should employ multiple sources of data whenever possible. In particular, researchers should avoid relying on parents or teachers as the sole source of data on children, as these studies rarely yield significant results. In studies dealing with factors that influence children's divorce adjustment, it is necessary to use different sources to measure independent and dependent variables.

6. Researchers frequently fail to use control variables or use them incorrectly. Researchers should include all variables in statistical models that are likely to be causes of both divorce and children's outcomes to rule out the possibility of spurious associations. Researchers should enter variables that mediate the effect of divorce on children (that is, variables that follow divorce in time) in statistical models only *after* checking for spuriousness (that is, after estimating the total effect of divorce on children).

REFERENCES

Achenbach, T.M., McConaughy, S.H., & Howell, C. T. (1987). Child/adolescent behavioral and emotional problems: Implications of cross-informant correlations for situational specificity. *Psychological Bulletin, 101,* 213-232.

Amato, P. R. (1987). Children's reactions to parental separation and divorce: The views of children and custodial mothers. *Australian Journal of Social Issues, 22,* 610-623.

Amato, P. R. (in press). Children's adjustment to divorce: Theories, hypotheses, and empirical support. *Journal of Marriage and the Family.*

Amato, P. R., & Keith, B. (1991a). Parental divorce and the well-being of children: A meta-analysis. *Psychological Bulletin, 110,* 26-46.

Amato, P. R., & Keith, B. (1991b). Consequences of parental divorce for adult well-being, A meta-analysis. *Journal of Marriage and the Family, 53,* 43-58.

Amato, P. R., & Ochiltree, G. (1986). Children becoming independent: An investigation of children's performance of practical life-skills. *Australian Journal of Psychology, 38,* 59-68.

Amato, P. R., & Ochiltree, G. (1987a). Child and adolescent competence in intact, one-parent, and stepfamilies: An Australian study. *Journal of Divorce, 10,* 75-95.

Amato, P. R., & Ochiltree, G. (1987b). Interviewing children about their families: A note on data quality. *Journal of Marriage and the Family, 49,* 669-675.

Ball, D. W., Newman, J. M., & Williams, J. S. (1984). Teachers' generalized expectations of children of divorce. *Psychological Reports, 54,* 347-353.

Barber, B. L., & Eccles, J. S. (1992). Long-term influence of divorce and single parenting on adolescent family- and work-related values, behaviors, and aspirations. *Psychological Bulletin, 111,* 108-126.

Berg, B., & Kelly, R. (1979). The measured self-esteem of children from broken, rejected, and accepted families. *Journal of Divorce, 2,* 363-369.

Cooper, J. E., Holman, J., & Braithwaite, V. A. (1983). Self-esteem and family cohesion: The child's perspective and adjustment. *Journal of Marriage and the Family, 45,* 153-160.

Demo, D. H. (1992). Parent-child relations: Assessing recent change. *Journal of Marriage and the Family, 54,* 104-117.

Demo, D. H., & Acock, A. C. (1988). The impact of divorce on children. *Journal of Marriage and the Family, 50,* 619-648.

Dunlop, R., & Burns, A. (1988). *'Don't feel the world is caving in.' Adolescents in divorcing families.* Melbourne, Australia: Australian Institute of Family Studies.

Etzioni, A. (1992, Oct. 7). Point of view. *Chronicle of Higher Education, 48.*

Emery, R. E. (1982). Interparental conflict and the children of discord and divorce. *Psychological Bulletin, 92,* 310-330.

Emery, R. E. (1988). *Marriage, divorce, and children's adjustment.* Newbury Park, CA: Sage.

Grych, J. H., & Fincham, F. D. (1990). Marital conflict and children's adjustment: A cognitive-contextual framework. *Psychological Bulletin, 108,* 267-290.

Guidubaldi, J., Cleminshaw, H. K., Perry, J. D., & McLoughlin, C. S. (1983). The impact of parental divorce on children: Report of the nationwide NASP study. *School Psychology Review, 12,* 300-323.

Hedges, L. V., & Olkin, I. (1985). *Statistical methods for meta-analysis.* San Diego, CA: Academic Press.

Hetherington, E. M., Cox, M., Cox, R. (1982). Effects of divorce on parents and children. In M. Lamb (Ed.), *Nontraditional families: Parenting and child development* (pp. 233-288). Hillsdale, NJ: Lawrence Erlbaum.

Hodges, W. F., Buchsbaum, H. K., & Tierney, C. W. (1984). Parent -child relationships and adjustment in preschool children in divorced and intact families. *Journal of Divorce, 7,* 43-57.

Huntley, D. K., Phelps, R. E., & Rehm, L. P. (1987). Depression in children from single-parent families. *Journal   of Divorce, 10,* 153-162.

Kalter, N., Kloner, A., Schreier, S., & Okla, K. (1989). Predictors of children's postdivorce adjustment. *American Journal of Orthopsychiatry, 59,* 605-618.

Kanoy, K. W., Cunningham, J. L., White, P., & Adams, S. J. (1984). Is family structure that critical? Family relationships of children with divorced and married parents. *Journal of Divorce, 8,* 97-106.

Kelly, R., & Berg, B. (1978). Measuring children's reactions to divorce. *Journal of Clinical Psychology, 34,* 215-221.

Kurdek, L. A., and Berg, B. 1983. Correlates of children's adjustment to their parents' divorces. In L. A. Kurdek (Ed.), *Children and divorce* (pp. 47-60). San Francisco: Jossey-Bass.

Kurdek, L. A., Blisk, D., & Siesky, A. E. (1981). Correlates of children's long-term adjustment to their parents' divorce. *Developmental Psychology, 17,* 565-579.

Kurdek, L. A., & Siesky, A. E. (1979). An interview study of parents' perceptions of their children's reactions and adjustment to divorce. *Journal of Divorce, 3,* 5-17.

Kurdek, L. A., & Siesky, A. E. (1980). Children's perceptions of their parents' divorce. *Journal of Divorce, 3,* 339-378.

Maccoby, E. E., & Martin, J. A. (1983). Socialization in the context of the family: Parent-child interaction. In E. M. Hetherington (Ed.), *Handbook of child psychology, Vol. IV: Socialization, personality and social development* (pp. 1-101). New York: Wiley.

Marotz-Baden, R., Adams, G. R., Buech, N., Munro, B., & Munro, G. (1979). Family form or family process? Reconsidering the deficit family model approach. *The Family Coordinator, 28,* 5-14.

Martin, T. C., & Bumpass, L. L. (1989). Recent trends in marital disruption. *Demography, 26,* 37-51.

Mitchell, A. K. (1983). Adolescents' experiences of parental separation and divorce. *Journal of Adolescence, 6,* 175-187.

Piers, E. V., & Harris, D. B. (1969). *Manual for the Piers-Harris Children's Self-Concept Scale.* Counselor Recordings and Tests, Nashville, TN.

Reinhard, D. W. (1977). The reactions of adolescent boys and girls to the divorce of their parents. *Journal of Clinical Child Psychology, 6,* 21-23.

Rollins, B. C., & Thomas, D. L. (1979). Parental support, power, and control techniques in the socialization of children. In W. R. Burr,

R. Hill, F. I. Nye, & I. L. Reiss (Eds.), *Contemporary theories about the family* (pp. 317-364). NY: The Free Press.

Santrock, J. W., & Tracy, R. L. (1978). Effects of children's family structure status on the development of stereotypes by teachers. *Journal of Educational Psychology, 70,* 754-757.

Spitze, G. (1988). Women's employment and family relations. *Journal of Marriage and the Family, 50,* 595-618.

Stephens, N., & Day, R. H. (1979). Sex role identity, parental identification, and self-concept of adolescent daughters from mother-absent, father-absent, and intact families. *The Journal of Psychology, 103,* 193-202.

U.S. Bureau of the Census. (1992). *Statistical abstract of the United States: 1989.* (112th ed.). Washington, DC: Author.

Wallerstein, J. S., & Kelly, J. B. (1980). *Surviving the breakup: How children and parents cope with divorce.* London: Grant McIntyre.

Wallerstein, J. S., & Blakeslee, S. (1989). *Second chances: Men, women, and children a decade after divorce.* NY: Ticknor and Fields.

Weed, J. A. (1980). National estimates of marriage dissolution and survivorship. *Vital and Health Statistics* (Ser. 3, No 19 IV). Washington, DC: U.S. Department of Health and Human Services.

Weiss, R. (1979). *Going it alone: The family life and social situation of the single parent.* New York: Basic Books.

Weitzman, L. J. (1985). *The divorce revolution.* NY: The Free Press.

White, L. K. (1990). Determinants of divorce: A review of research in the eighties. *Journal of Marriage and the Family, 52,* 904-912.

White, K. R. (1982). The relation between socioeconomic status and academic achievement. *Psychological Bulletin, 91,* 461-81.

FAMILY ASSESSMENT IN BEHAVIORAL PARENT TRAINING FOR ANTISOCIAL BEHAVIOR

Elaine Buterick Werth

University of Nebraska-Lincoln

Family assessment as a means of guiding research and practice in mental health and pathology has been carefully examined in the preceding chapters of this text. Individuals, whether healthy or disturbed, function in a network of social interactions, with the primary system of interaction being that of the family. Children, as part of that family system, are not only influenced by other family members within the system but also influence other members and, simultaneously, the dynamics of the total system. The complex network of social interchanges that comprise human functioning begin with the parent-child relationship (see Lerner & Spanier, 1978, for a dynamic-interactional model of development). The ongoing reciprocal interaction between individual family members and its effect on child development and behavior has become an area of increasing interest to researchers (Reid, 1978; Patterson, 1982; Wahler & Dumas, 1984; Hartup & Rubin, 1986; Laosa & Sigel, 1982).

The field of behavioral parent training, with the focus on parent-child interactions, has emerged from early research in applied behavioral analysis as an indirect treatment intervention, building on the skills of family members to instigate change in the management of child behaviors. Initially, empirical research in parent training consisted of investigation into the uni-directional linear effects of parent responses on child behavior. Early on, little attention was directed at exploration of the influence of child variables upon parent behavior. Research in parent training has since addressed the reciprocal nature of child behavior and parent management skills.

Until very recently, assessment of children has relied primarily on the individual child from a normative perspective to determine level of functioning, developmental status, personality characteristics, and normal and deviant behavior in order to guide clinical treatment and therapeutic processes. Within the past decade, the child assessment literature is placing an increasing emphasis on family variables and their influence on child health and pathology (Mash & Terdal, 1988; Prinz, 1986). Researchers and clinicians alike have long recognized the need to address childhood behaviors within the context of the environments in which they are manifest. The trend toward expanded assessment procedures that take into consideration family variables has also developed in response to the needs of children who exhibit antisocial behaviors and the needs of their families.

Research in the field of behavioral parent training has begun identifying family variables that place children at risk for the development of antisocial behavior patterns and has extended our understanding of the factors involved in the development, facilitation, and maintenance of various child behaviors. This understanding is especially instrumental in making determinations regarding normal and deviant functioning, prognosis for an individual and family, treatment planning, and treatment evaluation. Behavioral parent training, also referred to as child management training, is one of only a few treatment approaches that addresses the family rather than the individual child and has been found to be an effective form of treatment for children who exhibit antisocial behavior (Kazdin, 1987a). The present chapter investigates the family variables that have been found to correlate with conduct disorders and antisocial behavior in children and explores how parent management training has been used to assist families in the management of childhood behavior problems. Assessment techniques and procedures most frequently used in behavioral parent training to evaluate family interactional patterns in order to identify needs, guide the course of treatment, and determine program efficacy are described.

ANTISOCIAL BEHAVIOR IN CHILDREN

Just as there is a wide range of childhood behaviors considered normal at any age, the range of behaviors considered to be deviant is also broad. Both the determination of normality and the determination of deviancy are dependent upon contextual factors such as environment, expectations, and developmental level, as well as on the severity, intensity, and pervasiveness of the behaviors being considered (Kazdin, 1987a). In addition, what behaviors are seen as normal and what behaviors are viewed as deviant are dependent upon the perceptions of those observing or rating the behaviors. Certain antisocial behaviors are considered to be normal for a 2-year-old but are not acceptable for a 10-year-old (i.e., whining). Likewise, other behaviors such as hitting peers may be displayed normally at age 4 at a low level of intensity and because of contingencies in place in the environment, and may be extinguished before they escalate to higher levels of intensity or become pervasive. There are other behaviors, such as fire setting and cruelty to animals that are considered deviant solely on the basis of their severe ramifications, and very few occurrences of a particular behavior are enough to label the child as deviant or delinquent.

Antisocial behaviors are displayed at one time or another by almost every child and are defined by Kazdin (1987a) as violations of social rules and/or as actions against other people. Antisocial behavior becomes problematic when it is demonstrated repeatedly over long periods of time or when the intensity of the actions are severe. Conduct disorders refer to antisocial behaviors that are of clinical significance and not considered to be within the normal range of functioning (Kazdin, 1987a). For the purpose of this chapter, the terms antisocial behavior and conduct disorders will be used interchangeably and include classes of behavior that are deviant or aversive to others within a social context. These terms may be used to refer to any one or a combination of behaviors that involve breaking social rules and/or societal laws, including aggression, disruptive behavior, destructive behavior, truancy, and lying (Kazdin, Siegel, & Bass, 1992).

Conduct disorders in children have a far-reaching impact, not only for the child, but for the family, the school, the community, and society in general. Research has indicated that childhood conduct problems correlate with school achievement (Dishion, Loeber, Stouthamer-Loeber, & Patterson, 1984), social adjustment (McMahon & Forehand, 1988), self-esteem (Capaldi & Patterson, 1991), substance abuse (Kazdin, 1987a), depression (Patterson, Capaldi, & Bank, 1991), criminal behavior (Kazdin, 1987b), and other forms of adult antisocial behavior (Loeber, 1982). There is evidence to suggest the cycle of antisocial behavior and poor parenting is intergenerational and, therefore, the effects are not short-lived but chronic, persisting from one generation to the next (Elder, Caspi, & Downey, 1986; Kelso & Stewart, 1986; Robins, 1966).

ANTISOCIAL BEHAVIOR AND THE FAMILY

The parental role is of major importance in the process of socialization of young children. Parents through interactions with their children engage in behaviors that serve to extinguish or reinforce certain prosocial behaviors and other behaviors considered to be antisocial. Very young children typically exhibit high rates of aversive behaviors (Patterson, 1982), yet for a majority of youngsters most negative behaviors do not persist beyond early childhood. In the normal population, young children display numerous deviant and antisocial behaviors in their parents' presence at a surprisingly high rate. As children mature and acquire more appropriate means by which to achieve need fulfillment and to interact socially with others by means of parental responsiveness, the deviant behaviors diminish and are replaced with more socially appropriate behaviors (Pettit, Harrist, Bates, & Dodge, 1991). By the time most children reach elementary school age, appropriate social functioning has become the predominant mode by which they interact with other children, as well as, with adults.

There are a number of ecological, parental, and child variables that correlate with the development of deviant behaviors in childhood and later in adolescence and adulthood. Those variables range from molar or global to molecular in nature (Capaldi & Patterson, 1988). Research into the global correlates has revealed that families at highest risk for antisocial behavior are those with high levels of environmental stress (Wahler & Hann, 1986), low socioeconomic status (West, 1982), marital discord (Glueck & Glueck, 1968), multiple family transitions (Capaldi & Patterson, 1991), familial substance abuse or antisocial behavior (Kelso & Stewart, 1986), and parental depression (Biglan, Hops, & Sherman, 1987). It is important to note that many of the constructs that are related to antisocial behavior have complex paths of influence. For example, although it has been found that there is a higher incidence of antisocial behavior in families within the lower socioeconomic range, Werner (1987) observed that socioeconomic status per se was not the determining factor. Low socioeconomic status in combination with family instability correlates with delinquent behavior in children (Capaldi & Patterson, 1991).

Although these global variables correlate with a higher incidence of problem behaviors in children, they are variables that do not explain the direct causes of conduct disorders nor do they readily address the explicit nature of the problem in a manner that would lead to practical solutions. Investigation into global variables can alert practitioners as to who is most at risk for conduct disorders, whereas a micro-analysis of interactional patterns between parents and children in normal families and in families exhibiting behavioral concerns gives a much clearer picture of changes that can be made to ameliorate the faulty patterns of familial interaction that maintain antisocial behaviors.

Johnson, Wahl, Martin, & Johanssen (1973) found, in a normal population of 4- to 6-year-old children, that prosocial behaviors accounted for only 34% of their behaviors during interactions with other family members. Deviant behaviors were estimated to occur at a mean rate of more than once per minute. Johnson et al. then analyzed the consequences of these deviant behaviors and found that parents responded with positive consequences to their children's deviant behaviors as frequently and sometimes more frequently than with the use of negative consequences.

Pettit, Harrist, Bates, and Dodge (1991) conducted research to examine the family interaction variables that were associated with the development of social competence and antisocial behavior in young children. Parenting variables during the preschool years found to correlate with prosocial skills in kindergartners, included responsiveness and proactive involvement (Pettit et al., 1991). Preschool children, whose parents engaged them in more positive social interactions through contingent attention and teaching events were rated as being socially competent by their kindergarten teachers. Pettit and colleagues found that parental use of coerciveness and intrusiveness with preschoolers correlated with antisocial behavior in kindergarten age children. Parents who engaged in aversive interchanges with their preschool age children through noncontingent attention and negative affect had children whose kindergarten teachers rated them higher on aggressive behavior.

The implications for parents regarding the processes of child development, child management, and the resulting child behaviors are that they must not only be knowledgeable about the kinds of behaviors to be expected at different ages, but they must also know how to arrange contingencies to extinguish misbehavior and to accel-

erate the occurrence of appropriate behavior. Effective child management requires parents to recognize and reinforce acceptable social
behaviors when emitted by their child and to identify and efficiently
ignore or use mild forms of punishment for unacceptable behaviors.
Parents who are not knowledgeable about normal child development
and who have inept parenting skills may have unrealistic expectations and use inadequate methods to teach and manage child behavior. Consequently, they may fail to recognize and reinforce appropriate child behavior when it occurs or they may be more aware of
aversive behaviors and attend more frequently to the child when he
or she is engaging in inappropriate behavior, thus creating a pattern
of negative interactions with the child.

Several causal models have been developed to explain family
variables influencing the development and maintenance of antisocial
behaviors (Bank, Patterson, & Reid, 1987). Patterson and associates at
the Oregon Social Learning Center (OSLC) have engaged in extensive
research efforts since the 1960s to determine the causes and effects of
antisocial behavior in boys. Longitudinal studies have explored
variables associated with deviant child behaviors, family characteristics, and parent training intervention. In building their theoretical
models of the emergence of antisocial behavior in children and its
consequences, researchers at OSLC have continued to refine assessment techniques and to build constructs through a process referred to
as bootstrapping (Patterson & Bank, 1986). Their exemplary work has
offered researchers and clinicians a conceptual framework for understanding antisocial behavior and for designing effective treatment
interventions.

A basic training model developed by Patterson (1986) and colleagues traces the development of antisocial behavior from a framework of coercive family process. The coercive process (Patterson,
1982) consists of a series of aversive exchanges between the parents
and child that eventually result in the removal of the unpleasant or
aversive stimuli for both individuals. Typically, the pattern of coercive parent-child interchanges begins when the child is young and
appears to occur most often with children who have difficult temperaments and whose parents lack adequate child management skills
(Patterson, 1986).

The coercive interchange between parent and child may begin
with something as innocuous as a request by the parent directed at the
child. The child reacts by whining and refusing to comply. The
parent in turn reacts to the whining behavior and refusal by scolding
the child. As the parent and child continue to engage in this series of

exchanges, one of three outcomes may occur. The parent may disengage himself or herself from the situation, consequently resulting in negative reinforcement for the child who no longer is expected to comply with the initial request and for the parent who is no longer confronted with a whining child. The second outcome may be that the child eventually complies with the parent's request, thereby reinforcing the parent's scolding behavior. The third outcome, the worst case scenario, is that the intensity of the interchange escalates, with the parent yelling louder, the child screaming and crying, leading to the exchange of verbal and physical abuses, and eventually resulting in the termination of aversive parent and child behaviors.

Over an extended time period, as these patterns of coercive exchanges continue, both parent and child are negatively reinforced for their behaviors and the child is not taught appropriate social behavior, much less, given the opportunity to develop and practice the use of appropriate problem-solving skills. The final result is that the child continues to exhibit noncompliant and antisocial behaviors not only within the family setting, but also with peers, in school, and in the community, develops a poor self-concept, is rejected by peers, experiences school failure, develops associations with other antisocial adolescents, and eventually engages in criminal activity (Patterson, 1986).

There is evidence to suggest that child temperament may play a key role in placing children at risk for the development of antisocial behaviors (Elder, Caspi, & Downey, 1986; Thomas, Chess, Birch, Hertzig, & Korn, 1963) and that the coercive process may begin as early as infancy when infants who are irritable and difficult to pacify are reinforced by parental attention after lengthy crying episodes (Thomas, Chess, & Birch, 1968). In an attempt to quiet the infant, the parent's attending behavior is negatively reinforced by the cessation of crying. As the child gets older, the crying behavior is replaced by other forms of coercive behavior, which are terminated, at least for brief periods of time by the parents' responses. Elder, Caspi, and Downey (1986) studied data from hundreds of families over the course of four generations and found that an irritable temperament, characterized by high rates of temper-tantrums during childhood correlated with marital instability and explosive parenting style by those same individuals as adults. Temperament, therefore, may have implications for the immediate family and ramifications may be manifest intergenerationally.

Coercive parent-child interactions may be affected not only by behaviors of family members but also by parental social interactions with individuals outside the immediate family (Panaccione & Wahler, 1986). Wahler and Dumas (1984) have studied the parenting styles of insular mothers, mothers who have little or no social support through family and friends, and noninsular mothers, those who have an adequate support system. There are significant differences between the two groups in the frequency of aversive and nonaversive interactions with their child. Not only do insular mothers become involved more frequently in coercive processes with their child, but they engage in multiple coercive interchanges, with spouses, extended family members, friends, and representatives from community agencies. There appears to be a direct correlation between the number of daily coercive interchanges a mother experiences with other individuals and the frequency of aversive interactions she engages in with her child (Dumas, 1984). When designing parent training programs, the traditional assessment may be supplemented by collecting additional information regarding the parents' perceptions of their relationships with other family members, friends, and associates. If a pattern of multiple coercive exchanges has been established, parent training alone may be insufficient to meet the needs of the family and child.

PARENT TRAINING

The current trend in clinical child therapy and educational interventions for children emphasizes the importance of a systems approach to assessment and treatment (Bernstein, 1983; Christenson & Cleary, 1990; Christenson, Abery, & Weinberg, 1986; Dumas, 1984; Kramer, 1985, 1990; Patterson, 1986). Behavioral parent training is one of only a few interventions that draws on the family system to facilitate change and it has been found to be one of the most effective clinical interventions for children with conduct disorders (Kazdin, 1987a). An indirect means of intervention, behavioral parent training seeks to change maladaptive child behavior by changing the contingencies within the child's daily environment. The view that the child is influenced by his/her environment, that parents are the primary change agents in a child's environment, and that parents can learn the skills that will facilitate the development of socially appropriate behaviors for their children are basic premises upon which child management training is based. Empirical findings support the tenet that parents can acquire skills necessary to assist their children in alleviating numerous behavioral and performance deficits and excesses (Bank, Patterson, & Reid, 1987; Davies, McMahon, Flessati, & Tiedemann, 1984; Kazdin, Siegel, & Bass, 1992; Rickert, Sottolano, Parrish, Riley, Hunt, & Pelco, 1988). Consequently, the influence of effective parent training interventions may reach far beyond the immediate parent-child realm in which they are being employed. In fact, Ramsey, Walker, Shinn, O'Neill, & Stieber (1989) found a direct correlation between child management practices used by parents in the home setting and children's behavior in the school setting.

Assuming the primacy of the parent-child relationship as the foundation for all of the child's social interactions, it follows that compliance training initiated by parents for children who display high levels of noncompliant and antisocial behavior would serve to weaken the pattern of coercive interchanges and build more acceptable styles of social intercourse. Therefore, the most effective behavioral parent training programs for families of children with conduct disorders assist parents in acquiring the skills necessary to teach their children to comply with parental requests and household rules. Of course, this requires parents to make significant changes in how they respond to their child's appropriate behaviors and misbehaviors. A number of different approaches have been developed to accomplish this task and key components of several will be briefly reviewed.

Behavioral parent training for families of children with conduct disorders teaches parents to use effective child management skills based on social learning principles. A number of different parent training programs are available for use in clinical practice, many of which have been instrumental in affecting change in both parent and child behaviors (refer to Dangel & Polster, 1984 for an extensive review; Patterson, Reid, Jones, & Conger, 1975; Forehand & McMahon, 1981; Barkley, 1987; Webster-Stratton, 1984). Methods used for training parents vary but usually include a form of didactic instruction combined with modeling, role-playing, practice, and immediate performance feedback (Dangel & Polster, 1984; Rickert et al., 1988; Davies et al., 1984) presented in a group format or individual family instruction (Webster-Stratton, 1984). Self-administered videotape training programs have also been used and found to be an effective supplement to group and individual training (Webster-Stratton, Kolpacoff, & Hollinsworth, 1988).

The primary emphasis of training programs for parents of antisocial children is on changes in parent behaviors that will result in positive changes in the child's behavior. Parents learn how to respond to the child's appropriate and inappropriate behaviors in a contingent manner to increase prosocial skills and decrease antisocial behavior. They acquire skill in the effective use of reinforcement techniques and learn how to use mild forms of punishment to extinguish negative child behaviors. Not all parent training programs utilize the same techniques and methods to accomplish these goals; however, the end result, an increase in effective parenting skills and a decrease in antisocial child behavior, is most often achieved.

The pattern of coercive interaction that is typical of children with conduct disorders and their families is changed by parents who discontinue the reciprocal use of negative social behaviors. Parents learn to identify the types of behaviors their child is displaying and disengage themselves from the coercive cycle by ignoring mildly aversive child behaviors and using effective discipline techniques such as time-out and cost-response when more aversive behaviors are exhibited. Parents also acquire skill in eliciting child compliance by utilizing differential attention and they learn how to reinforce prosocial child behaviors using a variety of techniques including praise, positive physical contact, and token systems (Patterson et al., 1975; Dangel & Polster, 1984; Forehand & McMahon, 1981; Barkley, 1987).

OUTCOMES OF PARENT TRAINING

The efficacy of behavioral parent training in treating conduct disorders has been demonstrated in numerous studies (see Kazdin, 1985). Not only has parent training been instrumental in affecting behavioral changes for parent and child immediately following treatment, but studies have shown long term maintenance of results as well as generalization across settings and individuals (Bank, Marlowe, Reid, Patterson, & Weinrott, 1991; Webster-Stratton, 1990; Webster-Stratton, 1984; Webster-Stratton, Kolpacoff, & Hollinsworth, 1988). In addition to the effects on behavior, parent training has also been found to have positive impact on parental knowledge of behavioral concepts, attitude toward and perceptions of the targeted child, and maternal ratings of depression (McMahon, Forehand, & Griest, 1981; Patterson et al., 1975; Spitzer, Webster-Stratton, & Hollinsworth, 1991). Diverse populations of parents, including teenage parents (Hans, Bernstein, & Percansky, 1991), low-income parents (Strayhorn & Weidman, 1989), and child abuse perpetrators (Barone, Greene, & Lutzker, 1986), have been successfully trained to acquire functional parenting skills.

The ultimate determination of efficacy of any parent training program is the observed or perceived change of child behavior; however, the variables contributing to child behavior change must be determined. Because parent training procedures are developed based upon an indirect service delivery model and involve imparting information and teaching skills to parents, which in turn will be used to influence child behavior, assessment can be used to determine the

effect of trainer-parent interaction through measures of parental behavior change, parent-child interaction by assessing child behavior
change, and the dyadic parent-child relationship through observation
of parent and child interactions. In order to counterbalance potential
bias in data collection and to assess all relevant variables, multiple
methods and sources are often used to determine the extent of
behavior change and generalization across time, settings, behaviors,
and individuals (Patterson & Bank, 1986).

Behavioral observations of parent-child interaction in clinic and
home settings provide clinicians with information regarding the
acquisition of specific skills and changes in parent and child behaviors
following parent training. Pre-test/post-test comparisons of parent
training intervention have shown that parents have acquired skills in
the use of differential attention, giving instructions to elicit specific
child behaviors, teaching their child new skills, using time-out as a
discipline technique, and using token systems to increase compliance
(Budd & Fabry, 1984; Budd, Riner, & Brockman, 1983). Patterson et
al. (1975) reported that results of observations following family involvement in parent training showed that parents were able to use
punishment more effectively to decrease the occurrence of coercive
exchanges with their child and that children engaged in fewer aversive
behaviors during interactions with other family members. Observations conducted by Forehand and colleagues showed parent training
to be effective in increasing maternal use of rewards, attending to
child following appropriate behavior and contingent attention to
compliance, decreasing commands and questions, and increasing
child compliance to parental requests (Forehand & McMahon, 1981).

ASSESSMENT OF PARENT TRAINING

There are a multiplicity of measurement instruments used for
assessment in parent training in both research and clinical practice.
Normative assessment is used to measure child behavior, self-esteem,
parent perceptions and attitude, family demographics, and numerous
other child and parent variables. No standard assessment battery is
used in the parent training research or by clinicians, although similar
classes of dependent variables are generally assessed. Typically, a
combination of measures, most often child behavior rating scales, a
child self-report measure, a measure of parent attitude, and a parent
stress or depression index are commonly used to assess pathology
and the need for treatment, to determine the course of therapy, and to
evaluate treatment efficacy. These measures are convenient to use,
are readily accessible to clinicians and researchers, provide global

information regarding parent and child variables, and yield normative data. Although these instruments offer valuable information to
the clinician, they rely on inferences made by respondents regarding
parent and child variables which are considered as separate entities,
however, and do not provide information pertaining to patterns of
family interaction. For example, child behavior checklists completed
by parents and teachers may reveal that a child exhibits a high
frequency of externalizing behaviors, including fighting, uncoopera-
tive behavior, and destructive behavior. Parental assessments indicate that the mother's stress and depression indexes are high. This
information is useful, yet limited. It alerts the clinician to some of the
problems the family is experiencing, but it does not provide information regarding the specific interactional patterns between parent and
child or between child and other family members that may be sustain-
ing the antisocial behaviors. Direct assessment of molecular variables
through direct observation provides information regarding specific,
discrete units of behavior exhibited by individual family members as
they interact with one another. The observation can supply a record
of sequential behaviors revealing the parental antecedents to particular child behaviors and the parents' responses to those behaviors.
This information is useful in determining specific skills and behaviors
that are in need of modification.

The need exists for the use of both normative and idiographic
assessment in the design, implementation, and evaluation of treatment programs. Normative assessment generally identifies and measures molar variables and facilitates a summative evaluation of outcomes. The measures are generally global and rely on accurate
observations and recall of respondents over extended periods of time.
In addition, they do not address the interactional processes that are
central to understanding family functioning and disciplinary practices. Direct observation of those interactions in the form of formative, idiographic measures can help facilitate the progress of treatment by identifying specific units of behavior as they occur. The
frequency of occurrence of such molecular variables is measured, but
more importantly, a chain of events involving not only the target
individual, but others with whom that individual interacts can be
measured. The frequency and sequence of events can be used to
guide the treatment process. Ongoing measures of the frequency of
the behavior identified as being in need of change can alert clinicians
to the need to change training procedures if the rate of progress is
minimal. The clinician is able to monitor progress by determining the
change in parent-child interactions through direct observation of

those interactions. This type of formative assessment allows clinicians to identify and change procedures as needed based upon client progress or lack thereof.

The analysis of molecular variables can also assist in identifying the specific interventions and behavior changes that are responsible for specific outcomes. When global assessments are used to measure outcome, the resulting information may be useful in informing practice as to the efficacy of a particular treatment, but will leave many questions unanswered from an empirical perspective. That is to say, global assessments may inform clinicians about whether a particular treatment was effective or ineffective with certain clients, however, it does not necessarily provide information regarding the specific variables that were affected. Global measures provide information about broad behavioral or attitudinal variables that may or may not be directly applicable to the child/parent being studied or the intervention utilized. When assessment does not measure directly the behaviors or the skills being taught, then some form of generalization must occur for indirect measures to reflect changes. Behavior rating scales and measures of attitude are oftentimes completed by the very persons toward whom treatment is directed, possibly introducing bias into the assessment. Additionally, inferences must be made by those completing rating scales, thus further obscuring the assessment of discrete changes made as a result of the intervention. Each method of measuring child and family functioning has its place in assessment, dependent upon the rationale and goals of therapy. Global assessment provides information regarding more general child and family characteristics and correlates of antisocial behavior in the family. Micro-analysis of parent-child interaction offers researchers and clinicians information regarding specific communication and behavioral patterns that may be maintaining antisocial behavior.

Correlates of family functioning and conduct disorders in children have been analyzed by studying both molar and molecular variables. By studying the full range of variables associated with antisocial behavior, the child and family are viewed from multiple perspectives. The information obtained may then serve an explanatory function and pervasive effects for the entire family can be explored. Molar variables such as parental depression and socioeconomic status are not directly observable and may influence behavior indirectly. Molecular variables have a direct impact on an individual's behavior, are observable, and can be measured through observation. For example, the amount of time parents engage in monitoring of their children's behavior is highly correlated with antisocial behavior in children. The more supervision, the less likely is the appearance of antisocial behavior. Although molar variables tend to be relatively stable over time, molecular variables may change depending upon the developmental level of the child, environmental factors, and skill levels of the parents.

Hayes, Nelson, and Jarrett (1987) recommend that assessment used in clinical practice have treatment utility. Behavioral observation can be used to formatively guide treatment and to contribute to treatment outcome. The measurement of discrete observable behaviors lends itself to formative assessment of behavioral changes occurring during family interaction. Formative assessment can be of particular value in increasing the effectiveness of parent training for individual families. The reiterative process that occurs during formative assessment provides the clinician with continual data regarding client behavior. Rather than relying on subjective judgment, a systematic means of assessing discrete behavioral change enhances the credibility of the program. The structured observation systems discussed below are suitable for this type of assessment. As part of ongoing treatment, brief observations can be conducted during therapy sessions that allow the clinician to assess interactions between parent and child, to implement treatment strategies with clients, to assess and obtain feedback regarding the effect of those strategies, to make adjustments according to that feedback, and to continually monitor the progress of therapy by collecting ongoing, objective data regarding parent-child interactions. Modification is central to the formative assessment of a program in that the clinician is constantly striving to develop the most effective treatment for clients and therefore making changes as dictated by the clients' responses to therapy. The most effective treatment is based on the individual needs of the client and the use of monitoring and feedback provide important information regarding those needs (Patterson, 1982). Observational coding systems are the few assessment instruments currently used in parent training to assess and monitor family interactions.

Several observational systems have been developed to measure family interactions, to assess acquisition of parenting skills during therapy, and to determine the extent of behavior change exhibited by the child. Clients can also make observations and record and report data (Patterson, Reid, & Maerov, 1978). Client observation can be useful in checking the reliability of observations made by independent observers, to monitor the incidence of low-frequency behaviors, and to supplement intervention by incorporating a self-monitoring procedure or parent-child monitoring component. The following observational coding systems, developed for use in parent training programs, have been shown to have relatively high reliability and validity. They are described in order from least structured and intrusive to most structured. Generally, the less structure imposed during observations, the more varied the behaviors exhibited by the clients, whereas the more structured observation systems elicit specific behaviors of interest to the clinician.

Family Interaction Coding System

The Family Interaction Coding System (FICS; Patterson, Reid, & Maerov, 1978) was one of the first instruments developed for use with conduct disordered children to assess family interactions in the home setting. It is a comprehensive observational system that has been used extensively in research to assess interaction patterns that are typical of clinic-referred and non-clinic-referred families as well as in clinical practice to identify and evaluate family interaction patterns in need of modification.

Observations are done by an independent observer in the family's home. All family members are to be present during the observation and a minimal number of restrictions are reviewed with the family prior to being observed. These restrictions, regarding activities, the absence of non-family members, and interaction with the observer, were developed to facilitate the observation and to minimize extraneous behaviors not pertinent to assessment of family interactions. Each family member is observed during 5-minute intervals and his or her interactions with others are recorded. Duration and interval recording are used to collect data regarding interactions between family members.

The FICS yields a record of the frequency and duration of behavioral exchanges between the child and other family members. Data can be analyzed to produce a total deviant score and a total social score. The behaviors coded are categorized as first and second order, first order being more important diagnostically, clinically, and theoretically, and as verbal and nonverbal. The first order verbal behaviors that are subsumed within the total deviant category include: command negative, cry, humiliate, negativism, whine, and yell. First order nonverbal or verbal-deviant behaviors are destructiveness, disapproval, dependency, ignore, noncompliance, high rate (very physically active, repetitive behavior), tease, and physical negative. Other first order verbal and nonverbal behaviors include: command, laugh, approval, compliance, indulgence, play, physical positive, and work. Second order behaviors are to be coded only when it is inappropriate to code first order behaviors and include: talk, attention, normative (routine behavior), no response, receive, self-stimulation, and touch.

Extensive training is required to teach observers to use the observation and coding system. Once didactic instruction and readings are completed and observers have memorized code abbreviations and definitions, an average of 15 to 20 hours of videotape practice is required before field experience begins. Frequent reliability checks and retraining, when needed, are recommended (Reid, 1978).

Using a small sample of observer protocols, Reid (1978) found inter-observer reliability across the 29 behavioral codes to range from 30% agreement for the self-stimulation category to 96% agreement for the no response category, with a median percentage of 72 across all 29 behavioral code categories (Reid, 1978; Patterson, 1982).

Dyadic Parent-Child Interaction Coding System

Eyberg and colleagues developed a structured observation system, the Dyadic Parent-Child Interaction Coding System (DPICS), for use in clinical practice with conduct disorder families (Robinson & Eyberg, 1981). The DPICS assesses parent-child interactions during brief observation sessions. The child-directed interaction session is less structured and requires the parent and child to interact together in child-initiated play activities. During the parent-directed interaction session, the parent and child engage in an activity that the parent has chosen and for which the parent has established rules. Observations are also conducted during a brief clean-up session. Nineteen parent and child behavioral categories are used for the child-directed interactions and 22 categories are used during the parent-directed interactions. Observations are conducted during 5-minute sessions and continuous recording of the frequency of behavioral categories is done by an independent observer for a sequential account of parent-child interactions. The component behavioral categories are used to form the following variables: total praise, which includes labeled plus unlabeled praise; total deviant, which is the total of whine, cry, physical negative, smart talk, yell, and destructive; total commands, which consists of direct commands plus indirect commands; command ratio, which is the number of direct commands divided by the total number of commands; no opportunity ratio, the number of no opportunities divided by the total commands; compliance ratio, the number of direct commands divided by total commands; and non-compliance ratio, non-complies divided by total commands.

Observer training using the DPICS involves readings, practice observations using videotaped role-plays of interactions, and practice coding of real-life family interactions. Interobserver reliability was found to be high, with a mean reliability coefficient of .91 for parent behaviors and .92 for child behaviors. Studies of validity have demonstrated that the DPICS differentiates between families with conduct problems and normal families and also between children with conduct problems and their siblings (Robinson & Eyberg, 1981).

Behavioral Coding System

The behavioral coding systems used in the parent-training program developed by Forehand and McMahon (1981) are designed for use in clinic and home settings. Clinic observations, 5 minutes in length, are conducted in structured settings, whereas the 40-minute home observations are semistructured. Behavioral sequences during parent-child interactions are observed and recorded. The coding system includes target behaviors exhibited by the parent and child to assess parent skill in managing the child's behavior and the occurrence of contingent noncompliant, compliant, and inappropriate child behavior. The clinic observations incorporate a Child's Game condition and a Parent's Game condition within which the parent and child interact. The Child's Game is a free-play situation whereby the child determines the activities and rules of play. The Parent's Game is a command situation requiring the parent to select the activities and rules of play when parent and child interact. The observations, which last 5 minutes for both of the game conditions, serve a formative function by allowing clinicians to identify and measure the skills parents use in managing their child's behavior under different circumstances and within different contexts. Specific parent and child behaviors are coded and, through direct observation, therapists monitor the parent's use of child management skills during interaction with their child. The information is then used to develop a treatment program that assists the parent in decreasing ineffective behaviors and increasing the use of effective management techniques.

Data collection and recording are similar for both clinic observations and home observations; however, the conditions in place for the home observations are less structured. Parameters are set for the observation setting in the family's home to facilitate data collection and consistency across observations. Those parameters include a 40-minute duration for the observation, the parent and child stay in a two-room area and remain visible to the observer, restrictions are placed on activities involving board games, television, playing cards, and books, and on the presence of other people, telephone calls, and conversation between observer and the individuals being observed.

A sequential analysis of parent and child behaviors results from the observations. An interval recording system is used that allows for the recording of as many as 10 interactions within 30-second time segments. The behaviors coded and recorded include parent behaviors that serve as the antecedents to the child's behavior, the child's behavior, and the parent's response to that behavior. This sequence of interactions allows the therapist to determine the skills the parent is using to elicit and maintain compliant or noncompliant child behaviors. The analysis provides information about the rate and frequency of compliant child behavior and the parent's use of skills taught in the parent-training sessions.

Behavioral codes are included for the following parental antecedent behaviors: alpha and beta commands, warnings, questions, attends, and rewards. Child compliance and noncompliance are coded and recorded only when following the antecedent parent behavior. Also coded are consequences of attend, reward, or time-out imposed by the parent in response to the child's behavior and a notation is made to indicate whether the child's behavior is appropriate or inappropriate.

Observer training involves readings, discussion, didactic instruction, written exercises, demonstration, practice, and feedback. Small group instruction is used for training and typically a total of 20 to 25 hours is required for observers to achieve adequate levels of agreement. Forehand and associates have reported adequate levels of interobserver and test-retest reliability for this observation system (Forehand & Peed, 1979; Peed, Roberts, & Forehand, 1977).

Playroom Observations of Parent-Child Interaction

Barkley (1987) has made adaptations to the coding and observation system used by Forehand and McMahon (1981) for use in clinical training programs for parents of children whose behavior is difficult to manage. Modifications included slight changes in the behavioral categories and definitions of the coding system and different conditions during which parent-child interactions are observed. The three-step behavioral sequences of parent-child interaction beginning with parent antecedent and ending with parent response are observed and recorded during 1-minute time intervals. The coding form developed for use with this system facilitates observer coding by including abbreviations of the codes in each of the spaces designated for that coding interval.

One of the unique features of Barkley's observation system is the context in which the parent and child interact. Observations are conducted in a clinic playroom or in the family's home. The parent and child are given time to acclimate to the playroom, or the presence of the observer in the home, during the 5 minutes before the observation begins by engaging in unstructured play activities. Immediately prior to the observation, parents are provided with a list of 10 developmentally appropriate instructions to use with their child. Parent-child interactions are recorded for 10 minutes as the parent instructs the child to accomplish the tasks on the list. The instructions given to the child are one- and two-step commands, such as "put your shoes on" and "fold these clothes neatly and put them in the box."

Parent behaviors coded include the initial command and repeat commands given by the parent, child compliant, noncompliant or negative behavior, and parent approval or negative response to the child's behavior. Data analysis yields rate of parental commands per minute, rate of repeat commands per original command, percentage of total child compliance during the observation session, percentage of negative child responses for each command, rate of parent approvals per minute, and rate of parent negatives per minute.

Structured Observation System

The structured observation system developed by Budd and associates directly assesses parent-child interactions as parents demonstrate their skill mastery in the use of selected child management techniques (Budd, Riner, & Brockman, 1983). The observation system was designed as a standardized, formative assessment instrument to be used in conjunction with behavioral parent training to monitor parents' skill acquisition. It is especially suited for clinicians because it yields information pertinent to the needs of clients, minimal observer training is required for reliable use (Budd & Fabry, 1984); it can be used with diverse populations of parents, children, and behavior problems; it takes little time to administer; and it can be used frequently to monitor client progress (Budd, Riner, & Brockman, 1983).

Observations are conducted by independent observers in the family's home or in the clinic setting. Each observation ranges in length from 5 to 12 minutes, depending upon the technique being assessed. A set of five child management techniques frequently taught in parent training are used for the observation and include: instruction giving, differential attention, the use of a token system, teaching new skills, and the use of time-out. Each technique has been task analyzed to identify the sequence of component behaviors necessary for skill mastery. As parents engage in structured activities with their child, their mastery of the child management techniques is assessed and the child's behaviors are also recorded.

Ratings are then obtained for both parent and child behaviors according to the specific behaviors displayed during the observation period. Although child behavior is observed and noted, the emphasis of this system is assessment of change in parent behavior. Parent and child data are used to calculate the following parent scores: percentage of appropriate parent responses in comparison to the total number of available opportunities for instruction giving, teaching new skills and use of token systems and total number of praise and ignore responses contingent upon child behavior for differential attention. The assessment of the use of time-out is completed in a role-play situation with the use of a confederate, rather than with the child, and scoring is based on the total number of occurrences and nonoccurrences of correct parent behaviors compared to the total number of correct responses to yield an overall correct performance score.

Observer training is conducted through didactic instruction, videotaped practice sessions, and practice in families' home with an experienced observer. Adequate levels of observer reliability are generally achieved with approximately 2 to 8 hours of training per structured activity (Budd, Riner, & Brockman, 1983). The observation system can be learned independently with relative ease by parent trainers as demonstrated by Budd and Fabry (1984) who found the amount of training time to be considerably less than that estimated by Budd and her associates, with mean length of training being 1.3 to 5.5 hours per structured activity.

High levels of interobserver reliability have been reported for the system. Interobserver agreement was determined for the component behaviors for each of the structured activities. The mean percentage of agreement across component behaviors ranged from 82% on the teaching new skills activity to 94% on the differential attention activity, with a range of 63% to 100% agreement for component behaviors. The system was also found to be sensitive to changes in parent behavior resulting from parent training, with significant differences between pre-test and post-test scores on 50 out of a total of 53 behavioral components.

CONCLUSION

Childhood conduct disorders if left untreated have significant implications for families and society in general. Assessment of family interactions has revealed the importance of measuring not only disparate parent and child variables but of evaluating the contextual environment in which antisocial behavior develops and is maintained. There are numerous assessment instruments available for evaluating the effectiveness of behavioral parent training. Many of the assessments currently being used for parent training are normed paper-and-pencil tasks completed from the perspective of one individual for the purpose of evaluating separate child and parent characteristics, but they do not directly assess family functioning. The observation instruments described in this chapter are the most commonly used methods to assess the interactions between parents and child and are sensitive to changes in high frequency behaviors over time.

No one method of assessment can adequately sample the array of variables associated with the effective training of parents in the use of child management skills. It is not enough to assess changes in parents, children, dyadic interactions, or even multiple familial dynamics, alone. For any program to be successful, any positive changes must be generalize to other settings, other individuals, and over extended periods of time. A wide variety of assessment methods and techniques are needed to provide a comprehensive view of children and their families as they function within the family setting and within the community.

REFERENCES

Bank, L., Marlowe, J. H., Reid, J. B., Patterson, G. R., & Weinrott, M. R. (1991). A comparative evaluation of parent-training interventions for families of chronic delinquents. *Journal of Abnormal Psychology, 19*, 15-33.

Bank, L., Patterson, G. R., & Reid, J. B. (1987). Delinquency prevention through training parents in family management. *The Behavior Analyst, 10*, 75-82.

Barkley, R. A. (1987). *Defiant children: A clinician's manual for parent training*. New York: Guilford Press.

Barone, V. J., Greene, B. F., & Lutzker, J. R. (1986). Home safety for families being treated for child abuse and neglect. *Behavior Modification, 10*, 93-114.

Bernstein, G. S. (1983). Training behavior change agents: A conceptual analysis. *Behavior Therapy, 13*, 1-23.

Biglan, A., Hops, H., & Sherman, L. (1987). Coercive family processes and maternal depression. In R. D. Peters & R. J. McMahon (Eds.), *Marriages and families: Behavioral-systems approaches*. New York: Brunner-Mazel.

Budd, K. S., & Fabry, P. L. (1984). Behavioral assessment in applied parent training: Use of a structured observation system. In

E. J. Mash & L. G. Terdal (Eds.), *Behavioral assessment of childhood disorders* (2nd ed., pp. 417-442). New York: Guilford Press.

Budd, K. S., Riner, L. S., & Brockman, M. P. (1983). A structured observation system for clinical evaluation of parent training. *Behavioral Assessment, 5,* 373-393.

Capaldi, D. M., & Patterson, G. R. (1988). *Psychometric properties of fourteen latent constructs from the Oregon Youth Study.* New York: Springer-Verlag.

Capaldi, D. M., & Patterson, G. R. (1991). Relation of parental transitions to boys' adjustment problems: I. A linear hypothesis. II. Mothers at risk for transitions and unskilled parenting. *Developmental Psychology, 27,* 489-504.

Christenson, S., Abery, B., & Weinberg, R. A. (1986). An alternative model for the delivery of psychological services in the school community. In S. N. Elliott & J. C. Witt (Eds.), *The delivery of psychological services in the schools: Concepts, processes, and issues* (pp. 349-391). Hillsdale, NJ: Lawrence Erlbaum Associates, Inc.

Christenson, S. L., & Cleary, M. (1990). Consultation and the parent-educator partnership: A perspective. *Journal of Educational and Psychological Consultation, 1,* 219-241.

Dangel, R. F., & Polster, R. A. (Eds.). (1984). *Parent training: Foundations of research and practice.* New York: Guilford Press.

Davies, G. R., McMahon, R. J., Flessati, E. W., & Tiedemann, G. L. (1984). Verbal rationales and modeling as adjuncts to a parenting technique for child compliance. *Child Development, 55,* 1290-1298.

Dishion, T. J., Loeber, R., Stouthamer-Loeber, M., & Patterson, G. R. (1984). Skill deficits and male adolescent delinquency. *Journal of Abnormal Child Psychology, 12,* 37-54.

Dumas, J. E. (1984). Interactional correlates of treatment outcome in behavioral parent training. *Journal of Consulting and Clinical Psychology, 52,* 946-954.

Elder, G. H., Caspi, A., & Downey, G. (1986). Problem behavior and family relationships: Life course and intergenerational themes. In A. B. Sorensen, F. E. Weinert, & L. R. Sherrod (Eds.), *Human development and the life course: Multidisciplinary perspection* (pp. 293-340). Hillsdale, NJ: Lawrence Erlbaum Associates.

Forehand, R. L., & McMahon, R. J. (1981). *Helping the noncompliant child: A clinician's guide to parent training.* New York: Guilford.

Forehand, R. L., & Peed, S. (1979). Training parents to modify noncompliant behavior in their children. In A. J. Finch, Jr., & P. C. Kendall (Eds.), *Treatment and research in child psychopathology* (pp. 159-184). New York: Spectrum.

Glueck, S., & Glueck, E. (1968). *Delinquents and nondelinquents in perspective.* Cambridge, MA: Harvard University Press.

Hans, S. L., Bernstein, V. J., & Percansky, C. (1991). Adolescent parenting programs: Assessing parent-infant interaction. *Evaluation and Program Planning, 14,* 87-95.

Hartup, W., & Rubin, Z. (Eds.). (1986). *Relationships and development.* Hillsdale, NJ: Lawrence Erlbaum Associates.

Hayes, S. C., Nelson, R. O., & Jarrett, R. B. (1987, November). The treatment utility of assessment: A functional approach to evaluating assessment quality. *American Psychologist,* 963-974.

Johnson, S. M., Wahl, G., Martin, S., & Johanssen, S. (1973). How deviant is the normal child? A behavioral analysis of the preschool child and his family. In R. D. Rubin, J. P. Brady, & J. D. Henderson (Eds.), *Advances in behavior therapy* (vol. 4; pp. 37-54). New York: Academic Press.

Kazdin, A. E. (1985). *Treatment of antisocial behavior in children and adolescence.* Homewood, IL: Dorsey Press.

Kazdin, A. E. (1987a). *Conduct disorders in childhood and adolescence.* Newbury Park, CA: Sage.

Kazdin, A. E. (1987b). Treatment of antisocial behavior in children: Current status and future directions. *Psychological Bulletin, 102,* 187-203.

Kazdin, A. E., Siegel, T. C., & Bass, D. (1992). Cognitive problem-solving skills training and parent management training in the treatment of antisocial behavior in children. *Journal of Consulting and Clinical Psychology, 60,* 733-747.

Kelso, J., & Stewart, M. A. (1986). Factors which predict the persistence of aggressive conduct disorder. *Journal of Child Psychology and Psychiatry, 27,* 77-86.

Kramer, J. J. (1985). Best practices in parent training. In A. Thomas & J. Grimes (Eds.), *Best practices in school psychology* (pp. 263-273). Kent, OH: National Association of School Psychologists.

Kramer, J. J. (1990). Training parents as behavior change agents: Success, failures, and suggestons for school psychologists. In T. B. Gutkin & C. R. Reynolds (Eds.), *The handbook of school psychology* (2nd ed.; pp.683-702). New York: Wiley.

Laosa, L., & Sigel, I. (Eds.). (1982). *Families as learning environments for children.* New York: Plenum.

Lerner, R. M., & Spanier, G. B. (Eds.). (1978). *Child influences on marital and family interaction: A life-span perspective.* New York: Academic Press.

Loeber, R. (1982). The stability of antisocial child behavior. *Child Development, 53,* 1431-1446.

Mash, E. J., & Terdal, L. G. (Eds.). (1988). *Behavioral assessment of childhood disorders* (2nd ed.), New York: Guilford Press.

McMahon, R. J., & Forehand, R. (1988). Conduct disorders. In E. J. Mash & L. G. Terdal (Eds.), *Behavioral assessment of childhood disorders* (2nd ed.; pp. 105-153). New York: Guilford Press.

McMahon, R. J., Forehand, R., & Griest, D. L. (1981). Effects of knowledge of social learning principles on enhancing treatment outcomes and generalization in a parent training program. *Journal of Counseling and Clinical Psychology, 49*, 526-532.

Panaccione, V. F., & Wahler, R. G. (1986). Child behavior, maternal depression, and social coercion as factors in the quality of child care. *Journal of Abnormal Child Psychology, 14*, 263-278.

Patterson, G. R. (1982). *Coercive family process.* Eugene, OR: Castalia.

Patterson, G. R. (1986). Performance models for antisocial boys. *American Psychologist, 41*, 432-444.

Patterson, G. R., & Bank, L. (1986). Bookstrapping your way in the nomological thicket. *Behavioral Assessment, 8*, 49-73.

Patterson, G. R., Capaldi, D., & Bank, L. (1991). An early starter model for predicting delinquency. In D. J. Pepler & K. H. Rubin (Eds.), *The development and treatment of childhood aggression* (pp. 139-168). Hilldale, NJ: Lawrence Erlbaum Associates.

Patterson, G. R., Reid, J. B., Jones, R. R., & Conger, R. E. (1975). *A social learning approach to family inervention. Volume 1. Families with aggressive children.* Eugene, OR: Castalia.

Patterson, G. R., Reid, J. B., & Maerov, S. L. (1978). Development of the family interaction coding system (FICS). In J. B. Reid (Ed.), *Observation in home settings* (pp. 3-9). Eugene, OR: Castalia.

Peed, S., Roberts, M., & Forehand, R. (1977). Evaluation of the effectiveness of a standardized parent training program in altering the interaction of mothers and their noncompliant children. *Behavior Modification, 1*, 323-350.

Pettit, G. S., Harrist, A. W., Bates, J. E., & Dodge, K. A. (1991). Family interaction, social cognition and children's subsequent relations with peers in kindergarten. *Journal of Social and Personal Relationships, 8*, 383-402.

Prinz, R. (Ed.). (1986). *Advances in behavioral assessment of children and families.* Greenwich, CT: JAI Press.

Ramsey, E., Walker, H. M., Shinn, M., O'Neill, R. E., & Stieber, S. (1989). Parent management practices and school adjustment. *School Psychology Review, 18*, 513-525.

Reid, J. B. (Ed.). (1978). *Observation in home settings.* Eugene, OR: Castalia.

Rickert, V. I., Sottolano, D. C., Parrish, J. M., Riley, A. W., Hunt, F. M., & Pelco, L. E. (1988). Training parents to become better behavior managers: The need for a competency-based approach. *Behavior Modification, 12*, 475-496.(2)

Robins, L. N. (1966). *Deviant children grow up*. Baltimore: Williams & Wilkins.

Robinson, E. A., & Eyberg, S. M. (1981).The Dyadic Parent-Child Interaction Coding System: Standardization and validation. *Journal of Consulting and Clincal Psychology, 49*, 245-250.

Spitzer, A., Webster-Stratton, C., & Hollinsworth, T. (1991). Coping with conduct-problem children: Parents gaining knowledge and control. *Journal of Clinical Child Psychology, 20*, 413-417.

Strayhorn, J. M., & Weidman, C. S. (1989). Reduction of attention deficit and internalizing symptoms in preschoolers through parent-child interaction training. *Journal of the American Academy of Child and Adolescent Psychiatry, 28*, 888-896.

Thomas, A., Chess, S., & Birch, H. (1968). *Temperament and behavior disorders in children*. New York: New York University.

Thomas, A., Chess, S., Birch, H., Hertzig, M., & Korn, S. (1963). *Behavioral individuality in early childhood*. New York: New York University.

Wahler, R. G., & Dumas, J. E. (1984). Changing the observational coding styles of insular and noninsular mothers: A step toward maintenance of parent training effects. In R. F. Dangel & R. A. Polster (Eds.), *Parent training* (pp. 379-416). New York: Guilford Press.

Wahler, R. G., & Hann, D. M. (1986). A behavioral systems perspective in childhood psychopathology: Expanding the three-term operant contingency. In N. A. Krasnegor, J. D. Arasteh, & M. F. Cataldo (Eds.), *Child health behavior: A behavioral pediatrics perspective* (pp. 146-167). New York: John Wiley & Sons.

Webster-Stratton, C. (1984). Randomized trial of two parent-training programs for families with conduct-disordered children. *Journal of Consulting and Clinical Psychology, 52*, 666-678.

Webster-Stratton, C. (1990). Enhancing the effectiveness of self-administered videotape parent training for families with conduct-problem children. *Journal of Abnormal Psychology, 18*, 479-492.

Webster-Stratton, C., Kolpacoff, M., & Hollinsworth, T. (1988). Self-administered videotape therapy for families with conduct-problem children: Comparison with two cost-effective treatments and a control group. *Journal of Consulting and Clinical Psychology, 56*, 558-566.

Werner, E. E. (1987). Vulnerability and resiliency in children at risk for delinquency: A longitudinal study from birth to young adulthood. In J. D. Burchard & S. N. Burchard (Eds.), *Prevention of delinquent behavior: Primary prevention of psychopathology,* (vol. 10; pp. 16-43). Newbury Park, CA: SAGE.

West, D. J. (1982). *Delinquency: Its roots, careers and prospects.* Cambridge, MA: Harvard University Press.

Assessment Issues in Families of Individuals with Disabilities

Marjorie A. Padula

University of Nebraska-Lincoln

Mortality in mothers and infants has been reduced as medical science has advanced. The ability to extend the lives of individuals born with disabilities, or who become injured later in life, has steadily increased with advances in science. As a result, the existing population of individuals with special needs has grown, thereby increasing the numbers of families affected by a disability. In the past, individuals with severe disabilities may have been institutionalized. Now, although institutions still exist, greater numbers of individuals with disabilities are likely to be cared for in the home. What effect does this have on families and their functioning? How can families be helped to access their strengths? Accurate family assessments are a crucial component in the task of answering these and other critical questions regarding individuals with disabilities and their families.

Assessing the families of individuals with disabilities is a complex, multifaceted task. Not only must the family be assessed, a formidable task in itself, but the impact of the disability on the family, as well as on the individual with the disability, must also be factored into the assessment process. Depending on the type of disability, successful assessment may require creative approaches. Information from all family members may not be available due to the nature of the disability. For example, people with certain disabilities may be unable to describe their perceptions of their place in the family or their sense of family cohesiveness. As each family member has his or her own view of the family system, it is important to have as many members of the family as possible complete family assessment measures (Olson, McCubbin et al., 1992). Family assessment that is unable to include the perceptions of the individual with the disability will necessarily be limited in its comprehensiveness and usefulness.

The purpose of this chapter is to provide information regarding the assessment of families of individuals with disabilities. In addition to the background information provided initially, a brief review of the literature is included. Methods of assessment and specific standardized assessment devices are then described and reviewed for their usefulness in assessing families of individuals with disabilities. Finally, critical issues to consider in assessing these special families are discussed.

LITERATURE REVIEW

The vast majority of published research has as its focus the families of children with disabilities, particularly congenital disabilities (Yura, 1987; Benson & Gross, 1989; Lobato, Faust, & Spirito, 1989; Konstantareas, 1991). A much smaller amount of information is available regarding the families of adult individuals with disabilities acquired congenitally or through accident or injury later in life (Fohs, 1991; Jackson & Haverkamp, 1991).

Research surrounding the families of children with disabilities has perhaps been spurred by the involvement of government—first in the rights of children and later in the rights of children with disabilities. Not only do laws exist that provide services for school-aged individuals with disabilities, but Public Law 99-457 extends services to birth for children with disabilities. This law also serves to underline the importance of involving the family of the individual with a disability in both assessment and provision of services (Fewell, 1991) and reflects "the assumption that family functioning and child development are inextricably intertwined" (Frey, Greenberg, & Fewell, 1989, p. 240).

Government may again provide the impetus to study individuals with disabilities and their families. The recent enactment of the Americans with Disabilities Act (ADA) has drawn attention to the rights of all individuals with disabilities, particularly adults, and may spur interest in investigating the families of these individuals.

Studies regarding families containing individuals with disabilities have often been conducted in a somewhat noncohesive fashion. Researchers have studied the individual with the disability in relationship to various individuals and systems. These include studying the individual with the disability in relationship to: the family (Newman, 1991; Seligman & Darling, 1989; Roberts, 1984); the parents (Seligman & Darling, 1989); the mother (Dunst, Trivette, & Cross, 1986; Roberts, 1986; Vadasy & Fewell, 1986); the father (Meyer, 1986; Lamb & Meyer, 1991); the siblings (Bischoff & Tingstrom, 1991; Crnic & Leconte, 1986; Seligman & Darling, 1989; Seligman, 1991); single-parent families (Vadasy, 1986; Wikler, Haack, & Intagliata, 1984;); grandparents (Seligman & Darling, 1989; Seligman, 1991; Sonnek, 1986); and support networks and institutions (Darling, 1991; Stagg & Catron, 1986). Studies investigating cultural differences in response to family members with disabilities have also been conducted (Florian, 1989). In general, these studies show the presence of an individual with a disability has a decided impact that may be both positive and/or negative (Benson & Gross, 1989; Yura, 1987). This impact is felt in a variety of family and community areas including individual relationships, quality of life, and economics.

Type of disability is another area of focus seen in the literature. Researchers have looked at individuals with specific disabilities in relationship to the above listed individuals and systems, whereas others have studied the isolated individual effects of the disability. Disabling conditions researched include: juvenile rheumatoid arthritis (Varni, Wilcox, & Hanson, 1988); cystic fibrosis (Brinthaupt, 1991); spina bifida (Spaulding & Morgan, 1986); cerebral palsy (McCubbin, 1989); head/traumatic brain injury (Jackson & Haverkamp, 1991); Down's syndrome (Carr, 1988; Damrosch & Perry, 1989; Ryde-Brandt, 1991); mental retardation (Donovan, 1988; Gowen, Johnson-Martin, Goldman, & Appelbaum, 1989; Abbott & Meredith, 1986); developmental disabilities (Hampson, Beavers, & Hulgus, 1990; Thorin & Irvin, 1992; Trute & Hauch, 1988; Rimmerman & Portowicz, 1987); learning disabilities (Konstantareas, 1991; Konstantareas & Homatidis, 1989; Michaels & Lewandowski, 1990; Morrison & Zetlin, 1988, 1992); behavior disorders (Parker, Hill, & Goodnow, 1989); mental illness (Chafetz & Barnes, 1989; Medvene & Krauss, 1989); autism (Donovan, 1988; Konstantareas, 1991); visual impairments (Ammerman, VanHasselt, & Hersen, 1991; VanHasselt, Hersen, Moor, & Simon, 1986); hearing impairments (Strom, Daniels, & Jones, 1988; Warren & Hasenstab, 1986); and orthopedic impairments (Varni & Setoguchi, 1993). Comparisons of families containing children with congenital disabilities versus families containing children with acquired disabilities are also available (Bragg, Brown, & Berninger, 1992).

Ongoing research in the area of families containing individuals with disabilities is critical, as is research regarding the impact on a family when a previously healthy adult is disabled through illness or accident. Not only the families, but the individual who has become disabled, may need assistance in coping in ways that may be very different from those of families into which a disabled member is born. Family assessment instruments designed to measure the needs, strengths, and weaknesses of families containing individuals with disabilities will be critical to increased understanding and effective service provision.

METHODS OF ASSESSMENT

A variety of family assessment methods are described in the available research. These standardized and researcher-designed methods include behavioral observations and ratings, videotaped observations, role-play tests, projective tests, questionnaires and inventories, interviews, and surveys. Many of the family assessment measures used in the research, however, have been inadequately described, making it difficult, if not impossible, to make judgments regarding the reliability, validity, or generalizability of much of the reported research. This lack of information also makes it difficult to determine the potential usefulness or adequacy of the assessment device or procedure for clinical purposes.

Infrequently cited as assessment tools in the research, but believed by Seligman (1991) to be valuable in clinical assessment and treatment planning for families containing individuals with disabilities are genograms and ECO-MAPS. The genogram (McGoldrick & Gerson, 1986) allows a multi-generational and extended view of the family. The ECO-MAP (Hartman, 1978) is a diagrammatic portrayal of the interactions of the family and the community and may be essential to the understanding of some families containing individuals with disabilities because outside supports are often critical.

By far the most frequently cited method of collecting information from the families of individuals with disabilities has been self-report. Standardized or researcher-designed protocols, instruments, or forms have been used. The use of in-home, office, and phone interviews employing both open- and close-ended questions have been used to gather information. Most of the information collected has been provided by parents, although information has also been gathered from siblings and grandparents. The effects of situational variables and examiner variables on test outcome are well documented (Anastasi, 1988). There are dangers inherent in the use of self-report. The mood of the individual responding, his or her reaction to the interviewer, the type of interview, and the influence of seeing an interviewer face-to-face versus talking with an unknown caller or completing an anonymous form are only a few of the factors that may influence the type of response and information provided by family members.

Standardized and researcher-designed paper-and-pencil questionnaires or survey measures are frequently employed. A difficulty with many of these measures is their use of close-ended questions that may fail to uncover important variables of concern. Measures employing open-ended questions may elicit more information but may not provide enough information about constructs of particular interest. In addition, open-ended questions may tend to elicit responses which may be somewhat disjointed but reflect the immediate concerns of the individuals responding.

STANDARDIZED ASSESSMENT INSTRUMENTS

The most frequently mentioned standardized assessment instruments used with families of individuals with disabilities are the Questionnaire on Resources and Stress for Families with Chronically Ill or Handicapped Members (QRS; Holroyd, 1987), the Family Adaptability and Cohesion Scales (FACES II; Olson, Portner, & Bell, 1982; FACES III; Olson, Portner & Lavee, 1985), and the Family Environment Scale (FES; Moos, 1974). The Family Crisis Oriented Personal Evaluation Scales (F-COPES; McCubbin, Larsen, & Olson, 1992), Parent-Adolescent Communication Form (Barnes & Olson, 1985; 1992), and Family Strengths Scale (Olson, Larsen, & McCubbin, 1992) are mentioned infrequently in the literature, but may be useful for assessing some specific areas of interest in families of individuals with disabilities. The Parenting Stress Index (PSI; Abidin, 1983, 1990) and the Child Behavior Checklist (CBCL; Achenbach & Edelbrock, 1983) are frequently cited in the body of literature regarding families of children with disabilities; however, because they are not used in assessments of the entire family, they will not be reviewed here.

The Questionnaire on Resources and Stress for Families with Chronically Ill or Handicapped Members (QRS). The Questionnaire on Resources and Stress for Families with Chronically Ill or Handicapped Members (QRS; Holroyd, 1987) was constructed in order to measure stress in families caring for relatives with illness or disabilities. The questionnaire is designed for families containing individuals with disabilities of all ages, but there is a clear lack of studies with adult populations (Holroyd, 1988). It is, however, one of the most frequently cited instruments in published studies involving the assessment of families of children with disabilities.

The QRS purports to measure the impact of the disability or illness on the respondent of the questionnaire and on other members of the family. The questionnaire consists of 285 true/false items that are self-administered, generally takes less than an hour to complete, and requires a 6th grade reading level. There is a 66-item short form intended to be used as a broad screening device. The comments presented here are based on the long form as Holroyd (1987) has reported the long form is the more reliable instrument. According to Holroyd, the QRS can provide information to clinicians regarding the problem to address first, the families who should be the first to receive care, and can be used to measure treatment effects. Because the QRS was originally designed for use in public health settings (Holroyd, 1988) in order to identify families with social assistance needs, its application is limited.

Holroyd (1987) describes the questionnaire as covering three domains: personal problems for the respondent (seven scales), family problems (three scales), and problems of the individual in the family with the disability, referred to by Holroyd as the index case (five scales). Information regarding the internal consistency of the QRS scales was provided by Holroyd (1987) using the Kuder-Richardson-20 method. Overall, internal consistency is reported as .96. No information regarding test-retest or alternate test form reliability is provided. In a recent review of the QRS, Erickson (1992) noted the validity information on the QRS is limited: Content validity is established qualitatively rather than quantitatively through the ratings of items by 12 judges; criterion validity is difficult to obtain as there are no other standard instruments in this area and construct validity is not established. Norms for the long form are based on a very limited sample of 107 families with nondisabled children.

The personal problem scales collect information regarding poor health and mood, excess time demands, negative attitude toward index case, overprotection/dependency, lack of social support, overcommitment/martyrdom, and pessimism. The family problem scales collect information regarding lack of family integration, limits on family opportunity, and financial problems. The index case scales collect information regarding physical incapacitation, lack of activities for the index case, occupational limitations for index case, social obtrusiveness, and difficult personality characteristics.

A major drawback of the QRS is that it does not provide for input from the individual with the disability. The form is to be administered to any family member other than the disabled member. Accessing the view of the individual with the disability, in addition to the remainder of the family, would be critical to a complete assessment. In addition, this exclusion from the assessment process discounts the perceptions of the individual with the disability.

Respondents to items on the QRS are given initial instructions that the questionnaire taps into their feelings regarding the family member with the disability. The nature of the majority of the questions seem to assume pathology rather than strength. The questionnaire has blanks in many of the questions and the respondent is asked to imagine his or her disabled relative's name in the blanks, and to give their honest feelings and opinions in a true/false format. For example, Item 70 on the QRS reads "I am afraid that other members of the family will be hurt because they are related to _____ " (Holroyd, 1987).

Three QRS scales are purported to deal with family problems. Scale 8 consists of 23 items reported by the author to measure lack of family integration ($r = .78$). Scale 9 consists of 9 items reported by the author to measure limits on family opportunity ($r = .69$). Scale 10 consists of 17 items reported to measure financial problems ($r = .74$). An analysis of the items in these three scales, presented below, suggest some difficulties when using them with families of individuals with disabilities.

Scale 8 measures family integration problems such as difficulty getting along with the individual with the disability or with other family members. The majority of the Scale 8 items (15 of 23 items) include references to the individual with the disability, thus continuing the more traditional medical model focus on the identified patient, rather than a focus on the entire family system. The negative wording of some of the items may present problems for individuals asked to complete this questionnaire. For instance, Item 141 reads "Because of _____ our family has never enjoyed a meal" and Item 120 reads "Taking _____ on a vacation spoils pleasure for the whole family." Although the statement may be representative of their feelings, answering in the affirmative may be difficult for respondents, particularly parents. My clinical experience indicates that providing affirmative answers to questions such as these has the potential to produce conflicting feelings such as guilt, anger, and/or grief in some respondents. This type of item also serves to keep the focus on the individual with the disability as the source of problems. Eight of the items on this scale are family oriented rather than patient focused. Examples of these more family focused items include Item 10 "Members of our family praise each other's accomplishments" and Item 40 "Our family agrees on important matters." Items of this type are far too limited to provide a solid measure of family integration.

Scale 9 measures limits on family opportunity in a variety of areas including schooling, careers, social life, and the growth and development of other family members. The majority of the Scale 9 items (6 of 9 items) include direct references to the individual with the disability. Again the focus is on an identified patient rather than the entire family system. These items tend to focus on the possible negative effects of having an individual with a disability in the home. For instance, Item 6 reads "A member of my family has had to give up education (or a job) because of _____" and Item 32 reads "Other members of the family have to do without things because of _____." Even those items that do not have specific blanks for the name of the individual with the disability keep the focus on the family member with the disability. For instance, the wording of Item 236 seems to imply a problem: "Members of our family get to do the same kinds of things other families do."

Scale 10 items measure family financial problems that are a result of having an individual with a disability or chronic illness in the home. Fewer of these items (7 of 17 items) have specific references to the individual with the disability. However, these items do not measure family functioning, but are concretely geared to such things as family debt, income, amount spent on medical care, and other financial needs.

In summary, this analysis of the three QRS scales purported to measure family problems suggest these items have limited use. The items do provide information regarding how family members perceive the impact of having an individual with a disability in the home. The QRS provides a chance for family members to talk about lost opportunities and financial difficulty and can be used to provide information regarding the negative views of family members. However, the scales do not supply much information regarding family strengths that could be utilized in treatment. Nor does the questionnaire provide an opportunity for the individual with the disability to provide input. In addition, the wording of the questions assumes problems rather than solutions. The use of the word handicapped throughout the QRS is also unfortunate. Individuals with disabilities are entitled to have the focus put on their individuality and potentials before their disability.

Family Environment Scale (FES). Another instrument cited in the literature regarding families of individuals with disabilities is the Family Environment Scale (FES; Moos & Moos, 1986). The FES is composed of 10 subscales consisting of nine items each and is designed to measure family social environment. Moos (1974) believed family environments could be measured and that these environments would affect behavior. There are three forms of the FES. Form R, the Real Form, measures the perceptions of individuals regarding marital or family environments. Form I, the Ideal Form, measures individuals' perceptions regarding the ideal family environment. Form E, the Expectations Form, measures family setting expectations. Each form consists of 90 questions to be answered in a true-false manner. Both the Ideal and Expectations Forms were created by rewording the items and instructions on the Real Form.

Three dimensions are assessed by the FES: relationship, personal growth, and system maintenance (Moos, 1974). The relationship dimension consists of three subscales: cohesion, expressiveness, and conflict. The personal growth dimension consists of five subscales: independence, achievement orientation, intellectual-cultural orientation, active-recreational orientation, and moral-religious emphasis. The system maintenance dimension consists of two subscales: organization and control.

As the FES is a paper-and-pencil measure it does require reading. The second edition of the FES manual does not report the reading grade level required. The wording of the items is fairly straightforward, however, and some reviewers (Jacob & Tennenbaum, 1988) believe a minimum age of 10 is sufficient for completion. The problems that might be associated with administering the FES orally to family members who cannot read are not addressed in the manual.

The original normative sample for the FES was large for construction of Form R, the Real Form. A group of 1,125 normal families and a group of 500 distressed families were used (Moos & Moos, 1986). The distressed families consisted of families being seen at a psychiatric clinic and a probation and parole department; families containing an alcoholic member; families of general psychiatric patients; and families with a child in crisis, a runaway, or a delinquent. In a review of the FES, Busch-Rossnagel (1985) noted the FES norms provided limit the instrument's usefulness. Information regarding sample subgroups is not provided nor are significant differences between means of different family groups presented. Although families having individuals with psychiatric or emotional difficulties were part of the distressed family group used in the norming sample, families containing members with other types of disabilities were not included. This obviously limits the research and clinical usefulness of the FES with families containing one or more members with a disability. Another difficulty noted (Lambert, 1985) is the lack of profiles for the model family as criteria for correlation of the perceptions of family members regarding their own family.

The FES can be administered to all family members, including the individual with the disability. According to Moos and Moos (1983), the FES can be used not only to compare and describe the social environments of families, but also to contrast the perceptions of parents and children, and to look at actual as well as preferred family environments. Billings and Moos (1982) have maintained the instrument may be used to identify interventions but the FES manual does not give information regarding how this might be accomplished. Although the FES may be useful in identifying treatment issues for families of individuals with disabilities, it has its greatest usefulness in providing the perceptions of families regarding specific areas of family life. One of the drawbacks of the FES is its lack of sensitivity to the special needs that may be present in families of individuals with disabilities; it fails to address the strengths and weaknesses such families have as a result of living with an individual with a disability.

In a recent review of the FES, L'Abate and Bagarozzi (1993) reported inadequacies in the methodology employed in the development of the scale. They noted a lack of evidence for reliability and validity, pointing out that many of the 10 subscales are not statistically independent. Another criticism concerned the lack of grounding in a conceptual framework of family development, process, functioning, or family therapy theory. These methodological weaknesses put the value of the FES in question as anything other than a measure of the perceptions of others.

The Family Adaptability and Cohesion Scales (FACES). The Family Adaptability and Cohesion Scales (FACES II; Olson, Portner, & Bell, 1982; FACES III; Olson, Portner, & Lavee, 1985) are also cited in the literature regarding families of individuals with disabilities. See Halverson (Chapter 1 in this volume) for additional discussion of the FACES. FACES IV has been developed but the manual and completed assessment device are not yet available. Olson, McCubbin et al. (1992) have reported research regarding the reliability and validity of FACES IV is currently in progress. Although FACES III is the most recent FACES version available, Olson, McCubbin et al. recommend using FACES II for the following reasons: FACES II has higher alpha reliability at .90; FACES II adaptability, social desirability, and cohesion correlation are less problematic than for FACES III; and FACES II has higher concurrent validity. There are two forms of FACES II: a family version and a couples version. A Clinical Rating Scale (CRS) to be completed by clinicians observing the family has also been developed (Olson, 1989) to provide family ratings in the areas of cohesion, adaptability, and communication. Information presented here is concerned with the family version of FACES II unless otherwise indicated.

The theoretical basis of the FACES is the Circumplex Model of Marital and Family Systems originally proposed by Olson, Sprenkle, and Russell (1979). This model proposed that cohesion and adaptability were important dimensions of behavior in families. A third dimension, communication, was proposed as important in that it facilitates movement on the cohesion and adaptability dimensions. Olson, McCubbin et al. (1992) have provided information regarding the concepts upon which the FACES is built. Family cohesion is defined as the emotional bonding of individuals within the family. It appraises how members of the family are connected to or separated from the family. Family adaptability is concerned with the family's ability to change in a variety of areas including relationship rules and roles as well as power structures.

FACES II is a paper-and-pencil self-report measure that provides individual family members' perceptions of family functioning. According to Olson, McCubbin et al. (1992), the instrument requires about a seventh grade reading level. This eliminates children younger than about age 12 and individuals who are unable to read due to disability from completing the form. Information regarding the effects on validity and reliability due to administering the FACES II orally to accommodate a disability is not provided in the manual. Respondents are directed to read statements as they apply to their family and to rate the frequency of the behavior described on a scale ranging from 1 (almost never) to 5 (almost always). Olson, McCubbin et al. recommend that as many family members as possible take the instrument in order to capture as much of the family complexity as possible.

FACES II consists of two scales: cohesion (16 items) and adaptability (14 items). The initial FACES II consisted of 50 items and was administered to 2,412 adults in a national survey (Olson, McCubbin et al., 1992). The scale was reduced to 30 items based on reliability and factor analyses. The cohesion scale consists of 2 items in each of the following eight areas: emotional bonding, family boundaries, coalitions, time, space, friends, decision-making, and interests and recreation. The family adaptability scale consists of two or three items in each of the following six areas: assertiveness, leadership (control), discipline, negotiation, roles, and rules.

A major drawback to using this instrument with families of individuals with disabilities is that they were not included in the standardization population. This may not be significant for families of individuals with a mild or even moderate disability; however, if FACES II is to be used in families in which a family member has a severe disability, the family dynamics purportedly being assessed by the scales may look more pathological than they actually are. The more severe the disability the more necessary it may be for all family members to devote a considerable amount of time to caretaking tasks such as dressing, toileting, and feeding and to tasks aimed at keeping the family member safe. There is no vehicle in FACES II for measuring the healthiness of what may appear to be either an enmeshed or disconnected interaction, but may actually be highly functional behavior in a family coping with the demands of another family member's disability.

An analysis of FACES items suggests some problematic areas for use with families of individuals with disabilities including Item 4, "Each family member has input in major family decisions"; Item 9, "In our family, everyone goes his/her own way"; Item 29, "Family members pair up rather than do things as a total family"; Item 30, "Family members share interests and hobbies with each other"; and Item 22, "In our family, everyone shares responsibilities." Some difficulties with the above items are readily apparent. Major family decisions may be driven by medical concerns and perforce must be made primarily by parents. Individuals in families may go their own way or team up in pairs because one family member may be required as a caretaker and/or the individual with the disability may be incapable of joining many activities. Sharing interests, hobbies, and responsibilities may not be feasible for the same reason.

An advantage of FACES II is that it does take into account the view of the individual with the disability, provided they are capable of reading and understanding the questionnaire. Many items on FACES II are appropriate for families of individuals with disabilities. In addition, respondents are given the opportunity to rate items on a continuum from (1) almost never to (5) almost always. The opportunity to choose responses from a 5-point Likert scale is more likely to capture some of the differences present due to having an individual with a disability in the home than a true-false response format. However, an attempt to arrive at and interpret a final score from FACES II would not be useful in many cases. FACES II does provide both mean and discrepancy scores. These scores can be useful in discovering differences as well as in locating the family on major dimensions. Perhaps FACES II has its greatest usefulness in evaluating individual responses to items within the context of the disability and using items to plan treatment around specific areas that appear to be problematic.

Parent-Adolescent Communication Form. Another paper-and-pencil measure cited in the literature is the Parent-Adolescent Communication Form (Barnes & Olson, 1985, 1992) developed as an adjunct to the Family Adaptability and Cohesion Scales (FACES). Its theoretical base, the Circumplex Model of Family and Marital Systems (Olson et al., 1979) includes communication as an important component of family behavior. The Parent-Adolescent Communication Form is a 20-item self-report questionnaire with response choices on a 5-point Likert scale ranging from (1) strongly disagree to (5) strongly agree. There are three forms: the parent form, the adolescent and mother form, and the adolescent and father form. Differences in the forms are only in targeting the mother, father, or adolescent in each question. For example, Item 7 of the parent form reads "I am very satisfied with how my child and I talk together." On the adolescent and mother form, this item reads "I am very satisfied with how my mother and I talk together."

The instrument consists of two subscales, open family communication and problems in family communication, that are designed to measure content as well as process issues (Barnes & Olson, 1992). Cronbach's alpha was used to compute internal consistency of each scale (open family communication = .87; problems in family communication = .78; total scale = .88). Each subscale contains 10 items. The open family communication scale focuses on the positive dimensions of communication. It measures factual and emotional information exchanges, as well as the satisfaction and understanding experienced by participants in communication. The problems in the family communication scale look at the more problematic aspects of interactions. It measures negative interaction styles as well as caution and selectivity by the participants regarding what they communicate.

The norming sample for the Parent-Adolescent Communication Form consisted of adolescents who fell mainly in the age range 16–20 (Barnes & Olson, 1985; 1992). This raises the question of usefulness for the form with younger adolescents and developmentally delayed adolescents. No information regarding the use of families containing individuals with disabilities in the construction or refinement of the instrument is provided. This may limit the usefulness of the measure;

it certainly indicates caution must be exercised in using the norms provided to make decisions regarding the type of family communication evidenced by the instrument.

This form appears to have the potential for clinical usefulness in recognizing strengths and weaknesses in parent-adolescent communication patterns and in formulating treatment plans. Many of the items on this form appear to be both appropriate and useful for evaluating problem areas in communication between parents and adolescents in families coping with a disabling condition. However, it may not be appropriate for use with some families depending on the type of disability. For instance, a family with an individual with certain types of communication impairments may exhibit communication patterns that incorrectly appear to be dysfunctional. The items "I find it easy to discuss problems with my child" and "I am very satisfied with how my child and I talk together" on the Parent Form might be difficult for a parent to answer in the affirmative if their child was unable to express himself or herself due to a disabling condition. Therefore, the clinician might have difficulty evaluating the family communication patterns revealed by the assessment instrument.

Family Crisis Oriented Personal Evaluation Scales (F-COPES). The Family Crisis Oriented Personal Evaluation Scales (F-COPES; McCubbin et al., 1992) may prove to be particularly useful in treatment planning with families of individuals with disabilities. However, the clinical usefulness of F-COPES remains to be established (L'Abate & Bagarozzi, 1993). This paper-and-pencil questionnaire is based on the Double ABCX Model of Family Stress (McCubbin & Patterson, 1981) an outgrowth of Hill's (1949, 1958) ABCX model of family stress. The measure focuses on individual to family interaction and family to environment interactions, the hypothesis being that families with greater coping skills at both levels will be more successful in their adaptation to stress (McCubbin et al., 1992). Certainly families of individuals with disabilities often operate in a chronically stressful situation and it would be useful to determine where their strengths and weaknesses in coping skills lie.

F-COPES is a paper-and-pencil self-report questionnaire that can be administered to individuals above age 12 (Jacob & Tennenbaum, 1988). Two large samples ($N = 2,582$) consisting of husbands, wives, and adolescents were used in the construction of F-COPES. No information is provided regarding the use of families of individuals with disabilities in the construction of F-COPES. Nor is there information regarding oral administration and how this might affect results. Just as in the previous measures reviewed, these factors may limit the usefulness of F-COPES for assessing families containing individuals with disabilities.

F-COPES consists of 29 self-report items distributed over five scales: acquiring social support (9 items), reframing (8 items), seeking spiritual support (4 items), mobilizing the family to acquire and accept help (5 items), and passive appraisal (4 items). Reliability (Cronbach's alpha) for the five factors ranged from .63 to .83, with total scale alpha reliability of .86. Four-week test-retest reliability for the total scale is .81; test-retest for the five factors range from .61 to .95. (McCubbin et al., 1992).

Instructions for F-COPES ask respondents to decide how well the statements describe their attitudes and behavior when responding to difficulties or a problem in response to a stem. Responses are made on a 5-point Likert scale ranging from (1) strongly disagree to (5) strongly agree. Items are in response to the stem: "When we face problems or difficulties in our family, we respond by:" (McCubbin et al., 1992).

Many F-COPES items are geared to the family's response to new problems. Thus, the family's response to long-term disability is not really being tapped. However, the focus on new problems may be particularly useful for assessing families containing individuals with disabilities as they reach new developmental milestones or as the course of the disability changes. Information from family members in the area of acquiring social support may be particularly useful for families coping with disability or long-term illness. Much of the information could be used as an aid to planning treatment and distribution of community resources.

Family Strengths. The instruments discussed in the preceding sections do not adequately address family strength. Olson, Larsen, et al. (1992) developed a brief 12-item, paper-and-pencil, self-report questionnaire titled Family Strengths. The instrument consists of only two subscales, pride and accord. The authors limited the concept of family strengths to these two scales because they found "the expansive definition of family strengths makes them nearly impossible to measure" (Olson, Larsen et al., 1992, p. 60). Reliability using Cronbach's alpha was .83 for the total scale (pride = .88; accord = .72). Four week test-retest reliabilities were .58 for the total scale.

Respondents to the Family Strengths Scale are asked to rate items as they apply to their own family on a 5-point Likert scale ranging from (1) strongly disagree to (5) strongly agree. The pride scale consists of seven items designed to measure trust, respect, loyalty, and pride. The accord subscale consists of five items designed to measure the family's sense of competency.

This measure of family strengths may be useful as a research tool or as a screening measure in assessing global family strengths in families of individuals with disabilities. However, the need to access specific, as well as global strengths, is critical, especially if the information is to be used to improve understanding of, and clinical services for, families coping with a disability.

CRITICAL ISSUES IN THE ASSESSMENT OF FAMILIES OF INDIVIDUALS WITH DISABILITIES

Elman (1991) has outlined some critical areas to be assessed in families of individuals with disabilities. These include an assessment of individual family resources such as personality, ego strength, and health; as well as pragmatic family resources such as financial resources and support from extended family and community. If the individual with the disability is a child, age and sibling position should be considered as this may precipitate different family responses at different developmental milestones. Assessment should also include individual and family perceptions of events and responses.

Other critical areas of exploration have been noted by Seligman and Darling (1989). These include asking: To what extent does the family feel socially stigmatized? If the family feels socially stigmatized, it may be critically disabling to the system. What are the positive effects of having an individual with a disability in the family? How does the family's cultural background and socioeconomic class interact with other questions regarding the family containing an individual with a disability?

It is also important to assess the specific aspects of the disabling condition as the family assessment must always be done within the context of the particulars of the disability. Kazak (1986) has noted one of the most serious deficits in research regarding families of individuals with disabilities is the overgeneralization of results to other disabling conditions. Some important questions regarding the specifics of the disability are suggested by Elman (1991). Are there physical limitations? Do mental limitations accompany the physical difficulties? Is there a primary mental illness or mental retardation? What is the onset of the disability (i.e., birth or later)? Is the problem life threatening? How dependent will the individual with the disability be throughout the life cycle?

Fewell (1986a) reported the importance of determining the degree of severity of the disability when assessing the family. Is the disability mild, moderate, or severe? How will the type and severity of disability affect the family at critical periods of adjustment? What is the impact on parent-child interactions, siblings, family roles, family time, family finances, family relations with society?

The effects of having an individual with a disability in the family on grandparenting roles and on other extended family members has been discussed by Sonnek (1986). What are the effects on extended family members? What is the effect of extended family members on the family of the individual with the disability? What are the special considerations in assessing single-parent families (Wikler, Haack, & Intagliata, 1984; Vadasy, 1986)?

It is also critical to assess community supports in relationship to the family. If the individual with the disability is a child, what are the school supports and how do school interactions impact the family (Espinosa & Shearer, 1986)? What is the interaction of the religious community in the family system and how does that impact the family (Fewell, 1986b)? What is the impact of the therapeutic community on the family? The quality of the professional helping relationship with the family is known to be critical (Darling, 1991; Moeller, 1986). Are parent-professional relationships strained so that family members feel they are part of the problem, rather than the solution team (Upshur, 1991)? Does the family feel what Mallory (1986) termed "guilt by association" (p. 319); a situation where family members think helping professionals believe they are intellectually or emotionally deficient because they have a child with an intellectual or emotional disability in the family?

Family members with and without disabling conditions influence each other and the family system (Lyon & Lyon, 1991; Vadasy, 1986). How does each individual contribute to the family? This line of thinking leads to a number of questions regarding strengths. What are the family's strengths? What strengths have emerged as a result of having a family member with a disability in the home and how can they be capitalized upon? What benefits does the family member with the disability bring to the family? What has worked well for the family in the past and how can that be used in the present and future? These are all questions critical for planning effective family treatment.

CONCLUSION

There are obvious difficulties with the paper-and-pencil instruments reviewed in this chapter. Although the standardized assessments described access information regarding some areas of family functioning, they are far from complete. The difficulty in assessing family functioning, strengths, needs, and other variables of interest is compounded with the addition of a family member with a disability. If a major purpose of family assessment is to improve quality of life and service to families containing individuals with disabilities, it is crucially important for treatment professionals to look carefully at the multitude of issues discussed above. Perhaps Seligman and Darling (1989) were correct when they noted that only through long-term observation and discussion with family members regarding their strengths and needs, will true understanding of the family occur.

REFERENCES

Abbott, D., & Meredith, W. (1986). Strengths of parents with retarded children. *Family Relations Journal of Applied Family and Child Studies, 35*, 371-375.

Abidin, R. (1983). *Parenting Stress Index*. Charlottesville, VA: Pediatric Psychology Press.

Abidin, R. (1990). *Parenting Stress Index—Manual*. Charlottesville, VA: Pediatric Psychology Press.

Achenbach, T., & Edelbrock, C. (1983). *Manual for the Child Behavior Checklist and Revised Child Behavior Profile*. Burlington, VT: Department of Psychiatry, University of Vermont.

Ammerman, R., VanHasselt, V., & Hersen, M. (1991). Parent child problem solving interactions in families of visually impaired youth. *Journal of Pediatric Psychology, 16*, 87-101.

Anastasi, A. (1988). *Psychological testing* (6th ed.). NY: Macmillan.

Barnes, H., & Olson, D. (1992). Parent-adolescent communication. In D. Olson, H. McCubbin, H. Barnes, A. Larsen, M. Muxen, & M. Wilson (Eds.), *Family inventories* (2nd rev. ed., pp.29-44). St. Paul, MN: Family Social Science, University of Minnesota.

Barnes, H., & Olson, D. (1985). Parent adolescent communication and the circumplex model. *Child Development, 56*, 438-447.

Benson, B., & Gross, A. (1989). The effect of a congenitally handicapped child upon the marital dyad: A review of the literature. *Clinical Psychology Review, 9*, 747-758.

Billings, A. G., & Moos, R. H. (1982). Family environments and adaptation: A clinically applicable typology. *American Journal of Family Therapy, 10*, 26-38.

Bischoff, L., & Tingstrom, D. (1991). Siblings of children with disabilities: Psychological and behavioural characteristics. *Counseling Psychology Quarterly, 4*, 311-321.

Bragg, R., Brown, R., & Berninger, V. (1992). The impact of congenital and acquired disabilities on the family ststem: Implications for school counseling. *School Counselor, 39*, 292-299.

Brinthaupt, G. (1991). Pediatric chronic illness: Cystic fibrosis and parental adjustment. In M. Seligman (Ed.), *The family with a handicapped child* (2nd ed.; pp. 295- 336). Boston: Allyn & Bacon.

Busch-Rossnagel, N. (1985). Review of Family Environment Scale. In J. V. Mitchell, Jr. (Ed.), *The ninth mental measurements yearbook* (Vol. 1, pp. 574-575). Lincoln, NE: Buros Institute of Mental Measurements.

Carr, J. (1988). Six weeks to twenty-one years old: A longitudinal study of children with Down's syndrome and their families. *Journal of Child Psychology and Psychiatry and Allied Disciplines, 29,* 407-431.

Chafetz, L., & Barnes, L. (1989). Issues in psychiatric caregiving. *Archives of Psychiatric Nursing, 3,* 61-68.

Crnic, K., & Leconte, J. (1986). Understanding sibling needs and influences. In R. Fewell & P. Vadasy (Eds.), *Families of handicapped children: Needs and supports across the life span* (pp. 75-98). Austin, TX: Pro-Ed.

Damrosch, S., & Perry, L. (1989). Self-reported adjustment, chronic sorrow, and coping of parents of children with Down's syndrome. *Nursing Research, 38,* 25-30.

Darling, R. (1991). Parent-professional interaction: The roots of misunderstanding. In M. Seligman (Ed.), *The family with a handicapped child* (2nd ed.; pp. 119-150). Boston: Allyn & Bacon.

Donovan, A. (1988). Family stress and ways of coping with adolescents who have handicaps: Maternal perceptions. *American Journal on Mental Retardation, 92,* 502-509.

Dunst, C., Trivette, C., & Cross, A. (1986). Roles and support networks of mothers of handicapped children. In R. Fewell & P. Vadasy (Eds.), *Families of handicapped children: Needs and supports across the life span* (pp. 167-192). Austin, TX: Pro-Ed.

Elman, N. (1991). Family therapy. In M. Seligman (Ed.), *The family with a handicapped child* (2nd ed.; pp. 369-406). Boston: Allyn and Bacon.

Erickson, D. (1992). Review of the questionnaire on resources and stress. In J. Kramer & J. Conoley (Eds.), *The eleventh mental measurements yearbook* (pp. 735-737). Lincoln, NE: Buros Institute of Mental Measurements.

Espinosa, L., & Shearer, M. (1986). Family support in public school programs. In R. Fewell & P. Vadasy (Eds.), *Families of handicapped children: Needs and supports across the life span* (pp. 253-277). Austin, TX: Pro-Ed.

Fewell, R. (1986a). A handicapped child in the family. In R. Fewell & P. Vadasy (Eds.), *Families of handicapped children: Needs and supports across the life span* (pp. 3-34). Austin, TX: Pro-Ed.

Fewell, R. (1986b). Supports from religious organizaations and personal beliefs. In R. Fewell & P. Vadasy (Eds.), *Families of handi-*

capped children: Needs and supports across the life span (pp. 3-34). Austin, TX: Pro-Ed.

Fewell, R. (1991). Trends in the assessment of infants and toddlers with disabilities. *Exceptional Children, 58,* 166-173.

Florian, V. (1989). The cultural impact on the family dynamics of parents who have a child with a disability. *Journal of Comparative Family Studies, 20,* 97-111.

Fohs, M. (1991). Family systems assessment: Intervention with individuals having a chronic disability. *Career Development Quarterly, 39,* 304-311.

Frey, K., Greenberg, M., & Fewell, R. (1989). Stress and coping among parents of handicapped children: A multidimensional approach. *American Journal on Mental Retardation, 94,* 240-249.

Gowen, J., Johnson-Martin, N., Goldman, B., & Appelbaum, M. (1989). Feelings of depression and parenting competence of mothers of handicapped and nonhandicapped infants: A longitudinal study. *American Journal on Mental Retardation, 94,* 259-271.

Hampson, R., Beavers, W., & Hulgus, Y. (1990). Cross-ethnic family differences: Interactional assessment of white, black, and Mexican-American families. *Journal of Marital and Family Therapy, 16,* 307-319.

Hartman, A. (1978, October). Diagramatic assessment of family relationships. *Social Casework,* pp. 465-476.

Hill, R. (1949). *Families under stress.* New York: Harper & Row.

Hill, R. (1958). Generic features of families under stress. *Social Casework, 49,* 213-218.

Holroyd, J. (1987). *Manual for the Questionnaire on Resources and Stress for Families with Chronically Ill or Handicapped Members.* Brandon, VT: Clinical Psychology Publishing Co.

Holroyd, J. (1988). A review of criterion validation research on the Questionnaire on Resources and Stress for Families with Chronically Ill or Handicapped Members. *Journal of Clinical Psychology, 44,* 335-354.

Jackson, A., & Haverkamp, B. (1991). Family response to traumatic brain injury. *Counseling Psychology Quarterly, 4,* 355-366.

Jacob, T., & Tennenbaum, D. (1988). *Family asessment: Rationale, methods, and future directions.* New York: Plenum.

Kazak, A. (1986). Families with physically handicappped children: Social ecology and family systems. *Family Process, 25,* 265-282.

Konstantareas, M. (1991). Autistic, learning disabled and delayed children's impact on their parents. *Canadian Journal of Behavioural Science, 23,* 358-375.

Konstantareas, M., & Homatidis, S. (1989). Parental perception of learning disabled children's adjustment problems and related stress. *Journal of Abnormal Child Psychology, 17*, 177-186.

L'Abate, L., & Bagarozzi, D. (1993). *Sourcebook of marriage and family evaluation.* New York: Brunner/Mazel.

Lamb, M., & Meyer, D. (1991). Fathers of children with special needs. In M. Seligman (Ed.), *The family with a handicapped child* (2nd ed., pp. 151-180). Boston: Allyn & Bacon.

Lambert, N. (1985). Review of Family Environment Scale. In J. V. Mitchell, Jr. (Ed.), *The ninth mental measurements yearbook* (Vol. 1, pp. 574-575). Lincoln, NE: Buros Institute of Mental Measurements.

Lobato, D., Faust, D., & Spirito, A. (1989). Examining the effects of chronic disease and disability on children's sibling relationships. *Annual Progress in Child Psychiatry and Child Development,* 219-238.

Lyon, S., & Lyon, G. (1991). Collaboration with families of persons with severe disabilities. In M. Seligman (Ed.), *The family with a handicapped child* (2nd ed.; pp. 237-268). Boston: Allyn & Bacon.

Mallory, B. (1986). Interactions between community agencies and families over the life cycle. In R. Fewell & P. Vadasy (Eds.), *Families of handicapped children: Needs and supports across the life span* (pp. 317-356). Austin, TX: Pro-Ed.

McCubbin, M. (1989). Family stress and family strengths: A comparison of single- and two-parent famlies with handicapped children. *Research in Nursing and Health, 12*, 101-110.

McCubbin, H., Larsen, A., & Olson, D. (1992). F-COPES: Family crisis oriented personal evaluation scales. In D. Olson, H. McCubbin, H. Barnes, A. Larsen, M. Muxen, & M. Wilson (Eds.), *Family inventories* (2nd rev. ed.; pp. 121-137). St. Paul, MN: Family Social Science, University of Minnesota.

McCubbin, H., & Patterson, J. (1981). *Systematic assessment of family stress, resources, and coping: Tools for research, education, and clinical intervention.* St. Paul, MN: Family Social Science, University of Minnesota.

McGoldrick, M., & Gerson, R. (1986). *Genograms in family assessment.* New York: Norton.

Medvene, L., & Krauss, D. (1989). Causal attributions and parent-child relationships in a self-help group for families of the mentally ill. *Journal of Applied Social Psychology, 19*, 1413-1430.

Meyer, D. (1986). Fathers of handicappped children. In R. Fewell & P. Vadasy (Eds.), *Families of handicapped children: Needs and supports across the life span* (pp. 35-74). Austin, TX: Pro-Ed.

Michaels, C., & Lewandowski, L. (1990). Psychological adjustment and family functioning of boys with learning disabilities. *Journal of Learning Disabilities, 23,* 446-450.

Moeller, C. (1986). The effect of professionals on the family of a handicapped child. In R. Fewell & P. Vadasy (Eds.), *Families of handicapped children: Needs and supports across the life span* (pp. 149-166). Austin, TX: Pro-Ed.

Moos, R. H. (1974). *Family Environment Scale* (Form R). Palo Alto, CA: Consulting Psychologist Press.

Moos, R., & Moos, B. (1983). Clinical applications of the Family Environment Scale. In E. Filsinger (Ed.), *A sourcebook of marriage and family assessment* (pp. 253-273). Beverly Hills, CA: Sage.

Moos, R., & Moos, B. (1986). *Family Environment Scale manual* (2nd ed.). Palo Alto, CA: Consulting Psychologists Press.

Morrison, G., & Zetlin, A. (1988). Perceptions of communication, cohesion, and adaptability in families of adolescents with and without learning handicaps. *Journal of Abnormal Child Psychology, 16,* 675-685.

Morrison, G., & Zetlin, A. (1992). Family profiles of adaptability, cohesion, and communication for learning handicapped and nonhandicapped adolescents. *Journal of Youth and Adolescence, 21,* 225-240.

Newman, J. (1991). Handicapped persons and their families: Historical, legislative, and philosophical perspectives. In M. Seligman (Ed.), *The family with a handicapped child* (2nd ed.; pp. 1-26). Boston: Alllyn and Bacon.

Olson, D. (1989). *Clinical rating scale for Circumplex model* (rev. ed.). St. Paul, MN: Family Social Science, University of Minnesota.

Olson, D., Larsen, A., & McCubbin, H. (1992). Family strengths. In D. Olson, H. McCubbin, H. Barnes, A. Larsen, M. Muxen, & M. Wilson (Eds.), *Family inventories* (2nd rev. ed.; pp. 56-70), St. Paul, MN: Family Social Science, University of Minnesota.

Olson, D., McCubbin, H., Barnes, H., Larsen, A., Muxen, M., & Wilson, M. (1992). FACES II. In D. Olson, H. McCubbin, H. Barnes, A. Larsen, M. Muxen, & M. Wilson (Eds.), *Family inventories* (2nd rev. ed.; pp. 1-20). St. Paul, MN: Family Social Science, University of Minnesota.

Olson, D., Portner, J., & Bell, R. (1982). *FACES II: Family adaptability and cohesion evaluation scales.* St. Paul, MN: Family Social Science, University of Minnesota.

Olson, D., Portner, J., & Lavee, Y. (1985). *FACES III.* St. Paul, MN: Family Social Science, University of Minnesota.

Olson, D., Sprenkle, D., & Russell, C. (1979). Circumplex model of marital and family systems I: Cohesion and adaptability dimensions, family types and clinical application. *Family Process, 18,* 3-27.

Parker, T., Hill, J., & Goodnow, J. (1989). The impact of special needs children on their parents' perceptions of family structural interaction patterns. *Family Therapy, 16,* 259-270.

Rimmerman, A. & Portowicz, D. (1987). Analysis of resources and stress among parents of developmentally disabled children. *International Journal of Rehabilitation Research, 10,* 439-445.

Roberts, J. (1984). Families with infants and young children who have special needs. In J. Hansen & E. Coppersmith (Eds.), *Families with handicapped members,* Rockville, MD: Aspen.

Roberts, M. (1986). Three mothers: Life-span experiences. In R. Fewell & P. Vadasy (Eds.), *Families of handicapped children: Needs and supports across the life span* (pp. 193-220). Austin, TX: Pro-Ed.

Ryde-Brandt, B. (1991). Now it is time for your child to go to school, how do you feel? *International Journal of Disability, Development and Education, 38,* 45-58.

Seligman, M. (1991). Family systems and beyond: Conceptual issues. In M. Seligman (Ed.), *The family with a handicapped child* (2nd ed.; pp. 27-54). Boston: Allyn & Bacon.

Seligman, M., & Darling, R. (1989). *Ordinary families, special children.* New York: Guilford.

Sonnek, I. (1986). Grandparents and the extended family of handicapped children. In R. Fewell & P. Vadasy (Eds.), *Families of handicapped children: Needs and supports across the life span* (pp. 99-120). Austin, TX: Pro-Ed.

Spaulding, B., & Morgan, S. (1986). Spina bifida children and their parents: A population prone to family dysfunction. *Journal of Pediatric Psychology, 11,* 359-374.

Stagg, V., & Catron, T. (1986). Networks of social supports for parents of handicapped children. In R. Fewell & P. Vadasy (Eds.), *Families of handicapped children: Needs and supports across the life span* (pp. 279-296). Austin, TX: Pro-Ed.

Strom, R., Daniels, S., & Jones, E. (1988). Parent education for the deaf. *Education and Psychological Research, 8,* 117-128.

Thorin, E. & Irvin, L. (1992). Family stress associated with transition to adulthood of young people with severe disabilities. *Journal of the Association for Persons with Severe Handicaps, 17,* 31-39.

Trute, B. & Hauch, C. (1988). Building on family strength: A study of families with positive adjustment to the birth of a developmentally disabled child. *Journal of Marital and Family Therapy, 14,* 185-193.

Upshur, C. (1991). Families and the community service maze. In M. Seligman (Ed.), *The family with a handicapped child* (2nd ed.; pp. 91-118). Boston: Allyn & Bacon.

Vadasy, P. (1986). Single mothers: A social phenomenon and population in need. In R. Fewell & P. Vadasy (Eds.), *Families of handicapped children: Needs and supports across the life span* (pp. 221-249). Austin, TX: Pro-Ed.

Vadasy, P., & Fewell, R. (1986). Mothers of deaf-blind children. In R. Fewell & P. Vadasy (Eds.), *Families of handicapped children: Needs and supports across the life span* (pp. 121-148). Austin, TX: Pro-Ed.

VanHasselt, V., Hersen, M., Moor, L., & Simon, J. (1986). Assessment and treatment of families with visually handicapped children: A project description. *Journal of Visual Impairment and Blindness, 80,* 633-635.

Varni, J., & Setoguchi, Y. (1993). Effects of parental adjustment on the adaptation of children with congenital or acquired limb deficiencies. *Journal of Developmental and Behavioral Pediatrics, 14,* 13-20.

Varni, J., Wilcox, K., & Hanson, V. (1988). Mediating effects of family social support on child psychological adjustment in juvenile rheumatoid arthritis. *Health Psychology, 7,* 421-431.

Warren, C., & Hasenstab, S. (1986). Self-concept of severely to profoundly hearing impaired children. *Volta Review, 88,* 289-295.

Wikler, L., Haack, J., & Intagliata, J. (1984). Bearing the burden alone? Helping divorced mothers of children with developmental disabilities. In J. Hansen & E. Coppersmith (Eds.), *Families with handicappped members: The family therapy collections* (pp.44-62). Rockville, MD: Aspen.

Yura, M. (1987). Family subsystem functions and disabled children: Some conceptual issues. *Marriage and Family Review, 11,* 135-151.

Epilogue

The previous chapters have illustrated in great depth the intricacies of family assessment. The meaning of family across cultures, the effects of emotional, physical, and mental challenges on family functioning, and the frameworks useful in defining important family constructs have all been explored.

Although there are many measures for the many constructs that have been created to capture the meaning of family interaction, most are rather exploratory or useful only with limited populations. Clinical judgement and research acumen are required to be sure valid assessments are accomplished. There are significant challenges left to meet in designing assessment programs to illuminate important elements of family life such as marital quality, parent-child interactions, sibling interactions, the effects of stress associated with divorce, special needs children, or poor health.

Expert family assessment requires a clear grounding in a theory of families—a theory that can expand to include families from many cultural and groups. Measurement devices and approaches are most useful for clinical applications when they are embedded in such a theoretical network. Several such approaches may exist, but they remain untested across heterogeneous groups of families.

Expert family assessment requires a sensitivity to the myriad interactions that create family life. The skill of identifying which of those interactions make up a pattern with significant clinical importance is critical to meaningful assessment.

Although a human system in which almost everyone partakes, the family has clinical and theoretical mysteries yet unsolved. To what extent is the family environment shared? To what extent is each person's experience a unique variant of family patterns? What combination of individual attributes, interactional skills, and external stresses and supports makes for family success or dysfunction? How amenable to intervention are the many components of family life?

Perhaps an excellent book answers numerous questions while posing and framing many, many more. This is such a work.

Author Index

Subject Index

Test Index